POWER'S HUMAN FACE

For Mercy has a human heart,
Pity a human face,
And Love, the human form divine,
And Peace, the human dress.

from: *Songs of Innocence* by William Blake

POWER'S

Cruelty has a human heart,
And Jealousy a human face;
Terror the human form divine,
And Secrecy the human dress.

from: *Songs of Experience* by William Blake

HUMAN
FACE

A UNIQUE
AMERICAN
HISTORY

ARTHUR T. HADLEY

with an introduction by Howard R. Lamar

William Morrow & Company   New York 1965

Also by Arthur T. Hadley

Fiction:
THE JOY WAGON
DO I MAKE MYSELF CLEAR?

Non-fiction:
THE NATION'S SAFETY AND ARMS CONTROL

Drama:
WINTERKILL
THE FOUR MINUTE MILE

CONTENTS

For Kate, Arthur, Nick and my "old friend" George

INTRODUCTION

by Howard R. Lamar

Someone has aptly observed that the great national love of Americans is liberty, while their great national sport is politics. The two concerns bear an indissoluble relationship to one another, for as a free people Americans have always feared the concentration of great power in the hands of a single individual. They have watched with a particular fascination, therefore, the manner in which the thirty-five men who have served as President of the United States have used their limited constitutional powers. That same fascination has led Arthur T. Hadley to write *Power's Human Face*. With understandable inquisitiveness he, too, seeks to know how certain presidents imposed their unique personalities on the office and to answer the equally intriguing question: how does the office affect the men. Does power corrupt? Does the great crisis call forth the great man?

Beginning with Thomas Jefferson, whom Mr. Hadley calls our first modern president, he discovers that the Vir-

Howard R. Lamar is a Professor of History and the Director of Graduate Studies in History at Yale University.

ginian publicly abhorred the powers he rightly possessed as President, but that he used them nevertheless. Andrew Jackson's very personality gave the executive authority a new dimension. James Buchanan, faced with the possibility of disunion abdicated his responsibilities, while Lincoln, faced with the fact of disunion, fulfilled them magnificently. Teddy Roosevelt hugely enjoyed the presidential prerogatives every day he was in the White House. And, tragically, Woodrow Wilson let the power of the office carry him away from the political realities of his time.

It is this ever changing and intriguing human face of power which Mr. Hadley so vividly describes in the succeeding pages of this book. Sometimes the true visage is cleverly masked; sometimes it is contradictory when it speaks; often noble words and deeds pour forth, but occasionally the face appears as a study in tragic failure. Together the faces tell the old but endlessly engrossing story of man's leaders grappling with man's fate.

To say that *Power's Human Face* describes certain men who were concerned with the American presidency is a little misleading. Rather Mr. Hadley permits them and their contemporaries to supply their own lines and delineate their own characters by quoting selectively from their speeches, diaries, letters, and the words they spoke at press conferences. On occasion a close friend provides the insight, as in the sketch of Jefferson, when young John Quincy Adams commented on the Virginian's penchant for self-praise and exaggeration. In other instances, a one line slogan from the campaign of 1868: "Vote as you shot! Grant!" speaks volumes about the issues and bitter spirit of that election. On the eve of the Second World War the author simply lets the dialogue of one of FDR's press conferences demonstrate the masterful evasiveness which the President felt he had to employ to hide some of the secret policies of the government.

Mr. Hadley has also caught the Presidents in moments

of calm and anger, or when they were confiding their private thoughts to a friend. We see Thomas Jefferson, who once declared that "an honest man can feel no pleasure in the exercise of power over his fellow citizens," skillfully and pleasurably maneuvering Congress as if it were an obedient child, and in the meanwhile ruthlessly throwing out Federalist officeholders for partisan reasons.

If the calm and rational philosopher battled with the passionate and partisan political "pro" in Jefferson and made him seem contradictory, the power struggle involving Peggy Eaton, John C. Calhoun, and Martin Van Buren twisted a strong-willed Andrew Jackson into knots. In treating this curious mixture of issues involving a lady's virtue, social snobbery, and states' rights the garrulous Peggy does a large part of the talking herself in a set of delightfully revealing letters. At the same time the simple but dogged persistence of Old Hickory in trying to make Mrs. Eaton seem acceptable demonstrates afresh those qualities of will and determination which gave Jackson his reputation as a strong president and as a democrat with a small "d."

Mr. Hadley's talents are not confined to unifying revealing and dramatic quotations with a perceptive commentary. In *Power's Human Face* he does much more than that. To the initial dismay and eventual delight of the professional historian, he has also juxtaposed men, words, and situations, sometimes deliberately out of chronological order, to suggest the fundamental nature of a particular man. The narrative of Jackson's self-confident if furious determination to preserve the Union against South Carolina secessionists in 1832 is followed by one of the most compelling and eloquent vignettes in the book: a lady's report of President Buchanan's state of near hysteria and sense of helplessness when he learned in December 1860 that South Carolina had voted to secede from the Union. The unspoken contrast between Jackson and Buchanan is unforgettable.

And so the flashes of insight and understanding continue right up through the presidency of Harry S Truman. Many of the words and scenes Mr. Hadley uses will be familiar to every American: Lincoln in the White House telegraph office engaging in a word duel with General McClellan; Andrew Johnson obtusely battling the Radicals; Ulysses Grant being victimized by corrupt politicians, and William T. Sherman both politely and profanely declining over and over again to be president. Theodore Roosevelt and William Howard Taft engage anew in the well-known mutual bouts of character assassination which made the campaign of 1912 so disastrous for the two of them. Every reader will recognize the idealistic Wilson, the amorous Harding, the taciturn Coolidge, and the optimistic Hoover. In every case, however, Mr. Hadley gets beyond the familiar to the basic quality of a man or his concept of this offce. In reading of Teddy Roosevelt's consuming wish to be a powerful president, one suddenly understands not only why Roosevelt ceased to respect Taft, but why the former always asserted that Jefferson was a weak man and a terrible president·

As seemingly infinite as are the human aspects of power, that power itself has always been seen and endured by mankind in traditional forms whether it be the tyrant trying to usurp the hollow crown, or the elected president attempting to serve his fellow citizens. In his treatment of Franklin D. Roosevelt and Harry S Truman, though, Mr. Hadley traces the coming of a revolutionary new element which has affected the human use of power: the atomic bomb which the United States used in August 1945 to end the war with Japan. The words and actions which highlight the American presidency from 1932 to 1945 and relate to the building of the bomb, are already poignant and familiar to most adult Americans. But once again Mr. Hadley demonstrates his ability to get at essences and to provoke arresting associations. Under the pressure of world conflict, FDR reveals qualities of dissembling that John Quincy Adams saw in Jefferson. Truman's sense of heavy responsibility upon assuming office echoes Buchanan's remark that life in the White House was a nightmare, but his vigorous stand against the Dixiecrats makes him seem the true heir of Andrew Jackson.

Who before Truman, though, had faced a decision comparable to that of ordering an atomic bomb to be dropped? Buchanan had wept over the dissolution of the Union in 1861, and Wilson burst into tears in 1917 when he contemplated the sense of cruelty and hate which he and his administration would engender in the American people when they went to war against Germany. Truman's decision was more like that of Lincoln who, in ordering the troops to Sumter, made a decision which he knew would begin a frightful war of brothers. But even Lincoln's act did not take on the same awesome dimensions and fateful implications of Truman's decision in 1945. It is the impact of the atomic age of power on humanity itself which Mr. Hadley discusses in his final pages.

At the end of the War of 1812, Thomas Jefferson wrote Thomas Leiper, a Philadelphia merchant, that "I hope our wisdom will grow with power, and teach us that the less we use our power the greater we will be." To Truman and his successors in office, Jefferson the philosopher had at least posed an answer for the proper use of all power. The question remains: will one of his "pro" successors in office ever be able to make the answer a reality? It is about such fundamental questions as these—and the men who must consider them —that Arthur Hadley writes in his warm, imaginative and compassionate book, *Power's Human Face.*

NEW HAVEN, CONNECTICUT
April 19, 1965

I.. The "Pol" and the Philosopher

• • THOMAS JEFFERSON

1801–1809

This book catches certain Americans in the act of power. From Jefferson through Truman it aims to detail the different ways in which Americans have handled power; the human twists that give history so much of its excitement.

The method of this book is relatively unique. When I was a journalist I came to believe the best news story was one, if you were lucky enough to get it, where the reporter set the stage briefly and deftly and then let the people involved tell their story in their words. I have tried to treat history as news, to let those who fought for and wielded power speak for themselves as much as possible through what they said and wrote publicly and privately. Every sentence attributed to a man is in his own words. There are no chunks or paragraphs added. But I have selected with purpose as I did when a White House Correspondent or newspaper editor.

My goal has been to let the reader meet the famous of history in as intimate a manner as possible. To aid this face to face meeting, different speeches and various letters have been woven together or cut and obsolete words and phrases changed when necessary. But a man's "yes" has never been shifted to read "no" or "maybe." I have also sometimes altered time sequences. If a President's private letter, written three years after an event, shows he was being less than honest when he made a speech, I have put the letter right after the speech. This may disturb a few extreme academicians, but we see the man. We all get caught lying sometimes—even Presidents. References for all quotations are given in the notes at the book's end.

Unfortunately most of us are afraid of documents. If someone says to us, "Wouldn't you like to see the documents about this?" we immediately begin excuses why we must leave. Documents we feel are dull, heavy things best left to lawyers and antiquarians. Gold is there; but it would take us months of heavy spading to find it. So we too often only meet the famous of history in books written about them—not in their own words.

This need not be. The American democratic process has raised, cast up, let loose, boosted, allowed (pick your own verb), into power some extraordinary men—extraordinary in many ways. What they thought and felt privately, what power did to them and they with it, how those around them judged them and their actions makes fascinating reading when the personal narratives are culled and joined.

The background information in this book, the parts I have written, are used to move the reader behind scenes quickly. They are printed in the type you are reading now and set off from the rest of the book by a: • After the stage has been set—let those in power take over. I have not, for example, detailed the theme that Woodrow Wilson finally became a captive of power. This fact shouts from his own writings; and those around him saw and commented on it with the intimate agony of involvement. Nor have I analyzed the way Lincoln used humor. When Lincoln's stories are placed in the personal context in which they occurred, it becomes obvious he used humor both to gain his political ends and to relieve the horrible inner tensions the use of power created in him.

I hope no one will think that in stressing the human side of those in power I have aimed to debunk or make ludicrous. For someone who is perfect, a "superman," to become a hero does not require much. But when a man becomes a hero, that's a happening. Thomas Jefferson is not put down because he was a master politician, went against everything he believed to buy Louisiana, and tried to railroad a political rival, Aaron Burr, into jail. He is still a brilliant man who had the courage to turn down power when he could have been re-elected President for life. Nor is Andrew Jackson "debunked" because he could govern a country with force but was torn in two by a woman. Nor Franklin Roosevelt because he used the power of the Presidency to secretly battle Nazi Germany before Congress gave him the legal power to do so. Each was handling power in his way.

As these men used or refused to use power, they also changed America. Presidential power kept shifting and growing. Jefferson believed it wrong and would not spend federal money to build roads. Truman had the power to manufacture and use nuclear weapons. That story is also here. But mainly in these personal narratives by those in power, and by their contemporaries who helped or battled them, we can be an omniscient reporter on the inside of history. We can watch and question the famous in private and make judgments: What manner of men were they?

This book begins with Jefferson rather than Washington because Washington's problems were so removed from the present that they require a prohibitive amount of historical scene setting. For example, Washington spent a great deal of time and energy establishing himself and the Presidency as superior to the State Governors. But it was practically all done in a language and through political forms as alien to us as the problem itself. Jefferson on the contrary, a mere four years after Washington, appears almost modern.

Like the majority of men who reach great power, Jefferson had certain definite intellectual beliefs and emotional reactions to power and its effect on men. He distrusted power profoundly. Certain that power corrupted people and tended to be misused, he was the major figure behind the Constitution's Bill of Rights. He battled to make habeas corpus an integral part of the American judicial system.

While the States were voting to ratify the Constitution he wrote his friend James Madison, "The Constitution is a good canvas on which some strokes only want retouching. There is need for a bill of rights providing clearly for freedom of religion, freedom of the press, protection against standing armies, and the eternal unremitting force of the habeas corpus laws; and trials by jury."

Yet this man who so feared the effects of power sought power avidly most of his life. A major man, he embodied such major contradictions. Thoughtful and gentle, he was an intemperate hater—starting with General Washington—yet he couldn't bear to have enemies. Most of those who knew him well, enemies and friends, remarked on his infinite complexity.

Jefferson and John Adams, the second President of the United States, had been the committee of two to draft the Declaration of Independence. Adams had admired the articulate Virginia planter and they were then close friends. Later, politics came seriously between them. Jefferson was a Republican, the States' rights party that eventually evolved into the present Democratic party—which today, in spite of its Southern wing, stands for the strong central government Jefferson hated. Adams was a Federalist, the strong central government party which evolved into the present Republican party—which today stands against the federal involvement in individual affairs that Adams believed in.

In 1800, Jefferson, the Republican, ran against the incumbent Federalist President, John Adams. Jefferson held the high cards. Not only was he the more popular; but secretive and efficient John Adams had not been able to hold the Federalists together. They were divided both by the Presidential ambitions of Alexander Hamilton and the desire of a large faction of Federalists for a war against France.

Jefferson's speeches before and during the campaign display a modern quality of campaign logic. This includes the fact he could not admit he wanted to be President.

JEFFERSON   Mr. Adams and his Federalists wish to sap the Republic by fraud, destroy it by force, and elect an English monarchy in its place. The difference between the Federal and Republican parties is that the Federalists are rogues and the Republicans are honest men. The Federalists are monocrats while the Republicans are democrats, the hope of liberty and of the nation. . . .

Neither the splendor, the power nor the fame attached to the Presidency has any attraction for me. I am determined to retire from public office. There is no opening for future discussion. I will not be reasoned out of my decision. The subject has been thoroughly weighed. I wish to retire and that means from all office, high or low.

My age requires that I place my affairs in a clear state; and the little spice of ambition which I had in my younger days has long since evaporated. The question of my running is closed. I am proceeding in my agricultural plans with a slow but sure step. Last year my red clover had the most encouraging success.

• Jefferson loved to talk about his clover and his peas. Actually he was an inefficient farmer who lost money on his plantation at a time when most other planters were doing rather well. At politics he was far more successful. During the campaign he stated and restated his basic principles.

JEFFERSON   It is important that you understand what I deem the essential principles of government. They are equal and exact justice to all men of whatever state or persuasion;

Freedom of religion; Freedom of the press; and Freedom of the person. Also trial by juries impartially selected, this latter most important. When a person charged with an offense is placed in the possession of the judiciary authority, any interference on the part of the Chief Executive is open to censure.

Above all, I would rather construe the Constitution so narrowly as to oblige it to be amended from time to time than to construe it so broadly as to enable the President and the Senate to do things which the Constitution I believe forbids.

• *Jefferson defeated the divided Federalists easily. He had more trouble winning over a member of his own party, Aaron Burr, who with the help of Federalist votes almost became President when, under the complicated election procedures of the time, the election was thrown into the House of Representatives. Instead, as the man with the second largest number of votes, Burr, Jefferson's bitter political rival, became the Vice President. This situation was so confused that it led to the passage and ratification of the Twelfth Amendment to the Constitution in 1804, which by and large still determines the method of electing a President.*

In his inaugural speech Jefferson, publicly at least, buried the hatchet with the Federalists.

JEFFERSON   Called upon to undertake the duties of the First Executive of our country, I want to express my thanks for the favor with which, you my fellow citizens, have been pleased to grant me. Now, fellow citizens, that the contest of opinion through which we have just passed is over, let us unite with one heart and one mind. Let us restore social intercourse and banish political intolerance. We are all Republicans. We are all Federalists. Let us then with courage and confidence pursue our Federal and Republican principles, our attachment to the Union and representative government.

• *After his inaugural, Jefferson got down to the serious work of building a political party.*

JEFFERSON About the patronage of the Republican bank at Providence. I am in favor of making all banks Republican by sharing Government deposits among them according to how Republican they are. If the law forbids this we should amend it. . . .

Dear Governor Clinton, we still want an attorney and a marshall for your western district. Pray recommend two men to me. Let them be respectable but especially let them be Republican. . . . Dear Governor Gerry, please make out a list of Federalists still holding office in yours and neighboring states. There are too many of them left. . . . Mr. Barnes has been offered the Judgeship Mr. Green had expected. Mr. Green voted against me in the Senate on March 4th. . . .

I consent to the collector of Savannah recommended by General Jackson. I am glad also that the lighthouse keepers of Portsmouth and New York are now Republicans. . . . I am not satisfied with the recommendations of Mr. Neafville for Judge. They say nothing about his politics. . . . I am impressed that circumstances require a little something more for New York. The following is agreed by her Senators and representatives: David Gelston, Collector; Theodorus Bailey, Naval Affairs; M. L. Davis, Supervisor. . . .

Declarations by myself in favor of political tolerance and respect for the equal rights of the minority have been misconstructed into assurances that tenure of office was to be undisturbed. It is not.

● *The patronage axe fell on young John Quincy Adams, eldest son of Jefferson's rival the ex-President.* * *Without telling her husband, Abigail Adams, the ex-President's wife, wrote Jefferson an indignant note.*

* To one suddenly plunged into American history the Adamses can be confusing. They are John Adams, second President of the U. S.; his son John Quincy Adams, the sixth President; his son Charles Francis Adams, Minister to England during the Civil War; and finally his son Henry Adams, who wrote "the Education of——."

ABIGAIL ADAMS   Sir, I cannot avoid feeling a personal re-sentment. Soon after my eldest son's return from Europe, he was appointed Commissioner of Bankruptcy by the district judge. This is an office into which no political concerns enter, he is personally known to you, and possesses all the qualifica-tions you yourself had designated for that office.

As soon as Congress gave the appointments to the Presi-dent you removed him. This looked particularly pointed, though I have never heard from my son an expression of censure or disrespect towards you because of it. With pleasure I say he is not a blind follower of any party. I have written to you with the freedom and unreserve of former friendship to which I would gladly return if all that divided us were mere difference of opinion.

JEFFERSON   Your letter madam of the 18th of August has been received. I declare to you on my honor that this is the first knowledge I ever had that your son was a commissioner of bankruptcy. It may be thought that I ought to have known who the Commissioners were before I appointed others; but the judges as you well know are mostly Federalists and they had nominated Federalists exclusively. The Congress, dissatis-fied with this transferred the nominations to the President. Their object in passing the law was that he should correct the partiality of the judges. I therefore thought it proper, to fulfill the intentions of the law, to inquire only whom I ought to appoint.

Had I known your son was a commissioner it would have been a pleasure to have preferred him to some who were named in Boston. For both our political parties agree conscientiously in the same object, the public good; but they differ essentially in what they deem the means of promoting that good. I con-clude with a sincere prayer for your health and happiness and that of Mr. Adams.

ABIGAIL ADAMS   Sir, Affection may still linger in the Bosom, even after esteem has taken its flight. I am pleased to find that which respected my son all together unfounded. And I will do you the justice to say at this hour: that I believe you. However, here sir may I be permitted to pause, and ask you whether in your ardent zeal and desire to rectify what you consider to be the mistakes and abuses of former administrations, you are not led into measures still more fatal to the Constitution and more derogatory to your honor. Pardon me Sir, if I may say that I fear you are.

• *Master politician that he was, Jefferson handled Congress with the same skill as he built up his party.*

JEFFERSON Congress rises this day. They have carried into execution almost all the propositions submitted to them in my message. After the next election our majority in the Senate will be two to one. And it would not be for the public good to have it greater, a respectable minority is useful as censors. Indeed we Republicans shall now be so strong that we shall certainly split again; but the split must come under another name. That of Federalism has been so routed no party can rise under it.

• *Three years later the discharged Commissioner of Bankruptcy, John Quincy Adams, already a copious keeper of diaries, became a Senator, and now and then dined with President Jefferson.*

J. Q. ADAMS His itch for telling prodigies is unabated. Speaking of the cold he said he had seen Fahrenheit's thermometer in Paris at twenty degrees below for six weeks. "Never once in the whole time," said he "as high as zero, which is fifty degrees below the freezing point." Those were his words. He knows better than that, but he loves to excite wonder. Fahrenheit's thermometer never since Mr. Jefferson existed was at twenty degrees below zero in Paris. It was never for six weeks as low as twenty degrees above. Nor is Fahrenheit's zero fifty degrees below freezing, it is thirty-two.

He further observed that Spanish was a language so easy

to learn he had learned it with the help of a Don Quixote lent him by Mr. Cabot, and a grammar, in the course of a 19 day passage to Europe. His genius is certainly that of the French school. He imagines and believes he reasons. Also he tells nothing that does not redound to his own credit.

At an early age in life he became attached to one, William Small, a Scotsman and professor of mathematics at William and Mary. Small doubted the existence of God and Jefferson's loose morals necessarily followed. If not an absolute atheist he has no belief in future existence. All his ideas of obligation or retribution are bounded by this present life. The tendency of this condition is to produce duplicity.

• *Jefferson's favorite foreign country was France. And his favorite doctrine was the limits there should be on the powers of the President. Yet when Spain, beaten in war, ceded her vast Louisiana territories to France, Jefferson immediately realized the implications; and moved rapidly to meet them.*

JEFFERSON   The cession of Louisiana and the Floridas by Spain to France works most sorely on the U. S. It completely reverses all the political relations of the United States. Of all nations France is the one which hitherto has offered the fewest points on which we could have any conflict of right. But there is on the globe one single spot, the possessor of which is our natural and habitual enemy. It is New Orleans through which the produce of three-eighths of our territory must pass to market.

France placing herself in that door assumes to us the attitude of defiance. The impetuosity of her temper, the energy and restlessness of her character render it impossible that France and the U. S can long continue friends when they meet in so irritable a position.

• *Jefferson persuaded his friend James Monroe to go to France as a special envoy to try and purchase New Orleans. He also urged on the somewhat plodding Monroe the need for speed.*

JEFFERSON   As to the time of your going you cannot too much hasten it as the moment in France is critical. St. Domingo delays France's taking possession of Louisiana and her government is in the last distress for money for current purposes. You should arrange your affairs for an absence of one year at least. It will be necessary for you to stay in Washington some days on your way to New York.

• At the same time, through his French friends, Jefferson put pressure on the French government by threatening war. He wrote Dupont de Nemours in Paris:

JEFFERSON   Our circumstances are so imperious as to admit of no delay as to our course. The use of the Mississippi is so indispensable that we cannot hesitate one moment to hazard our existence for its maintenance. If we fail in this effort to put it beyond the reach of accident we see the destinies we have to run and prepare at once for them.

It may be said if this object be so all important to us, why do we not offer such a sum as to insure its purchase? The answer is simple. We are an agricultural people poor in money and owing great debts. The country too, which we wish to purchase is barren sand so we cannot make anything by a sale of the land to individuals. So it is peace alone which makes us desire it; and which ought to make the cession of it desirable to France.

• Napoleon was even more hard pressed for cash, and had less interest in the new territory than Jefferson realized. Instead of just selling part of Florida and the island of New Orleans he offered America the whole of the Louisiana territory from the Gulf to the Rockies for twelve million dollars. A treaty was quickly signed and Jefferson moved to lay the whole affair before Congress.

JEFFERSON   The treaty of purchase for Louisiana must of course be laid before both Houses. They I presume will see their duty to their country in ratifying and paying for it. They must then appeal to the Nation for an additional amendment to the Constitution approving their act. The Constitution makes no provision for incorporating foreign nations into our Union. In seizing the fugitive occurrence which so much advances the good of our country I have done an act beyond the Constitution. The Legislature must now ratify and pay for it; and then throw themselves upon the country. The country will support us. And the new amendment will confirm the Constitution more clearly by marking out its lines.

DEAR BRECKENRIDGE.   I wrote you six days ago on the subject of Louisiana and the constitutional provision that might be necessary to acquire it. Be so good as to consider that part of my letter on the constitutional question as confidential. Mr. Monroe reports from Paris that we must do without delay what we are bound to do; or there is reason to believe the French may declare the treaty void. What Congress shall think it necessary to do should be done with as little debate as possible and that in secret. All this strengthens the reasons for desiring the presence of every friend of the treaty on the first day of the coming session.

J. Q. ADAMS   Attended in the Senate the bill for enabling the President to take possession of Louisiana. I approve but how can he? Jefferson attained power by heading the attack on General Washington's administration under the banner of States rights. Elected President, the first thing he does is purchase Louisiana, an assumption of implied constitutional power greater than all the assumptions in the 12 years of Washington and my father put together.

I incline to the opinion that he is not altogether conscious of his own insincerity and deceives himself as well as others. His treatment of my father was double dealing, treacherous and false beyond all toleration; and he treated Washington no better. He is like the French lady who told her sister she did not know how it happened but she was the only one in the world who was always right.

He combines a rare and wondrous mixture of infidel philosophy and epicurean morals, of burning ambition and stoical self-control, of deep duplicity and generous sensibility, of ardent patriotism and passion for liberty against a pandering to public opinion and pliability of principle. His mind is of great compass and powerful resource yet coupled with a treacherous and inventive memory. This memory so panders to his will that to deceive others he begins by deceiving himself. His success seems to my imperfect vision a slur upon the moral government of the world.

JEFFERSON   To the Attorney General. On further consideration as to the amendment to our Constitution respecting Louisiana, I have thought it better instead to merely give Congress the same powers in the new territory they already have in other portions of the Union. The less that is said about the Constitutional difficulty the better. It is desirable and necessary to shut up the country for some time.

• *Did Jefferson realize the discrepancy between his view of power and what was happening? Did the strain tell on him or did he go blissfully on his way self-deceived as Adams believed? Jefferson wrote a close friend:*

JEFFERSON   After all my life having enjoyed the benefit of well formed organs of digestion I was recently taken with diarrhea, after having dined moderately on fish which had never before affected me. In the course of two or three weeks it wore me down by the frequency of calls; but then got so much better as to call on me but once a day; but still of watery consistency and distressing me with troublesome fluxes. However, I am improving and though the symptoms continue to a certain degree I enjoy good health.

What is remarkable, I find that while fish affects me, oysters and crabs do not. The stomach has never failed in the least.

The bowels alone are weak. I trouble you with these personal details because your friendship calls for them. I have found that riding is my remedy. A journey away from Washington brings back my health for some days. And daily rides of an hour or two keep me free from the visceral weakness. I hope my system may gradually recover its strength.

• *With Louisiana in his crown, a united political party behind him and his personal popularity, Jefferson was overwhelmingly re-elected. It seemed as if his second term would be full of even greater triumphs than his first. But one of the great real-life American mystery dramas intervened to draw Jefferson's energies. In 1805, at the start of Jefferson's second term, Aaron Burr was tried for treason. Burr was a leader of Jefferson's own party, Jefferson's bitter rival, a major political figure and a former Vice-President. The charge was that he had tried to carve out of the new Louisiana territory a nation for himself that he would rule as dictator.*

Was Burr guilty? Was the charge true? Jefferson passionately believed yes. So passionately indeed that he violated all his beliefs about habeas corpus and trial by jury. He held key witnesses incommunicado, sought to influence testimony, and maneuver Burr into being tried by a military court. However, a jury finally acquitted Burr—and historians have disagreed among themselves.

Before Burr came to trial, Jefferson sent Congress some selected bits of the evidence.

JEFFERSON   To the Senate and House of Representatives. I proceed to state information received touching on an illegal combination of private individuals against the peace and safety of the Union with the measures I have pursued for suppressing the same. The mass of the evidence I have received is chiefly in the form of letters containing rumors and conjectures and some of it is under the restriction of private correspondence. Therefore neither safety or justice permits exposing names except that of the principal actor, one heretofore distinguished by the favor of his country, a candidate for President of the United States, Aaron Burr, whose guilt is placed beyond question.

J. Q. ADAMS   I never believed Burr a fool. But he must be an idiot or a lunatic if he has really planned and attempted to execute the project imputed to him. But if his guilt is as clear as the noonday sun, the President ought not to have pronounced it so before a jury had tried him.

JEFFERSON   The anxiety and doubt in the public mind about Burr's guilt has been encouraged by tricks of judges to force a trial before it was possible to collect all the evidence. His most clamorous defenders are his accomplices. The federalists too give Burr their aid, making his cause their own, mortified only that he did not overturn the Union, rid them of this hateful Republican government and introduce their favorite monarchy. But he will be convicted fairly at Richmond for there is not a candid man in the United States who does not believe some, if not all, of Burr's acts have taken place.

• *Jefferson had arranged to have the trial take place in Richmond, Virginia, where his own political power was particularly strong, in an effort to make Burr's conviction certain. There were, however, quite a few who doubted Burr's guilt, among them a future leader of Jefferson's own party, Andrew Jackson. Jackson came to Richmond and denounced the trial. "I am more convinced every day," said Jackson, "that treason was never intended by Burr. I am sorry to say that this thing has assumed the shape of a political persecution."*

The irascible, quick-shooting, Andrew Jackson—not yet the hero of the Battle of New Orleans—had already much, if not all, his eventual fire. A Virginia State Senator reported to Washington: "As I was crossing the court-house green I heard a great noise of haranguing at some distance off. Inquiring what it was, I was told it was a great blackguard from Tennes-

see, one Andrew Jackson, who had come to the trial at Richmond, making a speech for Burr and damning Jefferson as a persecutor."

One of the key witnesses against Burr was a Doctor Bollman, whom Jefferson had held for a time in secret custody. Bollman, to speed his release, made certain statements to Jefferson, which Jefferson had sworn would never be used against him.

JEFFERSON To George Hayes, Prosecutor. While you are prosecuting Aaron Burr before the court I will trouble you from time to time in confidence with what occurs to me. I observe that the case of Marbury vs. Madison has been cited. It is my opinion that that case is against the law and therefore not law.

I am sending you some communications which Dr. Bollman on his arrival here in custody six months ago then gave me. My object is that you should know how to examine him and draw everything from him. Please keep the papers private to yourself and those who aid you as I assured Dr. Bollman that they would never be used against him. However, if he should prevaricate you may show them to him so that he shall see his prevarications will be marked. I will also forward you a pardon for him which may well remedy defects in his evidence. . . .

I have just heard the proceedings of the first day of Burr's trial. A jury of two Federals and ten Republicans was selected. This does not seem to be a fair representation of the state of Virginia. It shows the error of establishing judges for life. How in a state where there are not more than five federals, two of them should have been placed on one jury is difficult to explain as an accident. . . . Before an impartial jury Burr's conduct would convict himself, were not one word of testimony offered against him. But to what a state will our law be reduced by party feelings.

• *Chief Justice Marshall, a Federalist and enemy of Jefferson, was presiding over the trial. Jefferson stirred up popular feeling against Marshall, and Marshall tried to subpoena Jefferson. At this distance the conduct of all seems petty and demagogic. However the battle did prove that in the jungle of politics the Supreme Court can defend itself.*

JEFFERSON   To George Hayes. Three blank pardons have been made up and forwarded by the mail of yesterday. And three others go by that of this evening. Do you need further aid? . . .

Burr's acquittal is equivalent to a proclamation of immunity to every traitorous combination which may be formed to destroy the Union. However it will at least produce an amendment to the Constitution which while keeping judges independent of the Executive, will not leave them so of the nation.

J. Q. ADAMS   As my father cogently states: in substance Jefferson said that if Chief Justice Marshall should suffer Burr to escape, he, Jefferson would see that Judge Marshall was removed from office.

• *Jefferson often wrote friends how little he enjoyed power and being President. Did he believe this? Did he have many moments of depression? Or did he think he ought to feel that way? From the tone of his letters it is hard to tell.*

JEFFERSON   My dearest daughter, worn down here with pursuits in which I take no delight, surrounded by enemies and spies, catching and perverting every word which falls from my lips, and inventing where facts fail them, I pant for that society where all is peace and harmony, where we love and are beloved by every object we see. Not to have this is hard and it goes the harder when we see that the candle of life is burning out and the pleasures that we lose are lost forever. You and your sister and those dear to you are everything in my life.

Kiss your children for me, those dear little objects of our mutual love.

• A fascinating figure of those days was Mrs. Harrison Smith, a vivacious Washington hostess and friend of Jefferson. From the administration of Jefferson through those of Madison, Monroe and John Quincy Adams to Andrew Jackson she went everywhere and saw everything. Her notes and letters, whether about fleeing Washington during the war of 1812 or watching Jefferson's pet bird follow him up the White House stairs, have a life and vividness that raise gossip to history.

MRS. HARRISON SMITH   I once heard Mr. Jefferson exclaim that the only reason he wished he possessed the power of a despot was that he might save the noble trees scattered over the grounds of Washington that were daily falling as sacrifices to the cupidity of their owners or the necessity of the poor.

• As Jefferson's second term closed the pressure on him to run again was overwhelming. Still immensely popular in spite of the Burr trial, he probably could have been re-elected time after time had he so chosen. But to each entreaty that he run he made substantially the same moving answer.

JEFFERSON   That I should lay down my charge at a proper period is as much a duty as to have borne it faithfully. If some termination to the services of the Chief Executive be not fixed by the Constitution, or supplied by practice, his office, nominally four years, will in fact become for life, and history shows how easily that degenerates into an inheritance.

Believing that a representative Government responsible at short periods of election is that which produces the greatest sum of happiness to mankind, I feel it is a duty to do no act which shall impair that principle. General Washington set the example of voluntary retirement after eight years. I shall follow it. A few more precedents will oppose the obstacle of habit to anyone seeking to extend his term. Perhaps this obstacle may even be established by amendment of the Constitution.

Truth also requires me to add that I am sensible of that decline which advancing years brings on, and feeling their physical I ought not to doubt their mental effect. Happy if I am the first to perceive and to obey this admonition of nature, and to solicit a retreat from cares too great for the wearied faculties of age.

If I should be so fortunate as to carry into retirement the good will of my fellow citizens, it will close a service of forty years with the only reward it ever wished.

J. Q. ADAMS   He is one of the great men this country has produced. One of the men who have contributed largely to the formation of our national character; to much that is good and not a little that is evil. His Declaration of Independence is magnificent, laying open the first foundations of society. But he does not appear to be aware that it also lays open a precipice into which the slave holding planters of his country sooner or later must fall. The seeds of his Declaration are maturing. The harvest will be the terrible sublime.

MRS. HARRISON SMITH   As the term of his official life drew to a close he looked brighter and happier. On the morning of Mr. Madison's inauguration Mr. Madison asked Mr. Jefferson to ride to the capitol with him. Mr. Jefferson declined because he did not wish to divide the honors of the day. He followed at the rear of Mr. Madison's procession along Pennsylvania Avenue to the Capitol on horseback unattended. Arriving at the Capitol he dismounted, hitched his own horse to a post; and followed the multitude into the House of Representatives. A seat had been prepared for him next the new President. He declined.

JEFFERSON   Today I return to the people. My seat is with them.

II .. States Rights &
a Lady's Virtue
• • ANDREW JACKSON
1829–1837

General Andrew Jackson, hero of the battle of New Orleans, the lone American ground victory in the war of 1812, should have become President in 1825, four years before he actually took office. That he did not was a decisive event both in his own life and the political life of the nation.

In the election of 1824 General Jackson, then a Senator from Tennessee, had both a majority of the popular vote and the lead in the electoral college with 99 votes. John Quincy Adams, Monroe's Secretary of State, came second with 84 votes, then William H. Crawford, heir of the Virginia Dynasty, with 41, finally Senator Henry Clay trailed with 37. Since no candidate had received over half the votes in the electoral college, the election was thrown into the House of Representatives.

The House voted by States, each State having one vote. There were 24 States then in the Union and the winning candidate needed a simple majority of States to win, 13 being the magic number. Each State's one vote was cast as the majority of that State's congressmen voted. Thus if Pennsylvania which had 26 Congressmen was divided 10 votes for Jackson, 9 for

Adams, and 7 for Crawford, Pennsylvania cast one vote for Jackson, period. Both people at large and shrewd political observers figured the election in the bag for Jackson. But as Congressmen and other politicians began gathering in Washington in December of 1824, and the vote trading and bribery began, strange rumors swept the Capital. Supporters of Henry Clay, the gambling, drinking, swearing Kentuckian, were meeting with John Quincy Adams, the cold, isolated New England puritan.

Was there a deal? No one can be certain. Even Adams' usually loquacious diary is silent on the subject. But several strange things happened. Clay's supporters who wanted almost to a man to vote for Jackson were prevailed upon by Clay to vote for Adams, at least on the first ballot. On becoming President, Adams made his ancient enemy, Clay, Secretary of State, the traditional stepping stone to the Presidency. And for his entire term of office Adams acted in an above-politics, holier-than-thou, manner; exactly like a New Englander with something on his conscience.

The Clay-Adams alliance was not the only strange circumstance in Adams' victory over Jackson. The vote of New York was split 17 for Adams, 17 for other candidates. This meant that New York would be unable to cast her vote. Even with Clay's states which would start swinging to Jackson after the first ballot, Adams still had only 12 states, one short.

The key man in the New York delegation was an elderly, millionaire fuddy-duddy pledged to Crawford, General Van Rensselaer. Van Rensselaer didn't like Adams, but his vote was so vital and he was such a milksop that Senator Martin Van Buren, boss of New York, who had given his word his state would not go for Adams, was living in the same hotel room with him.

However Van Buren made the mistake of leaving Van Rensselaer when they got to the Capitol February 9, 1825, the day of the ballot. Webster and Clay got Van Rensselaer aside and convinced him there might be a revolution if the President was not elected on the first ballot. Still, the General didn't like Adams and had given his word. When the ballot box was passed to him, General Van Rensselaer dropped his head into his hands to pray for guidance before he voted. As he ended his prayer and took his hands from his eyes, feeling rather dizzy and faint, he saw at his feet a ballot bearing the name Adams. Being a pious man he voted God's way—at least Adams thought so. To the surprise of everyone New York went by one vote for Adams who, as a result, was elected on the first ballot —by 13 states.

Adams' cold, fussy manner, puritanical certainty and refusal to play politics made him an ineffective and unloved President. This was too bad. He was a brilliant, dedicated man. In the hard, second sight of history most of what he tried to do—from building roads and canals, through electoral and fiscal reform, to building a national science academy—turns out to have been wise. The tombstone he composed for his father shows grief and passion. It reads: "Beneath are deposited the mortal remains of John Adams, son of John and Susanna (Boylston) Adams, Second President of the United States. Born 19 October, 1735. On the Fourth of July 1776, he pledged his Life, Fortune, and sacred Honor to the INDEPENDENCE OF HIS COUNTRY.

"On the third of September, 1783, he affixed his seal to the definitive treaty with Great Britain, which acknowledged that independence and consummated the redemption of his pledge. On the Fourth of July, 1826, he was summoned to the Independence of Immortality, and to the JUDGMENT OF HIS GOD. This stone will bear witness to his piety; this town, his birthplace, to his munificence; history to his patriotism; posterity to the depth and compass of his mind."

I rather like the fact that he was summoned to the judgment of his God. Not your God, or my God, or John Smith's God; but his God. The Adamses were always rather sure about God. However, moral rectitude and good intentions can neither

run a country nor arrange a re-election. Man cannot live by the
word of God alone, and John Quincy Adams doled out little
bread. Four years later, in 1829, General Jackson was overwhelmingly elected President.

But those four years had been harsh for Jackson and
America. The General felt he had been cheated of the Presidency. He brooded and became bitter. The country, suspect-
ing a crooked deal between Clay and Adams, grew sullen and
divided. The campaign of 1824 had been just an ordinary two-
fisted, All-American mud slinger. The campaign of 1828 was
one of the two or three foulest in U.S. history. Leaflets were
circulated that denounced Jackson as a murderer, wife stealer,
looter, lecher, adulterer, and thief. Many of the attacks stressed
that Jackson and his wife had lived together, 40 years before,
while her divorce was not yet final. This type of violent attack
helped cause the death of his wife. The Jackson who finally
reached the Presidency was a vindictive, acid man, in bad
health; but a man whom the country loved.

While President, power appears to have changed Andrew
Jackson about as little as any man. Why? His own internal,
personal power was such, and his temper and temperament
were so strong, that the outside influences of power stopped
before him as if they had run head first into a steel wall. Jackson personified force. He supressed insurrection and secession, broke up the Bank of the United States which was a vast
autonomous powerhouse, developed the patronage system,
greatly increased the power of the Presidency while preaching
restricted Federal Government (like Jefferson he didn't see
the inconsistency), survived censure by Congress, collected
debts from France outstanding since her Revolution, was overwhelmingly re-elected in 1833, and in 1837 arranged to be followed as President by his personal choice, Martin Van Buren.
Yet "Old Hickory," this man of iron, who could put down the
threat of civil war with his left hand, was unable to control
his personal friends and was at the complete mercy of the
anger and intrigues of a woman. He could ride herd on Amer-

ica easily but was torn in two and almost let the country be torn in two by Peggy Eaton.

The Peggy Eaton affair and States Rights and Southern Secession are so woven together·as to be the same story and the same cloth. John C. Calhoun, South Carolina Senator and champion of States Rights, had become Vice President on the Jackson ticket. Through pressure he had been able to get three of his followers into the Cabinet. President Jackson, from Tennessee, appeared to be a States Rights man. Would he support Calhoun?

But the aristocratic Calhoun and his wife were snubbing Peggy Eaton, wife of Jackson's close friend Major Eaton whom he had made Secretary of War. However, Secretary of State Van Buren was championing Mrs. Eaton's cause as a method of destroying the power of Calhoun in the Administration. The force with which Jackson met the demands for more States Rights turned partly on his feelings for Calhoun. And these feelings turned on the Eaton affair.

General Jackson was a passionate man. This fact worried Thomas Jefferson who recorded his views on the man to be linked with him in history as co-founder of the Democratic Party.

JEFFERSON   I feel much alarmed at the prospect of seeing General Jackson President. He is one of the most unfit men I know of for such a place. He has had very little respect for laws or constitutions, and is in fact, an able military chief, nothing more. His passions are terrible.

When I was President of the Senate he was a Senator; and he could never speak on account of the rashness of his feelings. I have seen him attempt it repeatedly; and as often choke with rage. His passions are no doubt cooler now; he has been much tried since I knew him. But he is a dangerous man.

• Now that Andrew Jackson was President-elect, the doings of his friends were hot political gossip. Jefferson's hostess,

Mrs. Smith, still writing, records the first rumblings of the Eaton affair. What would historians do without her?

MRS. SMITH   Tonight Major Eaton, the bosom friend and almost adopted son of General Jackson is to be married to a lady whose reputation, her previous connection with him both before her husband's death and after, has totally destroyed. She is the daughter of O'Neil who kept a large tavern and boarding house. She has never been admitted into good society, is very handsome, of uninspiring character, silly and with a violent temper. She is, it is said, irresistible and carries whatever point she sets her mind on. The General's friends are very much disturbed.

PEGGY EATON   I never had a lover who was not a gentleman and who was not in a good position in society. My father was a right active tavern keeper; and no low, mean man ever dared from earliest childhood to intrude himself on me.

When Andrew Jackson advised John Eaton to marry me forthwith his own dear wife was dying inch by inch. And in less than a month before our marriage the political opponents of her husband had hunted that poor woman into the grave and embittered all the remainder of Andrew Jackson's life. He seemed to feel that every woman needed a defender. That's what he meant about me. This great old hater believed in my virtue as he believed in the virtue of his own wife.

• *Calmly, in his diary John Quincy Adams records his last days in office and the total breakup of his friendship with Jackson. Once they had been close. Adams had been the only member of Monroe's Cabinet to defend the General when a rash military action of his alarmed the British. Before he became a candidate in 1824, Jackson had supported Adams for the Presidency.*

J. Q. ADAMS   The President elect has arrived in this city and taken lodgings at Gadsby's hotel. Mrs. Jackson having died in December the General has signified his wish to avoid all displays of festivity or rejoicing and all magnificent parades.—He has not thought proper to hold any personal communication with me since his arrival.

MRS. SMITH   Oh what a gloom is cast over the triumph of General Jackson by the death of a wife fondly and excessively loved. Of a wife who could control the violence of his temper. It is said that she not only made him a happier but a better man. I fear not only the domestic circle but the public will suffer from this restraining and benign influence being withdrawn.

A similar case will occur to your mind perhaps in recollecting the history of Greece. It was Themistocles (I believe) who said: "My little son governs his mother, his mother governs me, I govern Athens, Athens governs Greece, Greece governs the world. So my boy governs the world."

JACKSON   I know 'tis unmanly to cry. But these tears are due her virtues. She has shed many for me. In memory of this dear saint, I can and do forgive all my enemies. But those vile wretches who have slandered her must look to God for mercy. The Almighty forgive her murderers, I never can.

J. Q. ADAMS   Consulted the members of my administrations whether I should attend the inauguration tomorrow. All were against it except Mr. Rush. About nine in the evening I left the President's house, and, with my son John and T. B. Adams, Jr., came out and joined the family at Meridian Hill.

• Adams walked glumly out of the White House and the next day, March 4th, 1829, the "Jackson Age" officially began.

MRS. SMITH   A national salute was fired early in the morning and ushered in the inauguration. But we did not go to the President's house 'til late when the crowd had lessened. Oh what a scene did we witness. The majesty of the people had disappeared and a rabble, a mob, of boys, Negroes, women, children, scrambling, fighting, romping. What a pity, what a pity. No arrangements had been made, no police officers placed on duty and the whole house had been inundated by the rabble mob.

The President after having literally been nearly pressed to death and almost suffocated had retreated out a back way and escaped to his lodgings at Gadsby's. Cut glass and china to the amount of several thousand dollars had been broken in the struggle and punch and other articles carried off in buckets. Ladies fainted, men were seen with bloody noses—those who got in could not get out by the door again but had to scramble out through the windows.

The noisy and disorderly rabble brought to my mind descriptions I had read of the mobs in the Tuilleries and at Versailles. But it was the People's day and the People's President and the People would rule.

• *In broken health and despondent over the death of his wife, Jackson began his term with unaccustomed lassitude. Hordes of office seekers pestered him for jobs, some supported by Van Buren others by Calhoun. Almost immediately the Peggy Eaton affair began.*

J. Q. ADAMS   Mr. Rush visited me and spoke about the President's message against the bank, the removals from office, and about Mrs. Peggy Eaton the wife of the Secretary of War, now the center of much political controversy and intrigue. Mrs. Eaton was the wife of a purser in the Navy named Timberlake. He being on service with the Mediterranean squadron, his wife lived with her father who ran a boarding house and tavern. General Jackson and Mr. Eaton were lodgers there.

When O'Neal's tavern failed and his house was sold it was purchased by Mr. Eaton. About a year and a half ago Timberlake died and very shortly after Eaton married his widow. He had lived with her openly during the life of her former husband whose death has been generally attributed to his dishonor. Calhoun, and three of Jackson's Cabinet members would not permit the females of their families to associate with Mr. Eaton's wife. And even Mrs. Donaldson wife to Jackson's private secretary has refused to visit her. Mr. Van Buren being a widower has become the champion for Eaton's wife. The President has taken up her cause as his own. The state of things is equally disgusting and ludicrous.

JACKSON   I know the reasons for their lies. It is a plot by Clay and Calhoun to separate Eaton and me. But by the eternal they shall not do it.

PEGGY EATON   It was the designs of politics that led to the slander of my fair frame; and not any frailty of mine that came in as an element to change the political history of the country.

• *Politics helped; but Peggy Eaton had run away with two men by the time she was 16. Though as she later explained these were but innocent larks. As for the other stories?*

Between pressure to remove Eaton, South Carolina's mounting threats to rebel against the new Federal Tariff, the press of office seekers, and the feud between Van Buren and Calhoun, Jackson was being sorely tried.

JACKSON   Am I to have no peace this side of the grave? All around me are troubles. People clamoring for a public tit from which to suck the treasury. Would you believe it, today, a lady who had once rolled in wealth and is an applicant for office and well recommended came in to see me destitute. To buy a morsel of bread to feed her children she had had to sell her thimble the day before. An office I had not to give and my cash was nearly out; but I could not withhold from her half the pittance I had with me. How I wish myself at the Hermitage to spend the remnant of my days beside the tomb of my beloved wife.

J. Q. ADAMS   The removals from office are continuing with great perseverance. The customs houses in Boston, New York and Philadelphia have been swept clear, also at Portsmouth and New Orleans. The new appointments are exclusively of violent partisans. Every editor of a slanderous newspaper is provided for.

JACKSON   In a country where offices are created solely for benefit of the people no one man has any intrinsic right to official station. Offices were not established to give support to particular men at public expense. The duties of all public offices are, or at least admit of being made, so plain and simple that men of intelligence may readily qualify themselves for their performance. No individual wrong is therefore done by removal.

• During Monroe's term as President, Jackson had written him a violent letter denouncing Monroe for giving out public jobs for reasons of party rather than merit. One of Jackson's private secretaries questioned him about the letter, asking: "About the letter you wrote to President Monroe, that politics should not influence appointments. How do you reconcile that doctrine with the conduct, sir, of your administration?"

Jackson replied quietly to the young man. "We are never too old to learn."

Finally the army of job seekers quit Washington. The Federal Government began to function again. And the President could give his total attention to the Eaton affair and South Carolina's attempt to lead the Southern States out of the Union.

Vice-President Calhoun, the South's chief spokesman, was no caricature southern politician but a brilliant intense dreamer whose own theories finally made him their captive. The ostensible issue between the North and South that was under debate was not yet slavery but the degree of force the Federal Government might employ to collect tariffs and so, by extension, to enforce any other law of which the States did not approve.

CALHOUN   I rise today to speak on the President's force bill. It has been called, here in this Senate it has been called, a measure of peace. Peace! Such peace as the wolf gives to the lamb—the kite to the dove—Russia gives Poland—or death its victim! A peace that comes by aweing a State into the abandonment of the exercise of every power which constitutes her a sovereign community.

It is to South Carolina a question of self preservation. And I proclaim it, should this bill pass, and an attempt be made to enforce it, it will be resisted at every hazard—even that of death itself. Death is not the greatest calamity. There are others still more terrible to the free and the brave. There is the loss of liberty and honor.

But Calhoun was too bright not to recognize the true divisions in the nation, and fanatic enough to admit it.

CALHOUN   The tariff and this bill are the occasion rather than the cause of the unhappy state of things. The truth can no longer be disguised that the peculiar domestic institutions of the southern states, and their soil, their climate and their industry has placed them in regard to taxation and appropriations in opposition to the majority of the Union. If there be no protective power against this danger in the reserved rights of States, the Southern States must in the end be forced to rebel or submit to having their interests sacrificed.

Jackson   They are trying to grind me. They are trying to grind me. Let them try.

• *From the other flank, Mrs. Smith recorded the sounds of the social battle.*

Mrs. Smith   As for the new lady what gossip, what prophesyings and apprehensions, what tittle-tattle.

A stand, a noble stand, I may say, has been made by the ladies of Washington; and not even the President's wishes can influence them to violate the respect due to virtue and visit one who has left her straight and narrow path. With the exception of two or three timid and insignificant personages, who trembled for their husbands' offices, not a lady has visited her; and far from being inducted into the President's house, she is, I am told, scarcely noted by the females of his family.

On three public occasions when she ventured out she was left alone and kept at a respectable distance by all virtuous and distinguished women. At the supper table, notwithstanding her proximity, she was not spoken to by them. These are facts you may rely on. Not rumors, facts, greatly to the honor of our sex.

J. Q. ADAMS   Three of his Cabinet have given large evening parties to which Mrs. Eaton is not invited. On the other hand the President makes her doubly conspicuous by an over display of notice.

At the last drawing room the night before last she had a crowd gathered about her. But Mrs. Donaldson, wife to the President's private secretary who lives at the President's house held no conversation with her. The administration is split into a blue and green faction upon this point of morals. Vice President Calhoun heads the moral party, Van Buren that of the frail sisterhood. He is notoriously engaged in lobbying for the Presidency by paying his court to Mrs. Eaton. Up to now the explosion has been deferred.

JACKSON   Having been informed by several members of Congress that there was a combination entered into by Ingham, Branch and Berrien, three members of my Cabinet to drive Major Eaton and his family out of society and by that meant to coerce me to dismiss him as Secretary of War, I sent and had a personal interview with those three gentlemen. I read to them from a paper in my own hand what I had heard, and told them if it was true I would hold them answerable to me.*

The Gentlemen replied that they would be the last man to do any act to injure the feelings or character of Major Eaton

* Jackson was saying, in a polite way, the President of the United States might challenge them to a duel.

and his family, that the parties given had no such thing in view, that they could not undertake to control their families, et cetera, et cetera, et cetera.

I protested against any such wish to control their social intercourse; but observed, that as they had disavowed any intention to wound the feelings of Major Eaton et cetera, et cetera, et cetera, I was bound to believe them—but the rumor had gone forth and it was believed by part of the community. Hereafter they might conduct themselves to maintain harmony in the Cabinet. For I had again to repeat that having brought Major Eaton into my Cabinet I would not part with him; and any attempt to degrade him I viewed, and should continue to view, as an indignity against myself.

• *The Eaton affair was now thoroughly entwined with politics. The Virginia legislature called for Eaton's resignation, saying "This game is too insignificant for a president." A group of Congressmen sent Jackson a petition that "Eaton must go or a hundred Congressmen go home unsatisfied." Jackson received the petition and thundered, "Let them come, let the whole hundred come. I would resign the Presidency sooner than desert my friend Eaton."*

Henry Clay, Adams' ex-secretary of State, back to being a leader in the Senate, also took up the anti-Jackson chant. He did this more to be against the President than from any passionate conviction in States Rights. When he made the following speech he was dressed all in black and even wore black gloves.

CLAY The eyes and hopes of the American people are anxiously turned to Congress. They feel they have been deceived and insulted; their confidence abused, their interests betrayed, and their liberties endangered. They see a rapid concentration of power in one man's hands.

The question is no longer what laws will Congress pass, but what will the executive not veto. We behold the usual incidents of approaching tyranny. The land is filled with spies and informers. People, especially officials, no longer dare speak

in the fearless tones of free men, but in the cautious whispers
of trembling slaves.

The symptoms of despotism are upon us; and if Congress
does not apply an instant and effective remedy the fatal collapse will soon come and we shall die—ignobly die, base, mean,
abject slaves—the scorn and contempt of mankind—unpitied,
unwept, unmourned.

CALHOUN   The South has been on the defensive throughout and borne for a long series of years indignities and encroachments on its rights and safety with a patience unex-
ampled. Yet she is basely charged with disunion and the north
is lauded as Union's advocate. We must learn to disregard
such unfounded and unjust charges; and manfully do our duty
to save the Union and ourselves if we can; and if not, save
ourselves. In doing so we would but follow the example of our
Washington in the great struggle which severed the Union
between the colonies and the mother country.

ADAMS   March 7. Mr. Calhoun's speech of 15th February,
upon the Enforcement bill, is published in the Telegraph. It
contains his system of nullification. His learning is shallow, his
mind argumentative, and his assumption of principle destitute of discernment. His insanity begins with his principles,
from which his deductions are ingeniously drawn.

• Time and again Jackson thought he had the Eaton affair
permanently solved. He wrote his close personal friend, General John Coffee:

JACKSON   Dear John—If you see any of those presently
slandering Mrs. Eaton you are at full liberty to show them
this letter. Major Eaton is now popular and will become one of
the most popular of all the heads of departments. Indeed I
am highly pleased with my Cabinet, they are able, amiable men
and the greatest harmony prevails.

Now I do know the originators of the falsehood about
Mrs. Eaton. They are the base satellites of Clay and Calhoun.

Their slanders are recoiling on their heads. The cloud is blowing over, although it has cost me some pangs. The world was mistaken in me. The attempt was made to induce me to abandon my friend, it failed. I would sink with honor in the grave before I would abandon my friend Eaton.

PEGGY EATON   All this terrible stew was kept up for more than a year. And I was made the unhappy occasion of breaking up harmony in the Cabinet. I never tried to make the Gentlemen of the Cabinet disagree. I knew nothing except from time to time as I wrung it out of Major Eaton or General Jackson.

General Jackson believed I was an uncommonly smart woman. He believed I was good—notwithstanding my freaks of temper. And then he believed I was persecuted.—I could fill a book with instances of his tenderness toward me.

I'll tell just one. It was in the midst of these Cabinet troubles that I projected a visit to relatives of my sister Mary, whose marriage had made her connected with many of the best families in Virginia. My horses were rather light for my fine carriage. Then my mother and my many servants, all with their baggage. . . .

• *Peggy Eaton then goes on to tell at great length how President Jackson lent her his own fine horses so she could visit her fine relatives in her fine carriage. When Peggy Eaton talked or wrote about her relatives or her possessions or her virtue she never tired of fulsome detail. Meanwhile the Eaton affair was reaching a climax at which the whole Cabinet would meet to formally consider Mrs. Eaton's virtue.*

JACKSON   Memorandum for the record. Be it remembered that last Tuesday evening I was in my parlour when the doorkeeper came in and informed me that my clergyman, the Reverend Campbell, wanted an interview with me. The Reverend Campbell then entered and detailed the information derived from a dead doctor, whom he called by the name of Craven, upon the subject of a miscarriage of Mrs. Timberlake, now Mrs. Eaton, in the absence of her husband under circumstances that made it manifest the child could not be his. I was astonished that this Presbyterian clergyman gave currency to this vile tale.

I inquired of him what date the dead doctor had given to this transaction, the date being important. He replied 1821. I asked him if he was aware of the situation he would be placed in, if on inquiry it should appear that Mr. Timberlake was in this country and never out of it in 1821.

I at once determined to make inquiry as to where Mr. Timberlake was in 1821. I accordingly went up to Major Eaton's. I asked Mrs. Eaton if she had the mercantile books of Mr. Timberlake. She said she had. I soon found from entries in the handwriting of Timberlake that he was in this country and in this city throughout 1821.

• *Martin Van Buren, "the little Magician," had been supporting Eaton and getting in with General Jackson. A windy fussbudget, Secretary of State, and master politician from upstate New York, Van Buren plucked at Jackson's feelings as an angel plucks a harp. With each new crisis in the Eaton affair, he became more intimate with the President.*

VAN BUREN   I would rather pull a tooth than say a word upon the Eaton subject. I have such a strong aversion to gossip that it is well known no one in this city hates it more. However, none is better advised upon the Eaton affair than I. Last Saturday I received a summons to attend at the President's house in the evening on business. On arrival I found there the whole Cabinet, except Major Eaton, and the President's minister, Reverend Campbell. The President then read his correspondence with Reverend Campbell and a protocol of his conversations with him.

JACKSON   Campbell acknowledged to me in the presence of my Cabinet, Mr. Van Buren, Mr. Ingham, Mr. Barry, Mr. Branch and Mr. Berrien that he entirely acquitted Major Eaton of the charge of improper or criminal conduct. Why this persecution of Mr. Eaton? I leave that to the decision of the moral and Christian world.

VAN BUREN He quit Mr. Campbell's church because he said the Reverend had not acted like a Christian and his preaching would be lost upon him. A quarrel between Eaton and Branch, from the supposition on the part of Eaton that Branch had not used Mrs. Eaton properly, was threatened. Also a duel. All the agency I have taken in the matter has been to prevent violence. The President has since that time talked freely and confidentially with me. He feels deeply for Eaton for the gossip continues.

• *But Major Eaton and his wife were becoming a liability to the whole Administration. Van Buren hit on a plan whereby putting his foot firmly on Eaton's neck he could vault into the Presidency. Van Buren's scheme was that he, Van Buren, would resign as Secretary of State. This would induce Eaton to resign and Jackson would then be politically free to reconstitute his whole Cabinet, ridding himself of the three Calhoun supporters: Berrien, Branch and Ingham.*

VAN BUREN A fit occasion to break the matter of my resignation as Secretary of State was only waited for and I looked to find one during one of my frequent rides with the General. Several, however, occurred without my having had the heart to broach the subject. My hesitation arose from my apprehension of the pain the communication would give him.

After passing Georgetown one day I missed one of my gloves; and begging him to go on, I returned to look for it. After finding it and putting my horse to a gallop to overtake my companion, I resolved I would open the subject forthwith. We were just turning off the Potomac Road and he was expressing a more cheerful view of our domestic broils:

"We shall soon have peace in Israel."

"No, General, there is just one thing can give you peace."

"What is that, sir?"

"My resignation."

"Never, Sir! By the Eternal! You know little of Andrew Jackson if you suppose him capable of consenting to such a humiliation of his friends by his enemies."

I was myself not a little confused by the vehemence of his exclamation, but after a few moments of silence to compose my thoughts I returned to the subject. I proceeded for four hours and we did not reach home 'til long after our usual dinner hour. He heard me through not only with patience but with deep interest. In return he asked me what were my views as to the future if he should accept my resignation. Ambassador to England was spoken of as probably the best.

—When I called at the White House the following day my mind was not free from serious misgivings. I had no sooner entered his room than I saw confirmation of my apprehensions in the usual signs of a sleepless night. He regarded me with an expression cold, formal and passionless, and said,

"Mr. Van Buren, I have made it a rule in life never to throw obstacles in the way of any man who desires to leave me. I shall not make your case an exception."

Without giving him time to say more I rose from my chair and standing directly before him, replied the matter had taken the turn I most feared. I ended by saying: "Now, sir, let me end General, that come what may I shall not leave your Cabinet until you shall say of your own motion without reference to any feeling of mine, 'It is best for us to part.' Feeling that I have now performed my whole duty I shall stay with pleasure." The President replied:

"Forgive me, friend, I have been too hasty. I know I have. Come back at one o'clock. We'll take another long ride and talk again in a better state of mind."

On the hour appointed we went again over the whole subject. On our return, he asked my permission to consult with Postmaster General Barry and Major Eaton. On the following day he told me that they had all considered the matter together and had come to the conclusion that I was right. They were to be with him that evening and he wished me to join them. After an hour or two with the President, the two adjourned to my house for supper.

Up to this time the idea of Eaton's resignation had not been thought of by anyone. It was a consummation devoutly to be wished but one I would have assumed to be hopeless. On the way to my house Eaton stopped and addressed us in these words. "Gentlemen this is all wrong. I am the man about whom all the trouble has been made. I, therefore, am the one that ought to resign." At supper he spoke of this again.

I excused myself from not having noticed his previous intimations on the grounds that his resignation had not been thought of. I said he must permit me to ask: What would Mrs. Eaton think? He answered promptly that he knew she would highly approve of it. At my suggestion we arranged to meet again at supper at my house the next evening. Major Eaton should in the meantime talk the matter over with his wife and report. His report fully confirmed his statement. It was forthwith agreed that we should both resign, with General Jackson's consent, which was obtained the following day.

JACKSON My dear General Coffee, you will see from the papers that I am engaged in reorganizing my Cabinet. The secret working of Clay, Calhoun and Co. is clearly developed. They believed I would not part from Van Buren and Eaton and that if I removed Ingham, the Secretary of the Treasury, it would arouse the whole state of Pennsylvania against me.

How little do they know me. And judging others by themselves, they could not believe that so much disinterested patriotism would dwell in the breasts of Van Buren and Eaton that they would resign office. They found themselves mistaken and by that one move on the political chessboard their coalition is checkmated. It has placed me in a situation to change my Cabinet and bring in men over whom the intrigues of Calhoun can have no influence.

J. Q. ADAMS   There is scarcely any other topic of conversation than the recent breaking up of the President's Cabinet. His correspondence with each of his ex-secretaries has been given out—one each day. Those of Van Buren and Eaton were published first. That with Ingham on Friday and that with Branch on Saturday. The letters of the last two were apparently written by Jackson himself; and they afford matter for much amusement. Ingham and Branch were not inclined to resign; and he was not willing to appear as having requested them to resign. He puts it upon the ground that his Cabinet was a unit, which has come together in great harmony, and, as two individuals of the unit had voluntarily withdrawn, he thought it necessary to reorganize the whole Cabinet.

JACKSON   This act of disinterested patriotism of Van Buren and Eaton must be long remembered by a grateful country. I now know both Van Buren and Calhoun. The first I know to be a pure Republican who has labored with an eye singly to promote the best interests of his country. Whilst the other, actuated alone by selfish ambition has secretly employed all his talents in intrigue and deception to disgrace my administration.

VAN BUREN   Sometime after our resignations were published, long enough to make Mrs. Eaton sensible to the change in her position, the President and myself paid her a visit. Our reception was formal and cold and what greatly surprised me was that the larger share of the chilling fell to the General. We soon quitted the house and I said to my companion: "There has been some mistake here." But I was satisfied we had stayed long enough to convince him that in his past anxiety over Mrs. Eaton he had at least overrated her sensibilities.

● *"The little Magician" had worked his most successful spell. The Eaton crisis had passed, though repercussions lingered for a time. Eaton challenged Berrien, Branch and*

Ingham to duel. They all hired bodyguards and declined. Then Eaton got a rifle and tried to bushwack Branch, but Branch was warned and left Washington. The Eatons were soon to follow.

MRS. SMITH   Mrs. Eaton cannot be forced or persuaded to leave Washington. Her triumph, for so she calls the dissolution of the Cabinet, her triumph she says is not yet complete. All her adversaries are not yet turned out of office and she must be received into society. She hopes and believes that next winter the new Cabinet ministers will open their doors to her. The truth is that in order to avoid this dilemma they are determined not to keep house or bring their families. Still it is hoped that she will soon leave town.

• Now safely Ambassador to England, Martin Van Buren continued to profess friendship for Eaton and advise the President.

VAN BUREN   I have derived the greatest satisfaction from your account of the state of Major Eaton's feelings and of the honors done him by those who know him best. The cruel and unmerited sufferings to which he has been exposed give him the strongest claim upon the public favor; and I have no doubt that in the end, the debt, which is so justly due him will be fully paid. I feel the office of Spanish ambassador excellent for him. Remember me affectionately to him and Mrs. Eaton when you write him and tell him it would give me sincere pleasure to hear from him.

• (Five years later, in the first week of his own administration, President Van Buren fired Major Eaton as Ambassador to Spain. And when Eaton came back in a rage, Van Buren was able to convince the Major he'd been relieved for his own good.)

The nullification crisis—could a state nullify, declare not binding on itself, a Federal law the state government didn't *like—now reached white heat. But the Southerners were faced with a new Jackson. Having brought peace to himself and the Cabinet he could turn all his energy toward thwarting his arch-enemy Calhoun.*

CALHOUN   This right of interposition be it called what it may, States rights, veto, nullification, or by any other name, I conceive to be the fundamental principle of our system, resting on facts historically as certain as our revolution itself. This is a political and moral truth; and I solemnly believe it to be the solid foundation of our system and of the Union itself.

JACKSON   Tell the nullifiers from me that they can talk and write and pass resolutions to their hearts' content. But if one drop of blood be shed in South Carolina in defiance of the laws of the United States, I will hang the first man of them I can get my hands on to the first tree I can find.

I repeat to the Union men, fear not. The union will be preserved. It is very late and my eyes grow dim. Keep me well advised. I keep no copy nor have I time to correct this letter. In haste. . . .

CALHOUN   No government based on the naked principle that the majority ought to rule can preserve its liberty even for a single generation. If the present usurpations continue it is the sacred duty of a State to nullify, to interpose—a duty to herself, to the Union, to present and future generations and to the cause of liberty throughout the world.

The rights of States is the remedy which the Constitution has provided to prevent encroachments by the Central Government. In them effective protection is afforded the minority against the oppression of the majority.

● *Earlier, to try and get the President on their side the Southerners had arranged a public Washington banquet to honor the beloved memory of Thomas Jefferson. Selections from Jefferson's writings were to be used in a series of pre-*

pared toasts to show that Jefferson historically was in favor of nullification. Afterwards the President was to be given an opportunity to make a toast himself and the Southerners hoped the surprised Jackson would commit himself to their cause.

They reckoned without both the temperament of Jackson and the wiles of Van Buren who was then still in town, and had a spy on the arrangements committee. The President was warned. After the prepared toasts lauding both Jefferson and States Rights, Jackson rose with his glass in his hand. Glaring directly at Calhoun he offered: "Our Union, it must be preserved."

The guests rose to drink. Calhoun's hand trembled so, he spilled some of his wine. Then after the guests had sat down Calhoun rose to offer his own toast. "Our Union, next to our liberty most dear."

The issue was joined. The State of South Carolina called a convention which declared that the tariff acts were "null and void" and not binding on South Carolina. Jackson cracked back with a proclamation from whose every sentence Presidential power explodes.

JACKSON   Whereas a convention assembled in the State of South Carolina has passed an ordinance by which they declare: "That the several acts of the Congress of the United States purporting to be laws for the imposing of duties and imposts on the importation of foreign commodities are unauthorized by the Constitution of the United States and are null and void and are no law." Whereas this said ordinance prescribes to the people of South Carolina a course of conduct in direct violation of their duty as citizens of the United States—Now, therefore I, Andrew Jackson, President of the United States, to preserve the bounds of our political existence from destruction, have thought proper to issue this my proclamation, declaring the course which duty shall require me to pursue.

I consider the power to annul a law of the United States

assumed by one State incompatible with the existence of the Union, contradicted expressly by the letter of the Constitution, unauthorized by its spirit, inconsistent with every principle on which it was founded and destructive of the great object for which it was formed. We are one people.

Fellow citizens of South Carolina, the laws of the United States must be executed. I have no discretionary power on that subject. My duty is emphatically proclaimed in the Constitution. Those who told you that you might peaceably prevent their execution deceived you; they could not have been deceived themselves. Their object is disunion. Disunion is treason. Are you really ready to incur its guilt? If you are, on the heads of the instigators of the act be the dreadful consequences, on their heads be the dishonor—but on yours may fall the punishment.

Fellow citizens of the United States, I rely with confidence on your undivided support in my determination to execute the laws and to preserve the Union. May the Great Ruler of Nations grant in His wise providence that those who have produced this crisis see their folly before they feel the misery of civil strife. Done in the year of the independence of the United States the fifty-seventh. Andrew Jackson. President.

• *But "Old Hickory" did more than just proclaim. For as his good friend Senator Benton remarked of him: "When Jackson begins to talk about hanging, people can begin to look for the ropes." Jackson began to organize the arming of a volunteer Army. He wrote the Secretary of War.*

JACKSON   We must be prepared for the crisis. The moment that we are informed that the legislature of South Carolina has passed laws to carry her rebellious ordinance into effect, which I suspect tomorrow, we must be prepared to act.

Tenders of service are coming to me daily; and from New York we can send to the Bay of Charlestown with steamers such numbers of troops as we may be pleased to order in four days. We will want three divisions of artillery each composed of nines, twelves and eighteen pounders. How many of these calibers are ready for field service? How many muskets with their complete equipments are ready for service? How many swords and pistols and what quantity of brass pieces for the field? As early tomorrow as possible I wish a report from the Ordinance Department on this subject.

• Jackson also moved politically to isolate South Carolina, forcing or cajoling the legislatures of other states to pass resolutions proclaiming their loyalty to the Union. He also promised an early revision of the tariff. Before such a vigorous use of Presidential power, South Carolina backed down.

CALHOUN Why do I waste my breath? I know it is all utterly vain. The day is gone; night approaches, and night is suitable to the despotism we have. There is a sort of destiny in this thing. All around us is melancholy evidence of a broken spirit ready to bow at the feet of power.

JACKSON There will be no bloodshed. I have in my study drawer a tender of one hundred and fifty thousand volunteers to aid me in the execution of the laws; and I have General Coffee to place at the head of a force to be called out in the west. When everything is ready I shall join them myself.

We shall cross the mountains into the upper part of South Carolina with a force, which, joined by the Union men of that State, will be so overwhelming as to render resistance hopeless. We will march through the State, seize the ringleaders, turn them over to the civil authorities and come home. You need not fear any bloodshed, gentlemen.

CALHOUN An action like this could never have been contemplated in the days of Pompey and Caesar and action like this could never have been perpetuated until the times of Caligula and Nero. What is left but to retire?

JACKSON   Nullification, the union of Calhoun and Clay, the South and the Southwest, supported by the corrupt and wicked of all parties, engages all my attention. The liberty of the people requires that wicked projects and evil combinations against the Government should be exposed and counteracted.

I met nullification at its threshold. My proclamation was well timed, as it at once opened the eyes of the people to the wicked designs of the nullifiers. The people investigated and saw that, although the tariff was made the ostensible object, a separation of the confederacy was the real purpose of the nullifiers.

Secession is, I think, for the present effectively and I hope forever put down. I thought I would have to hang some of them. And I would have done it.

• *At the end of his second term President Jackson took a trip to Massachusetts. Jackson had never been popular in that state and had become less so after he broke up the Bank of the United States and vetoed bills for improving commerce. The aging Jackson's visit to Massachusetts gives a final view of his blend of charm and power.*

Ex-President John Quincy Adams was still railing against the President. Adams was now a brilliant, cantankerous congressman, one of the principal champions of Negro freedom. Jackson's escort in Boston was young John Quincy, a cousin of John Quincy Adams—the Adamses were sort of the Kennedys of their time. Quincy, a proper Bostonian whose father was President of Harvard, hadn't wanted to act as Jackson's escort. However, he was soon captivated by "Old Hickory."

JOHN QUINCY   On his arrival, General Jackson's illness kept him closely confined to his bed in Boston for two days. My family physician, Dr. Warren, twice had him bled.

The morning of Wednesday the 25th was chilly and overcast, not at all the sort of day for an invalid to encounter the fatigue of travel and reception. At ten o'clock, nevertheless, the President appeared and took his seat in the barouche and was greeted with the acclamations which will always be forthcoming when democratic sovereignty is seen embodied in flesh and blood. Very little flesh in this case, however, and only such a trifle of blood as the doctors had thought not worth appropriating.

J. Q. ADAMS   I believe much of his illness is politic—part of his own policy, to suit his convenience and pleasure. He is one of our tribe of great men who turn disease to commodity, like John Randolph who for forty years was always dying. Jackson ever since he became a mark of public attention has been doing the same thing. He is so ravenous of notoriety that he craves the sympathy for sickness as a portion of his glory.

He is now alternately giving out he has chronic diarrhea and making Warren bleed him for pleurisy. At the same time he mounts the monument at Bunker's Hill to hear a fulsome address and receive two cannon balls. Then rides post to Lynn, Marblehead and Salem, receiving collations, deputations and addresses at them all, in one and the same day. Four-fifths of his sickness is trickery and the other fifth mere fatigue.

JOHN QUINCY   The General was full of conversation and his eye brighter than ever as we drove to Cambridge to get that doctorate whose bestowal occasioned many qualms to the high tone friends of Harvard. To many excellent persons it seemed a degrading mummery to dub a man Doctor of Laws who was credited with caring for no laws whatever which conflicted with his personal will. John Quincy Adams was especially disturbed at this academic recognition of Jackson and asked my father who was then President of Harvard whether there was no way of avoiding it.

J. Q. ADAMS   Called from my garden by a visit from Mr. Quincy. He told me that he planned to address the President in Latin and confer upon him the degree of Doctor of Laws; and he intimated that I should receive an invitation to be present at these ceremonies. I said that the personal relations in which President Jackson had chosen to place himself with me were such that I could hold no intercourse of a friendly character with him. I could therefore not accept an invitation to attend upon this occasion. And independent of that, as myself an affectionate child of our Alma Mater, Harvard, I would not be present to witness her disgrace in conferring her highest honors upon a barbarian who could not write a sentence of grammar and could hardly spell his own name. Mr. Quincy was sensible how utterly unworthy of honors Jackson was but thought it necessary to follow precedent and treat him as his predecessor, Mr. Monroe had been treated.

JOHN QUINCY Jackson's appearance before that Cambridge audience instantly produced a toleration which quickly merged into something like admiration and respect. The name of Andrew Jackson was indeed one to frighten naughty children with. But the person who went by it wrought a mysterious charm upon young and old—even on Beacon Street.

• The exercises which took place in the Harvard chapel were in Latin. Jackson being awarded his degree with these words: "Andrew Jackson bonis literis atque omnibus generosi animi affectibus penitus imbutum Utriusque Legis tum Naturae et Gentium tum civilis Doctorem honoris causa creaverunt."

Some Harvard wag seeking to embarrass the President called out from the audience, "Say something in Latin Doctor Jackson." The well bred sons of Harvard laughed and a voice cried again. "Say something in Latin Doctor Jackson."

The old man pivoted with the help of his cane and walked toward the audience. "E pluribus unum, my friend! The sine qua non."

III .. Power Abhors a Vacuum

• • *JAMES BUCHANAN*
1857–1861

A mere 15 years after President Jackson, slavery had become a *sine qua non* more important than union. And no Jackson ruled to hold the Union together. The major political parties had tried to straddle the slavery issue. Sane heads had tried compromise. The period between Jackson and Lincoln is full of famous compromises, like the Kansas-Nebraska Act which led to "bloody Kansas," each one leaving everybody a little madder than before. Congressman John Quincy Adams, the ex-President, was so incensed over the "Texas compromise" he spoke for three weeks. He had planned to speak longer, perhaps his sitting down was part of the compromise. Texas, California, Oregon, Utah, Kansas, Nebraska: all the new territories raised the question would they be slave or free? Underground railways, abolitionist newspapers, southern oratory divided the country.

First, a sample of the opinion of the time. What men were saying.

PRESIDENT FILLMORE   It is deeply regretted that in several instances officers of the Government in attempting to execute

the law for the return of fugitive slaves have been openly resisted and defeated by lawless and violent mobs. I regard it as
my duty in these cases to give all aid legally in my power for
the enforcement of laws. The act of Congress for the return of
fugitive slaves is one required by the Constitution; and is
obligatory upon every citizen of the United States.

CONGRESSMAN TOMBS OF GEORGIA   Sir, I have as much
attachment to the Union of these States as any freeman ought
to have. I am ready to concede and sacrifice for it whatever a
just and honorable man ought to sacrifice—but I do not hesitate to avow before this House and Country in the presence
of the living God, that if by your legislation you seek to drive
us and our slaves from the territories of California and New
Mexico and to abolish slavery in this District of Columbia;
then I am for disunion. And if my physical courage be equal to
the maintenance of my convictions of right and duty, I will
devote all I am and all I have on earth to its consummation.

JOHN BROWN   I have always been delighted with the doctrine that all men are created equal; and to my mind it is
like the Saviour's command, "Thou shalt love thy neighbor
as thyself." For how can we do that unless our neighbor is
equal to ourself? That is the doctrine, sir; and rather than have
that fall in the world, or in these States, it would be better for
a whole generation to die a violent death. Better that the
Union, that heaven and earth pass away than that one jot
or one tittle of this be not fulfilled.

SENATOR THADDEUS STEVENS OF PENNSYLVANIA   You and I
are free, while we fasten iron chains and rivet manacles on four
million of our fellow men; tear their wives and children from
them; sell them and doom them to perpetual bondage. Are we
not then despots, despots such as history will brand and God
abhors? How often have these walls of Congress been profaned
and the North insulted by the insolent threat that if we legis-

late against Southern will it should be disregarded, resisted to extremity and the Union destroyed. You Southerners have intimidated Congress too long.

• As in all family battles, the division between North and South extended to the children. Alert Southerners noticed that most of the schoolbooks came from New England. They quickly moved to produce texts more suitable for southern children: such as these excerpts from the "Elements of Algebra" by D. H. Hill, "approved for use in Southern Schools."

"A Yankee mixes a certain number of wooden nutmegs which cost him one quarter cent apiece with a quantity of real nutmegs worth 4 cents apiece and sells the whole assortment for $44; and gains $3.75 by the fraud. How many wooden nutmegs were there?

"The Buena Vista battlefield is 6 1/2 miles from Saltillo. Two Massachusetts volunteers ran away from the battle at the same time. One ran half a mile faster than the other and reached Saltillo 5 minutes and 54 seconds sooner than the other. Required: their respective rates of travel."

By now James Buchanan had become President, the fourth in a line of weak executives (Taylor, Fillmore, Pierce). He was a tall imposing figure, something of a Beau Brummel, and a most eligible bachelor. Mrs. Roger Pryor, the wife of an Alabama Congressman, describes his actions at the crucial moment of South Carolina's secession.

MRS. PRYOR   Among our first cards this winter was an invitation to the marriage of Mr. Bouligny, Congressman from Louisiana, and Miss Parker, daughter of a wealthy Washington grocer. Upon arriving at the house I found President Buchanan seated in an arm chair at one end of the drawing room, and the guests ranging themselves on either side. I stood behind his chair and observed he had aged much since the summer.

He had had much to bear. Unable to please either party,

he had been battered by both. "The President is pale with fear," said General Cass. "He divides his time equally between praying and crying. Such an imbecile was never seen before," said another. A lead editorial in the New York Tribune suggested he might be insane. The President kept his seat and I stood behind him as one and another came forward to greet him. Presently he looked over his shoulder and said:

"Madam, do you suppose the house is on fire. That commotion in the hall."

"I will inquire, Mr. President." I went out the nearest door and there in the entrance hall I found Mr. Lawrence Keitt, Congressman from South Carolina. He was leaping in the air, shaking a paper over his head, and exclaiming: "Thank God. Thank God. Thank God."

"Mr. Keitt," I asked, "are you crazy? The President hears you. What's the matter?"

"We've seceded! We've seceded! South Carolina's seceded! Here's the telegram. It's like being let out of school. Ahhh-Ha!" He jumped some more. I returned and bending over Mr. Buchanan's chair said in a low voice:

"Mr. Keitt has a telegram. South Carolina has seceded from the Union." The President looked at me. Then falling back and grasping the arms of his chair, whispered:

"Madam, I beg you, have my carriage called."

• Though the idea of an independent Nation of South Carolina seems to us now to border on farce, that State's "Ordinance of Secession from the Federal Union" is a moving document. The men who wrote it, like the men who were to die for it, believed.

We the people of South Carolina, by our delegates in Convention assembled, appealing to the Supreme Judge of the World for the rectitude of our intentions, have solemnly declared that the Union heretofore existing between this State and the other States of North America is dissolved; and that the State of South Carolina has resumed her position among the nations of the world, as a separate and independent State; with full power to levy war, conclude peace, contract alliances, establish commerce, and do all other acts and things which independent States may of right do.

• *Neither Buchanan's State's Rights political beliefs nor his temperament fitted him to face this crisis. He begged Congress to act. He temporized.*

BUCHANAN The fact cannot be disguised that we are in the midst of a great revolution. Therefore I commend the problem to Congress as the only tribunal possessing the power to meet the existing emergency. To them exclusively belongs the power to declare war or to authorize the employment of military force; and they alone possess the power to remove grievances which might lead to war and to secure peace and union to this distracted country. On Congress and Congress alone rests the responsibility. . . .

In heaven's name someone do something. Time is a great conservative power. The Union must and shall be preserved— by all Constitutional means. . . . Let us pause at this momentous point and afford the people an opportunity for reflection.

• *By "opportunity for reflection" Buchanan meant hold a national election. But there was little reflection in the election of 1860. The Republicans, who nominated Lincoln, condemned both slavery in the new territories and border ruffians; but would leave the "peculiar institution" alone in the South. The Democratic party split in two on slavery. The Southern Democrats walked out when the convention would not endorse slavery for the territories and nominated John C. Breckinridge of Kentucky. The Northern Democrats, who were rather more tolerant of slavery than the Republicans, nominated Lincoln's famous debate rival, Stephen A. Douglas. Senator Bell of Tennessee was put up by the National*

Constitutional Union, a pleasant party of benevolent ostrichs that Lincoln had a great time twitting.

Though campaign slogans always simplify, they also indicate the mood of the election. The Lincoln forces campaigned around such vote-getters as: "Link on to Lincoln!," "Old Abe will fence the Union in!," "Vote yourself a farm!," "Let Liberty be National, Slavery Sectional!" To help Lincoln with the western vote, pretty girls would ride a wagon beneath a banner proclaiming: "We girls link to Lincoln as our fathers clayed to Clay."

The opposition campaigned beneath such diverse devices as "Go for Douglas. The Little Giant!," "Bell-Everett and the Union Forever!," "Union and States Rights—Breckinridge and Lane!" And their hecklers taunted Lincoln speakers with the chant: "Free love, Free Niggers and Free women!" The voters themselves, fed up with rival slogans, coined one of their own. "Lincoln and Hamlin say you shan't! Breckinridge and Lane say you shall! Douglas and Johnson say do as you please! And Bell and Everett say nothing!"

Lincoln's looks also came in for comment in the following Democratic song:

> Tell us Abe's a second Webster
>   Or, if better, Henry Clay;
> That he's full of gentle humor
>   Placid as a summer's day.
>
> Tell again about the rails-split;
>   Seven miles or more per day
> How each night he seeks his closet
>   There to kneel alone and pray!
>
> Any lie you tell, we'll swallow—
>   Swallow any kind of mixture
> But oh don't we beg and pray you,
>   Don't for God's sake show his picture!

• *But Lincoln was quite able to turn his looks to his own advantage. "Nobody," he said, "ever expected me to be President. In my poor, lean, lank face nobody has ever seen that any cabbages were sprouting." The Lincoln forces too had their songs forecasting victory.*

One Abr'am there was who lived out in the West.
Esteemed by his neighbors the wisest and best;
And you'll see, on a time, if you follow my ditty,
How he took a straight walk up to Washington city.

Our Abr'am trudged on to Washington straight,
And reached the White House through the Avenue gate,
Old Buck and his cronies (some chaps from the South)
Sat round the East room rather down in the mouth.

Old Abe seized the knocker and gave such a thump
Buck thought the state ship had run into a stump;
He trembled all over and turned deadly pale,
"That noise," said he, "must have been made with a rail."

The Cabinet, frightened, sat still in their seats,
While Abr'am impatient the rapping repeats;
"I hope it ain't Abe," said old Buck, pale and grey.
"If it is, boys, there'll be here the devil to pay."

At last, tho' reluctant, Buck opened the door,
And found a chap waiting, six feet three or four;
"I've come my fine fellow," said Abe to the ring,
"To give you fair notice to vacate next spring."

• *Lincoln won the election. In part, the Democratic party split elected him; but his own vote-getting appeal with labor was also a major factor. Between his victory and his inauguration Lincoln moved like the politician he was to conciliate the South. "I denounce the lawless invasion by armed force of the soil of any sovereign state," he said, "no matter under what pretext, as the gravest of crimes." This is a period that those* biographers and historians who want to make Lincoln into a melancholy saint have a hard time explaining. President Buchanan reflected Lincoln's desire to compromise.

BUCHANAN   There is no difference in this matter between President elect Lincoln and myself.

At the beginning of these unhappy troubles I determined that no act of my administration should increase the excitement in either section of the country. If the political conflict were to end in civil war it was my determined purpose not to furnish an excuse for it by any act of mine. Entertaining this conviction I have refrained even from sending reinforcements to Major Anderson who commands Fort Sumter in Charleston Harbor. . . .

If South Carolina takes Fort Sumter it were better for me that a millstone were tied about my neck and I were cast into the Potomac. . . .

I have asked South Carolina to promise not to touch the fort.

• *Buchanan was no Andrew Jackson. Nor would time stand still. Major Robert Anderson, in command at Sumter, wrote the President:*

ANDERSON   Your Excellency, I need not say how anxious I am—indeed, determined, so far as honor will permit—to avoid collision with the citizens of South Carolina. Nothing, however, will be better calculated to prevent bloodshed than our being found in such an attitude that it would be madness and folly to attack us. For that there is a definite determination to leave the Union and obtain possession of this fort is apparent to all.

BUCHANAN   I have considered this question. I have made up my mind. The interests of the country do not demand a reinforcement of the forces at Sumter. I do not believe that a present necessity exists for a resort to force. It's impossible for me to risk a collision of arms in Charleston harbor.

• There was the rub. Buchanan and Lincoln might briefly sound the same when they talked compromise; but Lincoln was going to find it possible to risk a conflict of arms to save the Union. Indeed Buchanan's place in history rests not on what he was or did; but on what he left Lincoln. As the pressure on him mounted during his last days in office, Buchanan was more and more reduced to plain dither. His correspondence for the period has a pathetic ring: "Oh how I hope for the preservation of the Union." "No surrender and no reinforcement, that's my policy." "We have met the enemy and we are theirs." "I don't even get time to say my prayers."

On the day of his quitting office he turned to Lincoln with heartfelt relief and said, "My dear sir, if you are as happy on entering the White House as I on leaving, you are a very happy man indeed."

To which Lincoln replied, "Mr. President, I cannot say I will enter into it with much pleasure."

Lincoln took his oath of office.

LINCOLN   I, Abraham Lincoln, do solemnly swear that I will faithfully execute the Office of President of the United States of America. And will to the best of my ability preserve, protect, and defend the Constitution thereof. So help me God.

• A few months before, Jefferson Davis had placed his hand on a Bible and sworn:

DAVIS   I, Jefferson Davis, do solemnly swear that I will faithfully execute the office of President of the Confederate States of America. And will to the best of my ability preserve, protect, and defend the Constitution thereof. So help me God.

• The house was divided. President Lincoln went forward to deliver his inaugural address. As he began to speak he had trouble holding both his notes and his top hat. Stephen Douglas, his rival in debate and for the Presidency, stepped

up to hold it for him, then stood by the President's side
nodding agreement with the speech. Later Douglas was to rally
his Democratic party behind Lincoln and hold the all important state of Illinois, in which his political strength was
greatest, for the Union. In defeat he was indeed a "little giant."

Lincoln's inaugural held out the hand of friendship to the
South and contained the famous husband and wife metaphor.

LINCOLN Fellow citizens of the United States, apprehension seems to exist among the people of the Southern States
that by the accession of a Republican administration their
property and their peace are to be endangered. There has
never been any cause for such apprehension. I do but quote
from one of my own speeches when I declare that: "I have no
purpose directly or indirectly to interfere with the institution
of slavery in the States where it exists."

In contemplation of Universal Law and of the Constitution, I hold that the Union of these States is perpetual. It follows from this that no State upon its own mere motion can
lawfully get out of the Union. I therefore consider that the
Union is unbroken; and to the extent of my ability I shall take
care, as the Constitution expressly enjoins me, that the laws of
the Union be executed in all States. But there will be no invasion, no using of force.

Physically speaking we cannot separate. A husband and
wife may divorce and go out of the presence and beyond the
reach of each other; but the different parts of the country
cannot do this. They cannot but remain face to face; and intercourse must continue between them. In your hands, my dis-
satisfied fellow countrymen, and not mine, is the momentous
issue of civil war. Think calmly and well upon this whole subject. Nothing valuable can be lost by taking time. The government will not assail you. You can have no conflict without
yourselves being the aggressors. I am loathe to close. We are
not enemies but friends. We must not be enemies. Though

passions may have strained, they must not break our bonds of affection.

BUCHANAN   Good, good, good speech. There is no difference between President Lincoln and myself.

DAVIS   All we ask is to be let alone.

• *Lincoln's Secretary of the Navy, Gideon Welles of Maine, kept a diary. Energetic, honest and intelligent, Welles was one of Lincoln's great finds as a Cabinet official. He deployed the Navy efficiently and promoted not on political pull but on merit. This made him highly unpopular with Congress but materially shortened the war.*

WELLES   A strange state of things existed at this time in Washington. The atmosphere was thick with treason. The President had been smuggled through Baltimore to his inauguration in disguise. Party spirit and old party differences prevailed amidst accumulating dangers. Secession was considered by most persons as a political question, not as rebellion. Democrats to a large extent sympathized with the rebels more than with the administration. Not that they wished secession to be successful and the Union divided; but they hoped that President Lincoln and the Republicans would prove failures.

• *Senator Saulsbury of Delaware, a Democrat, described the President: "I never did see or converse with so weak and imbecile a man; the weakest man I ever knew in high place. If I wanted to paint a despot, a man perfectly regardless of every constitutional right of the people, I would paint the hideous, apelike form of Abraham Lincoln."*

One of Lincoln's own Republicans, Senator Fessenden, who was later to be one of the "heroic seven" to vote against the impeachment of President Andrew Johnson, was complaining openly. "We went for a rail-splitter and we got one."

WELLES   The Republicans on the other hand were scarcely less partisan and unreasonable. Crowds of them with the civil war about to burst thronged the anterooms of the President clamorous for the removal of all Democrats immediately from office.

LINCOLN   This making up a Cabinet. If the twelve apostles were to be chosen today, Christ would have to be certain they came from different parts of Israel.

• *A friend found Lincoln stalking through the White House, an expression of intense gloom on his face. "What's wrong, Mr. President," the friend inquired, "bad news from Fort Sumter?"*

"No," the President replied, "it's the post office at Jonesville, Missouri."

On April Fool's Day, Secretary of State Seward, a politician from New York who was the most powerful man in the Cabinet, presented Lincoln with the following ultimatum. Seward was secretly offering Jefferson Davis major concessions to get the Southern states back into the Union. He believed a foreign war would help reunite the country.

SEWARD   Some thoughts for the President's personal consideration.

First. We are at the end of a month's administration, and yet without a policy, either domestic or foreign.

Second. This, however, is not culpable, and it has even been unavoidable. The presence of the Senate, with the need to meet applications for patronage, have prevented attention to other and more grave matters.

Third. But further delay to adopt and prosecute our policies for both domestic and foreign affairs would not only bring scandal on the Administration, but danger upon the country.

I propose:

Change the question before the public from one upon slavery or about slavery, to a question about Union or disunion. In other words, from what would be regarded as a party question, to one of Patriotism or Union.

I would demand satisfaction from Spain and France, categorically, at once.

I would seek satisfaction from Great Britain and Russia, send secret agents into Canada, Mexico, and Central America, to rouse a vigorous spirit of independence against all European powers. And, if satisfactory explanations are not received from Spain and France, would convene Congress and declare war against them.

But whatever policy we adopt, there must be an energetic prosecution of it. For this purpose it must be somebody's business to pursue and direct it incessantly. Either the President must do it himself, and be all the while active in it, or devolve it upon some member of his Cabinet. Once adopted, debates on it must end, and all agree and abide.

It is not in my special province.

But I neither seek to evade nor assume responsibility.

LINCOLN   Sinners are calling the righteous to repentance. No. What must be done I must do. . . .

From the President to the Secretary of War. Sir, I desire that an expedition to move by sea be got ready to sail as early as April 6th for the resupply of Major Anderson at Fort Sumter. And that you cooperate with the Secretary of the Navy for that object. . . .

To Major Anderson, Commander Fort Sumter, by secret messenger. Hold out if possible till the arrival of the expedition. It is not, however, my intention to subject your command to any danger or hardship beyond what, in your judgment would be usual in military life. Beyond that I am confident that you will act as becomes a patriot and soldier.—Whenever, if at all, in your judgment, to save yourself and command a capitulation becomes necessary, you are authorized to make it.

• *The South learned the relief expedition was on its way. Confederate guns shelled Sumter. Anderson surrendered.*

By the President of the United States a Proclamation.
—Whereas the laws of the United States have been for some
time past and are now opposed and the execution thereof ob-
structed in certain States by combinations too powerful to be
suppressed by the ordinary course of judicial proceedings. Now
therefore, I Abraham Lincoln, President of the United States,
in virtue of the power vested in me by the Constitution hereby
do call forth the militia of the several States of the Union to
an aggregate number of 75,000 in order to suppress said combinations and cause the laws to be duly executed.

I appeal to all loyal citizens to favor, facilitate and aid this
effort to maintain the honor, the integrity, and the existence of
our National Union and popular government; and to redress
wrongs already long enough endured.

• *Seventy-five thousand volunteers. Wars have a bad habit
of starting small. Four years later Union dead alone would
number over four and one-half times this first call for volunteers.*

IV .. Lincoln Finds Lincoln

• • ABRAHAM LINCOLN
1861–1865

Two wars at once will finish most countries or men. Lincoln fought four. Against the South; against his incompetent generals, he tried Scott, McDowell, McClellan twice, Halleck, Pope, Burnside, Hooker and Meade before Grant; against the Congress that tried to use the war to dominate him; and finally against his own chilling doubts of self-ability. In addition he had the usual problems of politics, his administration was almost repudiated in 1862; a wife, Mary, who was partially mad; and an idolized son who died. He won all outer battles. The inner one was ended for him.

The threads of these four wars shuttle back and forth through Lincoln's handling of power. Perhaps no one ever understood him quite as well as a hospital orderly in Washington who used to go out of his way to watch the President drive by. Even before history had measured Lincoln, some leap of insight had revealed the President to the poet, Walt Whitman.

WHITMAN The first battle of Bull Run was one of the most singular fights on record. All battles and their results are far more matters of chance than is generally thought; but this was thoroughly a chance. Each side supposed it had won until the last moment. One had, in point of fact, just the same right to be routed as the other. By a chance the Union forces at the last moment exploded in a panic and fled from the field. The defeated troops commenced pouring into Washington over the Long Bridge at daylight on Monday.

The sun rises but shines not. The men appear, at first sparsely and shame-faced enough, then thicker, in the streets of Washington. They come along in disorderly mobs, some in squads, stragglers, companies. During the forenoon Washington gets all over motley with these defeated soldiers—queer looking objects. They drop down anywhere, on the steps of houses, up close by fences, on sidewalks, aside in some vacant lot, and deeply sleep. And on them sulkily drops the rain.

The worst is not only imminent; but already here. In a few hours, perhaps before the next meal, the Southern Generals with their victorious hordes will be upon us. The dream of humanity, the vaunted Union—lo! it seems already smashed like a china plate.

But the hour, the day, the night passed; and whatever returns, an hour, a day, a night like that can never again return. The President begins that very night to reorganize his forces. He endured that hour, that day—indeed a crucifixion day—it did not conquer him.

Lincoln Memorandum to myself. 1) Let the plan for making the blockade effective be pushed forward with all possible dispatch. 2) Let the volunteer forces at Fort Monroe be constantly drilled, disciplined and instructed. 3) Let Baltimore be held as now, with a gentle but firm and certain hand. 4) Let the forces in West Virginia act according to orders from General McClellan. 5) Let the forces late at Bull Run except the three months men, be reorganized as rapidly as possible in their camps here. 6) Give rather special attention to Missouri. . . .

I remember the evening of the day back in 1858 that decided the contest for the Senate between Mr. Douglas and myself. It was a night something like this: dark, rainy, and gloomy. Reading the returns at the telegraph office I ascertained that I had lost and started to go home. The path had been worn hog-backed and was slippery. Both my feet slipped from under me, but I recovered myself—for such an awkward fellow I am pretty sure footed—and lit clear. And I said to myself: "It's a slip; not a fall."

● *Three months before the battle of Bull Run a broken-down former regular army captain had begun his efforts to get more actively into the war.*

GRANT   Galena, Illinois, May 24th 1861. To the Adjutant General, Washington, D. C.

Sir, having served for 15 years in the regular army, including four years at West Point, and feeling it the duty of everyone who has been educated at Government expense to offer their services for the support of the government, I have the honor, very respectfully, to tender my services, until the close of the war. I would say, in view of my present age and length of service I feel myself competent to command a regiment, if the President should see fit to entrust one to me. A letter addressed to me at Springfield Illinois will reach me. I am very respectfully your obedient servant, Captain Ulysses S. Grant. . . .

I felt some hesitation in suggesting rank as high as the colonel of a regiment. But I had seen every Colonel who had been sworn in from the state of Illinois and felt that if they could command a regiment, I could also.

● *Even before the defeat, Lincoln had been having his troubles with Congress. The physical act of rebellion occurred while Congress was not in session. Lincoln moving with dispatch to meet the threat did a great many things for which the Congress wanted the credit or felt impinged on their* power. When Congress reconvened—Lincoln kept them out of session as long as he decently could—they made an issue of the fact Lincoln had suspended the writ of habeas corpus in certain strategically vital parts of the country. Lincoln fought back.

LINCOLN   Fellow Citizens of the Senate and House of Representatives. Having been convened on an extraordinary occasion your attention is not called to any ordinary subject of legislation. The assailants of the Government have forced upon the country the issue: "Immediate dissolution or blood." Congress had not anticipated and so had not provided for the emergency. In this emergency the President felt it his duty to employ with energy the extraordinary powers which the Constitution confides to him in cases of insurrection. He called into the field such military and naval forces, unauthorized by the existing laws, as seemed necessary. He instituted a blockade, and suspended the writ of habeas corpus in various places, and caused persons engaged in treasonable practices to be detained in military custody.

This last authority has purposely been exercised but very sparingly. Nevertheless the legality of what has been done under it is questioned. The attention of the country has been called to the proposition that I who am sworn to "take care that the laws be faithfully executed" should not myself violate them.

Are all the laws but one to go unexecuted and the Government itself to go to pieces lest that one be violated? But I do not believe that any law was violated. The Constitution itself states "the privilege of habeas corpus shall not be suspended unless in cases of rebellion the public safety may require it." Some insist that Congress and not the executive has this power. The Constitution is silent on this. Must I shoot a simple minded soldier boy who deserts, while I must not touch a hair of the wily agitator who induces him to desert?

I think in such a case to silence the agitator and save the boy is not only constitutional, but withal a great mercy.

The President in full view of his grave responsibility has so far done what he deemed his duty. You will now according to your own judgment, perform yours. . . .

It has been a rule of my life that if people would not step aside for me, I would step aside for them. Then you avoid collisions. Yet I shall show them at the other end of the avenue whether I am President or no.

• To a great extent the fortunes of war and the fortunes of Lincoln meshed. For those not civil war buffs a brief recapitulation of the war's ups and down may be helpful.

1861, July, Bull Run.

1862, February, Grant captures Fort Donelson; two months later is almost defeated at Shiloh. 1862, May–September, Lee inflicts a series of defeats on the Union Army during the Peninsular Campaign; McClellan is relieved; the disaster of the second Bull Run follows. Lee finally checked by the reappointed McClellan at Antietam. 1862, 22 September, the Emancipation Proclamation is issued. Winter 1862-63, a series of Union defeats under incompetent generals.

1863, 4 July, Grant takes Vicksburg; Lee is defeated by Meade at Gettysburg the same day, but escapes across the Potomac with his Army. 1863, September–November, George H. Thomas wins the Union victories of Chickamauga and Chattanooga.

1864, March, Grant made Commander of all Union forces. 1864, May, Grant begins the bloody Wilderness Campaign. 1864, September, Sherman takes Atlanta. 1864, November, Lincoln re-elected; Sherman marches to the sea.

1865, April, Grant takes Richmond; Lee surrenders.

But, both the South's defeat and the abolition of slavery were far away in the fall of 1861 as Grant approached his first battle.

GRANT   As my regiment approached the brow of the hill from which it was expected we could see the Rebel's camp and possibly find them ready formed to meet us, my heart kept getting higher and higher until it felt as though it was in my throat. I would have given anything to have been back in Galena, Illinois; but had not the moral courage to halt and consider what to do. I kept right on. When we reached a point from which the valley below was in full view I halted. The marks of a recent encampment were plainly visible but the troops were gone. My heart resumed its place. It occurred to me at once that the rebels had been as much afraid of me as I of them. This was a view I had not taken before. But one I never forgot afterwards.

LINCOLN   My paramount objective in this struggle is to save the Union; and is not either to save or destroy slavery. If I could save the Union without freeing any slave I would do it. And if I could save it by freeing all the slaves I would do it. And if I could save it by freeing some and leaving others alone, I would also do that. What I do about slavery I do because I believe it helps to save the Union.—This is no modification of my oft expressed personal wish that all men everywhere could be free. . . .

Whenever I hear anyone arguing for slavery, I feel a strong impulse to see it tried on him personally.

• *Lincoln spent a great many hours in the telegraph room of the War Department writing the telegrams and dispatches by which he controlled what he could of the war. These little scraps of orders and suggestions reveal a great deal of Lincoln.*

LINCOLN   Major General McClellan—can you not cut the Aquia Creek Railroad? Also what impression have you as to the entrenched works in front of Richmond? . . .

Major General Frémont—I see that you are at Moorefield. You were expressly ordered to march to Harrisonburg. What does this mean? . . .

General Meade—I am appealed to on behalf of William Thompson of Company K, 3rd Maryland Volunteers, said to be at Kelley's Ford, under sentence to be shot today as a deserter. He is represented to me to be very young, with symptoms of insanity. I am unwilling for any boy under 18 to be shot. Please postpone the execution until further order. . . .

General McDowell, Manassas Junction—You say General Geary's scouts report they find no enemy this side of the Blue Ridge. Neither do I. But have they been to the Blue Ridge to look for them? . . .

General McClellan—I am glad to learn of General Poreter's victory. If it was a total rout of the enemy, why was the Fredericksburg railroad not seized? . . .

Trying to move McClellan is like herding fleas across a barn yard. No matter how much you start out with, nothing reaches the other side.

• *McClellan's star was beginning to fall. In the West, Grant's was about to rise.*

GRANT To General S. B. Buckner, Confederate Army. Yours this date proposing armistice and appointment of Commissioners to settle the terms of capitulation of Fort Donelson just received. No terms except unconditional surrender can be accepted. I propose to move immediately upon your works. I am, sir, very respectfully, your obedient servant, U. S. Grant.

GENERAL S. B. BUCKNER To Brigadier General U. S. Grant. Sir: The distribution of the forces under my command, incident to the unexpected change of commanders and the overwhelming force under your command, compel me, notwithstanding the brilliant success of the Confederate arms yesterday, to accept the ungenerous and unchivalrous terms which you propose. Your very obedient servant, sir, S. B. Buckner.

• *"Unconditional surrender," the phrase made Grant famous in a nation starved for victory. Lincoln sent General*

Halleck, *later Chief of Staff, to inspect Grant's troops and report what Grant was like. Halleck was a gossipy, nervous man who constantly rubbed his elbows. He was called "old brains" because he could read French.*

HALLECK   I have visited Grant's brigade as you requested. It is much without discipline and order. I never saw a man more deficient in organization. Brave and able in the field, he has no idea of how to organize his forces before a battle or how to conduct the operation of a campaign.

LINCOLN   General Grant is a very meager writer or telegrapher, but a copious fighter. . . .

• *Over the telegraph, Lincoln continued to place his personal imprint on the increasingly impersonal and destructive war.*

LINCOLN   Private William B. Boyd, Company I, 5th Indiana Infantry. I pardon him. . . .

Major General Hurlbut. I understand you have under sentence of death a tall old man by the name of Henry F. Luckett. I personally knew him and did not think him a bad man. Please do not let him be executed unless upon further order from me. . . .

Mrs. Elizabeth Grimsley, Springfield, Illinois. I mail the papers to you today appointing your Johnny to the Naval School. . . .

Mrs. Lincoln, Philadelphia. Think you had better put Tad's pistol away. I had an ugly dream about him. . . .

Major General Wool, Baltimore. How certain is your information that Bragg is in the valley of the Shenandoah? . . .

Major General McClellan. How does it look? . . .

Major General Butterfield. Where is General Hooker? Where is General Sedgwick? Where is General Stoneman? . . .

Major General McClellan. You remember me speaking to you of what I call your overcautiousness. Are you not overcautious when you assume that you cannot do what the enemy is constantly doing? Should you not claim to be at least his equal in prowess and act upon the claim?

• *McClellan, fighting the Peninsula Campaign, was in the brush and swamps before Richmond being out-generaled by Lee. McClellan was handling his troops well but his nerve was not up to the strain of battle. He telegraphed the Secretary of War:*

McClellan   I shall draw back this side of Chickahominy, and I think I can withdraw all our material. Please understand that in this battle we have lost nothing but men. I wish to say to the President that I think he is wrong in regarding me as ungenerous when I say my force was too weak. I merely told a truth which today has been too plainly proved. If I save this Army now I tell you plainly I owe no thanks to you, the President or any other persons in Washington. You have done your best to sacrifice this Army.

Lincoln   I will hold McClellan's horse if he will only bring us success.

McClellan   If at this instant I had ten thousand fresh men, I could gain a victory tomorrow.

Lincoln   I give you all I can; and act on the presumption that you will do the best with what you have, while you continue, ungenerously, I think, to assume that I could give you more if I would. . . .

It's called the Army of the Potomac, but that's a great mistake. It's really just McClellan's bodyguard.

• *Concerned over McClellan's failure to take Richmond and fed up with his carping, Lincoln relieved him. A series of Union disasters followed of which the most prominent was the Second Bull Run. Lee next broke away from the Union Army, swung north, and crossed the Potomac. In desperation Lincoln put McClellan back in charge of the demoralized*

*troops. McClellan defeated Lee at Antietam and had Lee
trapped against the Potomac; but he failed to press the advantage and Lee escaped.*

LINCOLN   General McClellan, I have just read your dispatch about sore-tongued and fatigued horses. Will you pardon
me for asking what the horses of your Army have done since
Antietam that fatigues anything? We have sent the Army
every fresh horse we could, 7981. I suppose the river is rising
and I am glad to believe that you are crossing. . . . And I feel
badly about those horses. I can make generals any day; but a
horse costs the government 125 dollars. . . .

What shall I do? What shall I do? The treasury has no
money and the secretary tells me he can raise no more. The
people are impatient. The general won't move. The bottom
is out of the tub.

• *Exasperated, Lincoln relieved McClellan for the final
time.*

LINCOLN   By direction of the President it is ordered that
Major General McClellan be relieved from Command of the
Army of the Potomac and that Major General Burnside take
command of that Army.

• *Burnside was a rash incompetent, and the disaster of
Fredericksburg followed. Lincoln bound up the psychological
wounds of the Army as best he could and replaced Burnside
with Hooker, a cautious incompetent.*

LINCOLN   To the Army of the Potomac. I have just read
your General's report of the battle of Fredericksburg. Although
you were not successful the attempt was not an error, nor the
failure other than accident. The consummate skill and success
with which you crossed and recrossed the river in the face of
the enemy show that you possess all the qualities of a great
army. . . .

Often I, who am not especially a brave man, have had

to sustain the sinking courage of these professional fighters in critical times. . . .

Major General Hooker. General, I have relieved General Burnside and placed you at the head of the Army of the Potomac. I have done this; but I think it best for you to know that there are some things in which I am not quite satisfied with you. I have heard, in such a way as to believe it, of your recently saying that both the Army and the government needed a dictator. Of course it was not for this, but in spite of it, that I have given you the command. Only those generals who gain success can set up as Dictators.

What I now ask of you is military success and I will risk the dictatorship. I much fear that the spirit that you aided in infusing into the Army while Burnside commanded, of criticizing all orders will now turn on you. Napoleon himself could not get any good out of an Army while such a spirit prevails.

Now beware of rashness, but with energy and sleepless vigilance go forward and give us victories. . . .

The arrogance of Generals. The arrogance. I get asked why I put up with it. Well, I feel about that a good deal as a man I once knew, who I'll call Jones, used to feel about his wife. He was one of your meek men; and had the reputation of being badly henpecked. At last, one day, his wife was seen switching him out of the house. A day or two afterward a friend met him on the street.

"Jones," the friend said, "I've always stood up for you; but I'm not going to do it any longer. A man who will stand quietly and take a switching from his wife deserves to be horse whipped."

Jones looked up with a wink; and patted his friend on the back. "Now don't," said he. "Why it didn't hurt me any; and you've no idea what a power of good it did Sarah Ann."

• One of the many fevers endemic in Washington during the war killed Lincoln's second son, his favorite and beloved Willie.

LINCOLN My boy is gone. He is actually gone. Willie. Why is it? Why is it?

My poor boy. He was too good for this earth. God has called him home. I know that he is much better off in heaven; but then I loved him so. It is hard, hard to have him die. . . .

And father cardinal I have heard you say that we shall see and know our friends again in heaven; if that be true I shall see my boy again . . . Did you ever dream—dream of a lost friend and feel that you were holding sweet communion with that friend, and yet have a sad consciousness that it was not a reality? Just so I dream of my dead boy, Willie.

• *The public rooms of the White House were always thronged with politicians and citizens wanting things. Hour after hour Lincoln listened. Towards the end of one day an elderly woman came in while Lincoln and the Secretary of War were talking.*

"Mr. President, I feel so embarrassed, I never spoke to a President before. But I am a good Union woman down in Maryland and my son is badly wounded in the hospital and I have been trying to get him out but somehow I can't. They said I had better come to you. When the war first broke out I gave my first son to God and then told him he might go and fight the rebels. Now if you will let me take him home I will nurse him up. Just as soon as he gets well enough, just as soon, so shall he go back. He's a good boy and don't want to shirk service."

"God bless you, yes yes." Lincoln replied, signing an order to release her son from the hospital. Outside the door of the President's study the woman turned to the Secretary of War.

"How those secessionists lie, back home. How they lie. They said he was ugly. He's the handsomest man in the world."

With congressional elections and the war going against him, Lincoln described what led up to the Emancipation Proclamation.

LINCOLN   By midsummer 1862 things had gone from bad to worse. I felt we had about played our last card: time to change the tactics or lose the game! I now determined upon the emancipation policy and without the knowledge of the Cabinet I drafted the proclamation.

After much anxious thought I called a Cabinet meeting upon the subject. I said to the Cabinet I had resolved upon this step, I had not called them to ask their advice, but that suggestions would be in order after they had heard the proclamation read. Various suggestions were offered. Secretary Chase wished the language stronger. Postmaster General Blair felt it would cost the Administration the fall elections.

Nothing however was offered that I had not already anticipated until Secretary Seward spoke. He said in substance: "I approve; but, after our repeated defeats won't emancipation be viewed as a shriek for help? Why not postpone it until a military success."

That was an aspect that in all my thoughts I had entirely overlooked. So I put the draft of the proclamation aside waiting for a victory. From time to time I added or changed a line. Well the next news we had was Pope's disaster at Second Bull Run. Things looked darker than ever. Finally came the battle of Antietam. I determined not to wait longer.

THE PROCLAMATION:

I, Abraham Lincoln, do order and declare that all persons held as slaves are and henceforward shall be free; and that the executive government of the United States will recognize and maintain the freedom of said persons. Upon this act, sincerely believed to be an act of justice, warranted by the Constitution upon military necessity, I invoke the considerate judgment of mankind and the gracious favor of Almighty God.

• *Not every one in the North was enthusiastic.*

Honest old Abe, when the war first began,
Denied abolition was part of his plan;

Honest old Abe has since made a decree,
The war must go on 'till the slaves are all free.
As both can't be honest, will some one tell how,
If honest Abe then, he is honest Abe now?

● *A great many letters against the Proclamation reached the
White House. To one of these Lincoln replied:*

LINCOLN   You write that you will not fight to free Negroes.
Some of them seem willing to fight for you; but no matter.
Fight you, then, exclusively to save the Union. I issued the
proclamation on purpose to aid you in saving the Union.
Whenever you shall have conquered all resistance to the Union, if I shall urge you to continue fighting, it will be an apt
time for you to declare you will not fight to free Negroes. . . .

I am a slow walker. But I never walk back. . . . I feel a
presentiment that I shall not outlast the Rebellion. When it is
over my work will be done. . . .

Dear Mary, tell Tad the goats and his father are very well,
especially the goats.

● *Militarily, things continued dark.*

GRANT   Shiloh was the severest battle fought in the West
during the war and few in the East equalled it for hard fighting. I saw an open field on the second day over which the
Confederates had made repeated charges, so covered with
dead that it would have been possible to walk across the clear-
ing in any direction, stepping on dead bodies. Union and
Confederate troops were mingled together in about equal
proportions. Up to then I believed the South would collapse
suddenly and soon if a decisive victory could be gained over
any one of its armies. After Shiloh I gave up all idea of saving
the Union except by complete conquest.

LINCOLN   I don't know what to make of Grant, he's such
a quiet little fellow. The only way I know he's around is by
the way he makes things git.

WHITMAN

Year that trembled and reeled beneath me!
Your summer wind was warm enough, yet the air I breathed
    froze me,
A thick gloom fell through the sunshine and darkened me,
Must I change my triumphant songs? said I to myself,
Must I indeed learn to chant the cold dirges of the baffled?
And sullen hymns of defeat.

● *Doubting his own abilities, worn down by a string of defeats, Lincoln began to sag.*

LINCOLN Oh it's terrible, terrible, terrible. This war is eating my life out. Look at me. I wish I had never been born. A fire in my front and rear and a Congress that wishes to get rid of me. How willingly would I change places with the soldier who sleeps on the ground.

● *A friend watching the President's deepening despondency asked him if there was no way he could get away for a few weeks and play the hermit. Lincoln answered: "Two or three weeks would do me no good. I cannot fly from my thoughts. I have left Washington at times to visit the Army. It's a relief. But nothing touches the tired spot." Some while later he told a group of friends who were trying to cheer him up, "I do not need sympathy nearly so much as I need success."*

Grant, maneuvering to clear the Mississippi River, expressed the mood of the country.

GRANT At this time the North had become very much discouraged. Many strong Union men believed the war must prove a failure. The elections of 1862 had gone against Lincoln. Voluntary enlistments had all but ceased and the draft had been resorted to to fill up our ranks. It was my judgment that any backward movement from Vicksburg would be interpreted as a defeat, the draft would be resisted, desertions ensue and the power to capture and punish deserters lost. There was nothing left but to go forward to decisive victory.

LINCOLN   If Grant only does the right thing down there, why Grant is my man and I am his for the rest of the war.

• *Grant, in a brilliant campaign against a larger force, did the right thing. On July 4th he took Vicksburg, the last Southern fort blocking the Mississippi. Lincoln realized the victory's significance. He said: "I cannot tell you my joy over the result. It is great! It is great! The father of waters again goes unvexed to the sea." Continued criticism of Grant for drinking and wasting lives he brushed aside with the words, "If only I could find another general like him."*

SHERMAN   Hold the God-damn fort, I'm coming. . . .

You might as well appeal against the thunderstorm as against the terrible hardships of war. . . . War is cruel, you cannot refine it. I am tired and sick of it. Its glory is all moonshine. It is only those who have neither fired a shot nor heard the shrieks of the wounded who cry aloud for more blood. . . .

War is hell. . . .

I am a damn sight smarter than Grant. I know a great deal more about war. But I'll tell you where he beats me and where he beats the world. He don't give a damn for what the enemy does out of his sight, but it scares me like hell. . . .

General Grant is a great General. He stood by me when I was crazy and I stood by him when he was drunk; and now, sir, we stand by each other always.

GRANT   General Sherman is the finest General I know.

• *Some five or six years before, a red-headed, half-mad, business failure who was afraid to face his family was wandering along the St. Louis waterfront planning suicide. He looked up and saw slumped on a wagon a drunken wood seller. The two derelicts recognized each other. They had overlapped at West Point. The red-head, Sherman, and the wood seller,*

Grant, passed the afternoon together and parted. Now they were together again. Is history more than chance?

The same day that Grant took Vicksburg, General Meade defeated Lee at Gettysburg, checking the last drive north of the Army of Northern Virginia. But Meade repeated the error of most Union generals. He did not press his advantage.

LINCOLN   General Meade. You fought and beat the enemy at Gettysburg. Now please do not let Lee off without being hurt. . . .

Do not let Lee cross the river! . . .

When I think of General Meade's attitude toward Lee I'll be hanged if I can think of anything else than an old woman trying to shoo her geese across a creek.

Lee has escaped! What can I do? What? What General is any better than Meade?

Half a year later Lincoln answered that question of his in this way:

LINCOLN   General Grant, the Nation's appreciation of what you have done, and its reliance upon you for what remains to be done are now presented with this commission constituting you lieutenant general in the Army of the United States. You are assigned to command the Armies of the United States. I scarcely need to add that with what I speak here for the nation goes my own hearty personal concurrence.

GRANT   Mr. President, I accept this commission with gratitude.

LINCOLN   Major General Sherman: The State election of Indiana occurs on the 11th of October and the loss of it to friends of the Government would go far towards losing the whole Union cause. The bad effect upon the November election, and especially the giving of the State Government to those who will oppose the war, are too much to risk, if it can be avoided. The draft proceeds, notwithstanding its strong tendency to lose us the State.

Indiana is the only important state voting in October whose soldiers cannot vote in the field. Anything you can safely do to let her soldiers go home and vote in the State election will be greatly to the point. They need not remain for the Presidential election but may return to you at once. This is in no sense an order. . . .

I have been pressed to stop the draft. But what is the Presidency to me if I have no country?

• *Sherman maneuvering his army from Tennessee into Georgia could not spare the men. But he did something far better than that for Lincoln. On the 2nd of September he took Atlanta. News of the victory fired the North and turned the political tide decisively toward Lincoln. Not everyone was as enthusiastic about the war as the writer of the following popular song. But it is unlikely that the song would have been written or sung six months before.*

We are springing to the call of our brothers gone before,
Shouting the battle cry of Freedom,
And we'll fill the vacant ranks with a million free men
        more.
Shouting the battle cry of Freedom.

The Union forever, hurrah, boys, hurrah!
Down with the traitor, up with the star,
While we rally round the flag, boys, rally once again,
Shouting the battle cry of Freedom.

Yes for Liberty and Union we are springing to the fight,
Shouting the battle cry of Freedom,
And the victory shall be ours for we're rising in our might,
Shouting the battle cry of Freedom.

The Union forever, hurrah, boys, hurrah!
Down with the traitor, up with the star,
While we rally round the flag, boys, rally once again,
Shouting the battle cry of Freedom.

• *Earlier, a week and a half before the fall of Atlanta, Lincoln wrote his famous gloomy memorandum.*

LINCOLN   This morning as for some days past it seems exceedingly probable that this Administration will not be reelected. Then it will be my duty to so cooperate with the President-elect as to save the Union between the election and the inauguration; as he will have secured his election on such ground that he cannot possibly save it afterwards.

• *Lincoln folded the memorandum and pasted it shut in such a way that its contents could not be read. Then he got his entire Cabinet to write their names across the back without knowing what it said. In this way he pledged himself and them to loyally help the new Administration. Sherman's victory at Atlanta made the pledge unnecessary.*

After taking Atlanta, Sherman reasoned that the South would be forced to surrender if its heartland was destroyed. He therefore cut loose from his base of supplies at Atlanta and began his march to the sea. As he marched he lived off the land and destroyed food and military supplies, particularly the railroads. That campaign and his subsequent march up the coast to join Grant mark him as one of the five or six great commanders of history.

SHERMAN   We rode out of Atlanta by the Decatur road filled with the marching troops and wagons of the 14th Corps. We reined to look behind at Atlanta smouldering in ruins, the black smoke rising high in the air, and hanging like a pall over the ruined city. Then we turned our horses' heads to the East and the sea.

GRANT   Sherman's army is now somewhat in the condition of a mole when he disappears under a lawn. You can here and there trace his track; but you are not quite certain where he will come out till you see his head.

SHERMAN   The afternoon was unusually raw and cold. When we camped my orderly was at hand with his invariable saddle-bags, which contained a change of underclothing, my maps, a flask of whiskey, and a bunch of cigars. Taking a drink and lighting a cigar, I walked down the main road and found a good, double-hewed log house, in one room of which Colonel Poe, Dr. Moore, and others, had started a fire.

Looking around the room, I saw a small box, like a candle-box, marked "Howell Cobb," and, in inquiring of a Negro, found that we were at the plantation of General Howell Cobb, of Georgia, one of the leading rebels of the South, then a general in the Southern army, and who had been Secretary of the United States Treasury in Mr. Buchanan's time. Of course, we confiscated his property, and found it rich in corn, beans, pea-nuts, and sorghum-molasses.

I sent out word to explain whose plantation it was, and instructed the soldiers to spare nothing. That night huge bonfires consumed the fence-rails, kept our soldiers warm, and the teamsters and men, as well as the slaves, carried off an immense quantity of corn and provisions of all sorts.

Lieutenant George Snelling, who commanded my escort, was a Georgian, and recognized in an old Negro in the room a favorite slave of his uncle, who resided about six miles off; but the old slave did not at first recognize his young master in our uniform. His attention was then drawn to Snelling's face, when he fell on his knees and thanked God that he had found his young master alive and along with the Yankees.

Snelling inquired all about his uncle and the family, asked my permission to go and pay his uncle a visit, which I granted, of course, and the next morning he described to me his visit. The uncle was not cordial by any means to find his nephew in the ranks of the host that was desolating the land; and Snelling came back, having exchanged his tired horse for a fresher one out of his uncle's stables.

• *The "march to the sea" was successful. Sherman reached the coast at Savannah a few days before Christmas. Lincoln wrote Sherman his thanks. But even in a letter of thanks he couldn't resist giving his two trusted combat commanders a small push.*

LINCOLN   Many, many thanks for your Christmas gift, the capture of Savannah. When you were leaving Atlanta for the Atlantic coast, I was anxious if not fearful; but feeling that you were the better judge, and remembering "nothing risked, nothing gained" I did not interfere. Now the undertaking being a success, the honor is all yours.

But what next? I suppose it will be safer if I leave General Grant and yourself to decide.

• *An introspective, artistic genius whose ravenous energy, before it found its outlet in war, had several times driven him to insanity, Sherman had no illusions about himself or his victory. He remarked: "Like one who has walked a narrow plank, I look back and wonder if I really did it." He turned his men north to march up the coast and link with Grant: a more difficult military feat than the "march to the sea"—though not as poetic.*

Grant had begun his fight toward Richmond back in May. All through the summer and winter he kept Lee pinned. He was losing men but inching forward. And he pressed Lee so closely that Lee could spare no one to reinforce the troops battling Sherman. Grant held the South by the nose while Sherman kicked them in the tail.

GRANT   Soon after midnight the Army of the Potomac moved out of its position to start upon the new campaign. Victory was not to be accomplished, however, without as desperate fighting as the world has ever witnessed. The losses inflicted and endured were destined to be severe; but the armies now confronting each other had already been in deadly conflict for three years with immense losses. They had confronted each other so long without any decisive result that they hardly knew which could whip.

• While the fighting continued, the war between Congress and the President, particularly the Republicans in Congress, grew more bitter. The intellectual issue was reconstruction: how should the vanquished South be treated. Lincoln wanted to bring the Southern States back into the Union as full fledged members as rapidly as possible. Led by the "Radical Republicans" who wanted a tough peace, most of Congress disagreed. Senators and Congressmen wanted to run the country without being bothered with returned Southern legislators. Then there was the question: should the South be forced to pay the North a huge sum of money to atone for her war guilt. Also at what speed should the Negroes be given the vote. Several Northern States like Ohio passed laws preventing Negroes from voting at the same time their Congressmen and Senators were demanding immediate, total enfranchisement of all Negroes in the South.

The leaders of the opposition to Lincoln, the men who wanted to grind the South, were two "Radical" members of his own party: Senator "Bluff Ben" Wade of Ohio and Senator Charles Sumner of Massachusetts. Sumner had once been beaten with a cane on the floor of the Senate by an irate Southern Congressman.

SUMNER   I take the ground, sir, that you can both punish the Rebels as traitors and make war with them as belligerants. These men are enemies; and we must treat them as enemies.

WADE   The conflict is directly between slavery and liberty and the rebels are red-handed traitors. If you would find a prototype for their brutality you must turn your back upon civilized history and repair to an oligarchy of cannibals or to barbarous Africa, kept in barbarism by an oligarchy of menstealers.

The rebels are public enemies and should be dealt with as such.

LINCOLN   Let the rebels go. Let them all go, officers and all. I want submission and no more bloodshed. Let them have their horses to plow with and their guns to shoot crows with. They won't take up arms again. I want no one punished. We want these people to return to their allegiance to the Union and submit to the laws. Again I say give them the most liberal and honorable terms.

WADE   That's a silly performance. Think of telling the rebels they may fight as long as they like and then take a pardon when they've had enough.

• A delegation of Republican Senators, determined to subjugate Lincoln, called on the President. The principal scalps they were after were Secretary of State Seward's and Postmaster General Blair's.

SENATOR   Mr. President, we are going to reelect you. But we want you to promise, to make us a solemn promise, that you will reorganize your cabinet and in particular leave all Democrats out.

LINCOLN   Senator, I'm sorry to be compelled to deny your request to make such a promise. Even if I myself were inclined to make it I have no right to do so. Do the voters elect a man to be a mere puppet? I confess I desire to be reelected. God knows I do not want this labor and responsibility for another four years, yet I have the common pride of humanity and would like to have what I have done endorsed. But I have the courage to refuse the office if I must take it on such terms that I cannot be President if I am elected.

SENATOR   Sir, you are within one mile of Hell.

LINCOLN   Yes, yes, it is less than a mile to the Senate. . . .
    Although I may be stronger, yet if all the rest oppose I must give way. Old Hickory had as much iron in his neck as anybody; but he did sometimes. If the strongest horse in the team would go ahead he cannot, if all the rest hold back.

SUMNER   Jurisdiction over the rebel states belongs to Congress. And by the laws of war the conqueror may seize for his own use everything that belongs to the enemy. These things may be retained to pay the expenses of the war and the damage caused by it. Towns, cities, provinces may be held as punishment for this unjust war.

WADE   Every inch of rebel property should be held and sold to reimburse all the costs of the war. Their land if sold would produce enough to pay all the costs of the war, all damages to private property of loyal men, and create an ample fund to pay pensions to wounded soldiers and the bereaved friends of the slain. Who will object to this?

LINCOLN   In the Constitution of the United States it is provided that the President "shall have the power to grant pardons for offenses against the United States." Therefore I, Abraham Lincoln, President of the United States, do proclaim to all persons who have participated in the existing rebellion and who desire to resume their allegiance that a full pardon is hereby granted to each of them, with the restoration of all rights of property upon the condition that every such person shall take an oath to faithfully support the United States. . . .

Die when I may, I want it said of me by those who know me, I always plucked a thistle and planted a flower, when I thought a flower would grow.

SUMNER   Talk of one man power, here it is with a vengeance.

WADE   The President ought not to be permitted to handle this great question of reconstruction. Under the Constitution it does not belong to him. It belongs to us in Congress.

SUMNER   Rebels and rebel states will not be readmitted to the Union except under laws which Congress shall impose and on the conditions which Congress may require.

LINCOLN A traveler on the frontier found himself out of his reckoning one night in the most inhospitable region. A terrific thunderstorm came up to add to his trouble. He floundered along until his horse at length gave out. The lightning afforded him the only clue to his way, but the peals of thunder were frightful. One bolt which crashed to earth beneath him brought him to his knees. By no means a praying man, his petition was short. "Oh Lord, if it is all the same to you, give us a little more light and a little less noise."

• *Opposition to the President reached its height in the Wade-Davis Manifesto. Davis was a Republican Congressman from Ohio. In this document the Republicans detailed just why they didn't like the leader of their own party:*

The President has greatly presumed on the forebearance which the supporters of his Administration have so long practiced. He must understand that our support is of a cause and not of a man. That the authority of Congress is paramount and must be respected.

The whole body of Union men in Congress will not submit to his rash and unconstitutional legislation. If he wishes our support he must confine himself to his executive duties— to obey and execute, not make, the laws; and leave political reorganization to Congress.

LINCOLN To be wounded in the house of one's friends is perhaps the most grievous affliction that can befall a man. . . .

For my own part, I desire so to conduct the affairs of this administration that if at the end, when I come to lay down the reins of power I shall have lost every other friend on earth, I shall at least have one friend left; and that friend shall be down inside of me.

• *The war ground on.*

GRANT If you see the President, tell him from me that whatever happens, there will be no turning back.

LINCOLN   I have seen your dispatch of yesterday expressing your unwillingness to break your hold where you are. Neither am I willing. Hold on with a bulldog grip and chew and choke as much as possible.

GRANT   I propose to fight it out on this line if it takes all summer.

• *In his second inaugural Lincoln once again reached Periclean heights. It is worth noting that probably the noblest funeral orations we know were delivered by men, both democratically elected, who were damned in their time as too political.**

LINCOLN   Fellow countrymen: At this second appearing to take the oath of the presidential office there is less occasion for an extended address than there was at the first.

On that occasion corresponding to this four years ago all thoughts were anxiously directed to an impending civil war. All dreaded it, all parties sought to avert it; but one of them would make war rather than let the nation survive, and the other would accept war rather than let it perish, and the war came . . .

Neither party expected for the war the magnitude or the duration which it has already attained. Neither anticipated that the cause of the conflict might cease with or even before the conflict itself should cease. Each looked for an easier triumph and a result less fundamental and astounding. Both read the same Bible and pray to the same God, and each invokes His aid against the other. It may seem strange that any men should dare to ask a just God's assistance in wringing their bread from the sweat of other men's faces, but let us judge not, that we be not judged. The prayers of both sides could not be answered. That of neither has been answered fully. . . .

* Pericles' funeral oration over the Athenians killed in the first year of the Peloponnesian War occurs in Thucydides' History, at the end of the first chapter of Book II.

Now, with malice toward none, with charity for all, with firmness in the right as God gives us to see the right, let us strive on to finish the work we are in, to bind up the nation's wounds, to care for him who shall have borne the battle and for his widow and his orphan, to do all which may achieve and cherish a just and lasting peace among ourselves and with all nations.

GRANT   We now have a continuous line of troops and in a few hours will be entrenched from the Appomattox below Petersburg to the river above. The whole captures since the Army started out will amount to about twelve thousand men and probably fifty pieces of artillery. All looks remarkably well. . . .

The enemy made a stand at Burke's station. We attacked them with two divisions of the Sixth Army Corps and routed them handsomely, making a connection with the cavalry. We have captured several thousand more prisoners and fourteen pieces of artillery. If the thing be pressed, I think Lee will surrender.

LINCOLN   Let the thing be pressed.

• *The thing was pressed. Three days later Lee surrendered at Appomattox. For Lincoln too, unknown, the end was near. Gideon Welles, still Secretary of the Navy, recorded it.*

WELLES   When I went to the Cabinet meeting on Friday the 14th of April, General Grant who had just arrived from Appomattox was with the President. The President remarked that we must soon begin to act on the great question of reconstruction now before us; and that he was glad Congress was not in session. He was asked "What about Jefferson Davis?" which reminded him of a story.

LINCOLN   You know, there was a boy in Springfield who saved up his money and bought a raccoon. After the novelty wore off, this coon became an awful nuisance. He was leading this coon through the streets one day and had his hands full to keep clear of the little vixen who had torn his clothes half off. At length all fagged out he sat down on the curb. A passing man was stopped by the child's woeful face and asked him what was the matter.

"Oh," the boy replied, "this coon is such a trouble to me."

"Why don't you get rid of him then?" the man asked.

"Shhhh," said the boy. "Don't you see he's gnawing his rope off. I'm a goin' to let him do it. Then I'll go home and tell the folks: he got away from me."

I hope Jeff Davis gets away and I don't know it.

WELLES   Grant and the President were hourly expecting to hear from General Sherman pursuing Johnson in Virginia. The President remarked that the news would come soon.

LINCOLN   I had this strange dream again last night; and judging from the past we shall have great news very soon. I think it must be from Sherman for my thoughts are in that direction.

WELLES   I inquired what this remarkable dream could be. The President said it related to my element, the water. That he seemed to be in a singular, indescribable vessel, but always the same. He was moving in it with great rapidity, unable to control it, toward a dark and indefinite shore. He had had this dream preceding the firing on Sumter, Bull Run, Antietam, Gettysburg, Stone River, Vicksburg and several other great battles. Victory did not always follow this dream but the events and results were important.

LINCOLN   You know a lot of the stories they tell about me I didn't say. But I did say when I had the small pox: "Now let the office seekers come, for at last I have something I can give all of them."

I am very sure that if I do not go away from here a wiser

man, I shall go away a better man, from having learned here what a poor sort of man I am.

● *His last recorded words at the White House were: "Allow Mr. Ashmer and friend to come in at nine A.M. tomorrow."*

WELLES I had retired to bed about half past ten on the evening of the 14th and was just getting to sleep when Mrs. Welles said someone was at our door. Sitting up in bed, I heard a voice twice call to John, my son, whose sleeping room was on the second floor directly over the front entrance. I arose at once and raised a window, when my messenger, James Smith, called to me that Mr. Lincoln had been shot. "Where?" I inquired. James said he was at Ford's Theater on Tenth Street.

I immediately dressed myself and, against the earnest remonstrance and appeals of my wife, set out for the theater. The streets were full of people. Not only the sidewalks but the carriageway was to some extent occupied, all or nearly all hurrying toward Tenth Street. When I entered that street I found it pretty closely packed.

The President had been carried across the street from the theater to the house of a Mr. Peterson. I entered by ascending a flight of steps above the basement and passed through a long hall to the rear, where the President lay extended on a bed, breathing heavily. Several surgeons were present, at least six, I should think more. Among them I was glad to observe Dr. Hall, who, however, soon left. I inquired of Doctor Hall, as I entered, the true condition of the President. He replied the President was dead to all intents, although he might live three hours or perhaps longer.

The giant sufferer lay extended diagonally across the bed, which was not long enough for him. He had been stripped of his clothes. His large arms, which were occasionally exposed, were of a size which one would scarce have expected from his spare appearance. His slow, full respiration lifted the sheets with each breath that he took. His features were calm and striking. I had never seen them appear to better advantage than for the first hour, perhaps, that I was there. After that his right eye began to swell and that part of his face became discolored.

The room was small and overcrowded. The surgeons and members of the Cabinet were as many as should have been in the room, but there were many more, and the hall and other rooms in the front or main house were full. One of these rooms was occupied by Mrs. Lincoln and her attendants. About once an hour Mrs. Lincoln would repair to the bedside of her dying husband and with lamentation and tears remain until overcome by emotion.

About 6 A.M. I experienced a feeling of faintness and for the first time after entering the room a little past eleven, I left it and the house and took a short walk in the open air. It was a dark and gloomy morning, and rain set in before I returned to the house some fifteen minutes later.

Again I went into the room where the dying President was rapidly drawing near the closing moments. His wife soon after made her last visit to him. The death struggle had begun. The respiration of the President became suspended at intervals and at last entirely ceased at twenty-two minutes past seven. . . .

• Whitman produced the epitaph:

This dust was once the man
Gentle, plain, just, and resolute, under whose
    cautious hand,
Was saved the Union of these States.

V .. Andrew Johnson vs. Congress

• • ANDREW JOHNSON
1865–1869

Most men who become Vice President become so for poor reasons. Andrew Johnson was no exception. Lincoln needed a border Democrat to strengthen the Republican ticket by emphasizing the Unionism rather than the Republicanism of the Party. Andrew Johnson was a Democrat from Tennessee. The only Southern Senator to remain faithful to the Union, he had bravely returned to Tennessee and helped hold large portions of that State loyal. He was the obvious choice.

Johnson was famous for being rough, tough, and popular. Though a Democrat, his statement: "Treason is a crime and must be made odious," had endeared him to the Radical Republicans. After Lincoln's assassination the powerful Republican leaders thought they could work with Johnson. They were wrong.

First, there was the character of Johnson. He was prickly, arrogant, thick-headed; self-doubtful and self-assertive by turns. He had been drunk when he was sworn in as Vice President. But he was not a man who took orders. Also, though as a poor planter Johnson hated the rich Southern aristocracy, he had no use for the Negro either. He identified with the vast majority of Southerners: farmers, hardworking, impoverished, prejudiced like himself.

Second, perhaps no President could have got on with that Congress: Thaddeus Stevens, Charles Sumner, Ben Butler, Ben Wade and others. They were vindictive, inflated men determined to return to the days of figurehead Presidents such as Fillmore, Pierce and Buchanan when Congress ruled. Also there was money involved. Vast crooked fortunes were being made by carpetbaggers in the South, speculators in the East and land grabbers in the West. Congress wanted that juice trickling down their jaws alone. It was a period when a great many legislators were voting themselves and their friends private fortunes from public funds.

The great concern of the founding fathers had been that the President would dictate to Congress. The Constitution was designed primarily to hold the Chief Executive in check. Now in the aftermath of war, the balance almost tipped the other way, and allowed Congress to take over the Executive by making him removable at their pleasure. The United States lurched toward becoming a French-type republic, then halted at the brink. The battleground was how the South should be reconstructed. But the issue was who would rule: President or Congress.

Congress led off by sending the President a bill on Negro voting.

CONGRESS   An act of Congress to establish a bureau for the relief of Freedmen and Refugees.

JOHNSON   Vetoed. I have examined with care the bill entitled "An act to establish a bureau for the relief of freedmen and refugees." Having with much regret come to the conclusion that it would not be consistent with the public welfare to give my approval to the measure, I return the bill to the Senate with my objections to its becoming a law.

STEVENS Andrew Johnson must learn that as Congress shall order, he must obey. There is no escape from it.

• *Next, Congress tried to make it impossible for the President to discharge any members of his Cabinet without the approval of the Senate. Several Cabinet members, notably Edward M. Stanton, Lincoln's Secretary of War, were plotting with Congress behind the President's back.*

CONGRESS An act of Congress regulating the tenure of certain civil offices.

JOHNSON Vetoed! I have carefully examined the bill to regulate the tenure of certain offices. The bill provides that the President may not remove certain cabinet officers without the consent of the Senate. The bill in my judgment conflicts with the Constitution.

• *Johnson had been following Lincoln's policy of appointing civilian governors for the rebel states almost immediately. Congress now struck at this.*

CONGRESS An act of Congress to provide for the more efficient government of the rebel states. Be it enacted that the said rebel states shall be divided into military districts and made subject to the military authority of the United States.

JOHNSON Vetoed! This bill places the people of ten states under the absolute domination of military rulers. It declares that there exists in those states no legal governments and no adequate protection for life or property. This is not true.

SUMNER The issue is one man power versus Congress. Until now it has always been supposed that the Legislative gave the law to the Executive. Now the President madly undertakes to give the law to the legislative. What makes this irrational assumption more astonishing is that the actual President, besides being the creature of an accident, is inferior in ability and character, while the present House of Representatives, there is every reason to believe, is the best that has sat since the formation of the Constitution.

JOHNSON   You're a mean looking sneak.

CONGRESS   An act of Congress to protect all persons in the United States in their civil rights.

JOHNSON   Vetoed! I regret that this bill contains provisions which I cannot approve consistent to my sense of duty to the whole people of the United States.

STEVENS   Congress is the sovereign power because the people speak through them. He's sunk below any other President.

JOHNSON   Congress is trying to break up the government. If they'd support reconciliation every state would be anchored in the Union.

STEVENS   You all remember that in Egypt the Lord sent frogs, locusts, murrain and lice. Almost all of these have been sent upon us. We have been oppressed with taxes and debts. And he has sent us more than lice. He has afflicted us with Andrew Johnson.

JOHNSON   Frauds! Assumed Congressmen! I care not for dignity when I'm attacked by gangs of hirelings and traducers.

• *Things were going from bad to worse for Johnson. He had angered Grant, the popular hero. There had been several fatal riots in the South as Southerners prevented Negroes from holding political rallies. These riots made Johnson's lenient policies suspect. Then the President went on a whistle stop campaign to carry his case to the people. Unfortunately hecklers in the audience kept getting under his skin. He would lose his temper and lash out verbally in a manner that made him ridiculous and petty. (The parodies of Johnson's speeches on this trip by Lincoln's favorite humorist, Patrolium V. Nasby, rank as satire with Swift.) Meanwhile Congress kept hammering away at the President.*

CONGRESS   An act of Congress supplementary to an act to provide for the more efficient government of the rebel states.

JOHNSON   Vetoed! If universal suffrage for blacks is the sine qua non, the work of reconstruction may as well begin in Ohio as in North Carolina.

SUMNER   Johnson is an insolent drunken brute in comparison with which Caligula's horse was respectable.

CONGRESS   A further act of Congress supplementary to an act to provide for a more efficient government for the rebel states.

JOHNSON   Vetoed! Your President is the Tribune of the people and thank God I am. I intend to assert the power the people have placed in me.

WADE   To admit the States on President Johnson's plan is to voluntarily with our eyes open to surrender our political rights into the hands of those traitors we have just conquered.

● *This was the problem. Wade was being unusually honest. If the Southern States were readmitted, their Senators would hold the balance of power in the Senate and be able to turn the Republicans out.*

JOHNSON   Tyranny and despotism can be exercised by many more rigorously and more severely than one.

STEVENS   The Rebel States will with their allies in the North control Congress and occupy the White House. Where will we be?

JOHNSON   If I pardoned traitors I have only obeyed the injunction of the scripture—to forgive the repentant.

SUMNER   I doubt if in all history there is any ruler who in the same brief space of time has done so much evil. There have been emperors and satraps who exercised tyrannical power but the facilities of communication now lend swiftness to all evil. Next to Jefferson Davis stands Andrew Johnson as the Republic's worst enemy.

• *A few years later as chairman of the Foreign Relations Committee, Sumner was to seriously argue that Britain should cede Canada to the United States to pay for having sympathized with the South in the Civil War.*

JOHNSON   Because I refuse to hang eight million people, I'm called a traitor.

SUMNER   With the assassination of Lincoln the rebellion vaulted into the President's chair. Jefferson Davis was then in the dungeon of Fortress Monroe, but Andrew Johnson, that Judas, was doing his work.

JOHNSON   I have been called Judas Iscariot. Judas! If I've played Judas then who has been my Christ that I've played Judas with? Was it that arrogant bastard Thad Stevens!? What Senator stands forth as Jesus Christ?

WADE   Johnson was guilty of the assassination of President Lincoln.

JOHNSON   Bloody assassin yourself!

• *Certain of victory, Congress decided to put its power to the ultimate test. The House passed a resolution: "Resolved that Andrew Johnson, President of the United States, be impeached for high crimes and misdemeanors," which came before the Senate. In accordance with the Constitution, the Senate transformed itself into what it believed was a court of justice with the Chief Justice of the United States presiding. The indictment against the President was long and legalistic but there was no substance. A key clause read: "That said Andrew Johnson, President of the United States, unmindful of the duties of his office did ridicule and attempt to bring* into disgrace Congress. And that he did make and deliver with a loud voice certain intemperate, inflammatory and scandalous harangues about Congress."

Hardly a "high crime" even today. Yet everyone was certain the President would be impeached. Johnson and the loyal members of his Cabinet, the faithful Gideon Welles among them, considered what he would do when troops came to arrest him.

At the end of six weeks of charges and counter charges—Johnson was defended by a team of famous lawyers—Congressman John Bingham of Ohio summed up before the Senate for the impeachment of the President. Famous as an orator, wit and patriot, Judge Bingham spoke for three days.

BINGHAM   I know I stand in the presence of men who may be called today the living fathers of the Republic; and I ask you, Senators, to consider that we stand this day pleading for the violated majesty of the law by the graves of half a million murdered, martyred, hero patriots, who met death in battle by the sacrifice of themselves for their country, the Constitution and the laws, and provided by their sublime example that all must obey the law; that none are above the law; that no man lives for himself alone, but each for all; that some may die in order that the State may live; that the citizen is best for today but the Commonwealth is for all time; and that no position however high, no patronage however great, can be permitted to shelter crime to the peril of the Republic.

It only remains for me, Senators, to thank you, as I do, for the honor you have done me by your kind attention and to demand in the name of the House of Representatives and of this great Senate, and of the people, judgment against the accused for his high crimes and misdemeanors in office whereof he stands impeached, and of which, before God and man, he is clearly guilty.

• Congressman George W. Julian, one of the floor managers of the impeachment, described the final moments.

JULIAN The final vote was postponed till the sixteenth, owing to Senator Howard's illness, and on the morning of that day the friends of impeachment felt more confident. The vote was first taken on the eleventh article. The galleries were packed, and an indescribable anxiety was written on every face. Some of the members of the House near me grew pale and sick under the burden of suspense. Such stillness prevailed that the breathing in the galleries could be heard at the announcement of each Senator's vote.

As the name of Senator Fowler was reached the Chief Justice propounded to him the prescribed question: "How say you, is the respondent, Andrew Johnson, President of the United States, guilty or not guilty of a high misdemeanor, as charged in this article of impeachment?", the Senator, in evident excitement, inadvertently answered "guilty," and thus lent a momentary relief to the friends of impeachment; but this was immediately dissipated by correcting his vote on the statement of the Chief Justice that he did not understand the Senator's response to the question.

Nearly all hope of conviction fled when Senator Ross of Kansas voted "not guilty." And a long breathing of disappointment and despair followed the like vote of Van Winkle of West Virginia, which settled the case in favor of the President.

• *Fessenden, the first of the seven Republican Senators to cross party lines and vote in favor of the President gave his reasons.*

FESSENDEN To dispose the elected President of a great nation on the slight grounds presented here would be an abuse of the power conferred upon the Senate. To construe his acts as high crimes would, when the passions of the hour have had time to cool, be looked upon with wonder if not with derision. Worse than this, it would inflict a wound upon our government which might eventually destroy it.

One manager of impeachment has gone so far as to

threaten with infamy every Senator who shall now vote for the President's acquittal. I should consider myself undeserving of the confidence of just and intelligent people, if for the sake of securing popular favor I should disregard the convictions of my judgment and my conscience. —Not guilty.

● *Johnson was saved by one vote. Otherwise Ben Wade, president of the Senate and one of Johnson's judges, would have become President. The Congress had already passed laws, which the Supreme Court had tamely accepted, that the Supreme Court could not interfere in reconstruction. Congress would have ruled. Already the House had imprisoned a hostile witness in a specially constructed dungeon beneath the Capitol. Still, seven Senators had been able to both recognize the Nation's welfare and put that welfare above their own love of power. Perhaps a successful Democracy is continually just saved by such a few. As the following popular song of the time shows, it wasn't easy.*

> We had old Andy done that day,
>   Seven men! Oh! Seven men!
> Until you threw our chance away,
>   Seven men! Oh! Seven men!
>
> We'll not forget 'til we are grey,
>   How all our hopes around us lay
> When you refused by us to stay,
>   Seven men! Oh! Seven men!
>
> Alas! Alas!—for Fessenden
>   Seven men! Oh! Seven men!
> He will not have the chance again,
>   Seven men! Oh! Seven men!
>
> Perhaps you thought the thing was play,
> But if you did, just let us say:
> We'll hang you for your vote that day.
>   Seven men! Oh! Seven men!

• The threats were not merely words. Fessenden died of a heart attack under the strain of fighting for vindication. Ross was so brutally beaten on his return to Kansas that he never fully recovered. But after the vote, though hatreds remained, the political storm began to subside. Johnson's term had less than a year to run and already the Radical Republicans were planning to sweep the country with General Grant as a figurehead leader behind whom they could consolidate their power: a strategy that was to prove successful.

And what of Johnson? Here the picture is not all dark. At the Democratic Presidential Convention of 1868, the year of his attempted impeachment, he received the second highest number of votes. Had a handful more delegates been for him the country would have witnessed the campaign of a Republican President running to succeed himself on the Democratic ticket.

Johnson retired to his home town of Greenville, Tennessee: "An old man, weary with the cares of state, has come to lay his bones among you"; and immediately began to campaign. Tennessee was a state bitterly divided between ex-Confederates, Democrats, Republicans and Radical Republicans. Twice Johnson was defeated for the Senate and once for Congress. During some of his speeches his bodyguard stood around him with pistols cocked. Finally, in 1875, after a week of bitter political fighting, the Tennessee Senate appointed him U.S. Senator on the 54th ballot*—again by one vote. He returned to Washington vindicated and almost universally praised. Four months later, while visiting his daughter in Tennessee, he died.

* Senators were not directly elected until 1913.

VI.. The General, the Cowboy & the Judge

• • *WILLIAM T. SHERMAN*

• • *THEODORE ROOSEVELT*

• • *WILLIAM H. TAFT*

1868–1913

In the 33 years between the attempted impeachment of Andrew Johnson and the administration of Theodore Roosevelt there was crookedness, grime, occasional high service; but no political lustre. The power of the country was not in Washington. It was in New York, Chicago, Pittsburgh, Cleveland and other great cities where the industrialization of America was taking place. Congress and the President stood back while the spoils were divided. Now they would favor one group, now another, on rare occasions they even acted in the public interest; but they themselves were not the power.

The speeches and campaign songs of this period have a garish ring as if every four years America engaged not in a for-real election but rather in some Brechtian burlesque of the political act. In the boss-saturated atmosphere of the day most of the public politicians were puppets dancing on the strings of this or that special interest in sham battle over bogus issues. Were a writer to try and satirize those times he could not do it more perfectly than the era's songs and speeches themselves. Henry Adams, grandson of diary-writing John Quincy, summed up the era in his autobiography: "No period so thoroughly ordinary had been known in American politics since Christopher Columbus first disturbed the balance of American society."

In keeping with the times, General Sherman, perhaps the country's outstanding figure of power, refused to live in Washington. "Washington is corrupt as Hell, made so by the looseness and extravagance of war," he wrote. "I will avoid it as a pest house." Avoid it he did. No other American has ever been under such intense pressure to become President for so long and has so consistently said "No." There would have been no doubt of his election. Sherman realized that. Indeed, if Sherman had said "yes" in 1880 he might very possibly have been the candidate of both parties.

Undoubtedly, Sherman was influenced in his determination not to be a candidate by what happened as President to his friend Grant. But in addition, Sherman's reasons lay deeper. Having found himself after much struggle he did not wish again to jeopardize himself. He had that most un-American trait, the ability to recognize that the step up to something bigger was not necessarily for him: that he was happiest where he was. He could say: "No."

The period started with Grant and high hopes. People thought General Grant would be another Washington. They learned fast. Scandals replaced war as government's main business. There were the Gould gold scandal, the Credit Mobilier scandal, the Whiskey Ring scandal, the Gas Ring scandal, the Railroad scandal and the Navy Department frauds.

From the beginning Sherman had urged his own course on Grant.

SHERMAN   I have written Grant a long letter and begged him to adhere to his resolution to leave Washington. He's now deservedly the hero, belabored with praise by those who a short time ago accused him of all the sins in the calendar; and who next week will turn against him if so blows the popular breeze.

• *Grant accepted the Republican nomination and went on to run under the slogans of:*

> Patient of Toil
> Serene amidst alarms
> Inflexible in faith
> Invincible in arms.
> Grant! Grant! Grant!

• *Or more simply:*

> Vote as you shot! Grant!

• *The slogans of his opponents show the same logic:*

> No North!
> No South!
> Union Inseparable
> Seymour and Blair!

• *Also:*

> White men and Liberty—Seymour and Blair.

• *Grant was blessed (?) with a great many campaign songs.*

> Our Chieftain's bound to win the day,
>   Hurrah, Hurrah!
> And drive the night of gloom away,
>   Hurrah, Hurrah!
> He'll bring a day of joy and peace—
> From all misrule our land release,
>   And we'll all feel safe,
> When General Grant takes the helm
>   Boom! Boom!

Get ready for the jubilee
   Hurrah, Hurrah!
We'll give the hero three times three,
   Hurrah, Hurrah!
The laurel wreath is circling now
About his brave and loyal brow
   And we'll all feel secure,
When General Grant wins the day.
   Boom! Boom!

● *Grant won; and the unhappy first term began. As he him-self described it later:*

GRANT   It was my fortune, or misfortune, to be called to the office of Chief Executive without any previous political training. From the age of 17 I had never even witnessed the excitement attending a Presidential campaign but twice; and at but one of them was I eligible as a voter.

Under such circumstances it is reasonable to suppose that errors of judgment must have occurred, mistakes have been made as all can see and admit. But it seems to me oftener in the selection of assistants—in nearly every case selected without a personal acquaintance with the appointee, but upon the recommendations of the representatives chosen by the people.

History shows that no administration from the time of Washington has been free from these mistakes. I have acted in every instance from a conscientious desire to do what was right, constitutional, within the law, and for the very best interests of the whole people. Failures have been errors of judgment not of intent.

● *With Grant's first term a mess, both parties looked toward Sherman.*

SHERMAN   Some fool seems to have used my name for President. If forced to choose between the penitentiary and the White House for four years, I would say: the penitentiary, thank you. Of military titles I now have the maximum. I have commanded one hundred thousand men in battle successfully. That's enough. Soldiers should mind their own business. . . .

I care no more for the squabbles about the Presidency than I do for the causes of the Schleswig-Holstein difficulty.

● *Grant was renominated and ran against the editor of the New York Tribune, the eccentric political liberal, Horace Greeley.*

> So boys a final bumper
>   While we in chorus chant,
> For our next President we nominate
>   Our own Ulysses Grant;
> And if asked what state he hails from
>   This our sole reply shall be
> From near Appomattox Court House
>   With its famous apple tree.

● *The Greeley campaign slogans were:*

> Peace to the Nation
> Power to the People
> Purity to the Government

● *Or more simply:*

> Down with Grant
> Useless Grant!

● *Grant won. Gideon Welles, the aging diarist, summed up the whole affair with the words: "A crooked stick may be made available to beat a mad dog."*

SHERMAN   I've never seen Grant more troubled than since he's been in Washington. He's been compelled to read of himself as a sneak and a deceiver. It's ruined his children. I think these eight years will make him miserable 'til the end of his life. If it's done that with one so prudent as he is, what would be the result with one so careless, so outspoken as I am.—Never—I wouldn't be Grant for a million dollars.

● *In 1876 both parties wanted Sherman.*

SHERMAN   I see the Herald and others are in full blast for me as President. In no event and under no circumstances will I ever be a candidate for President or any other political office. And I mean every word of it. Goddamn it! I've seen power poison so many otherwise good characters that I'm more obstinate than ever. I will not be used for political ends.

● *The Republicans nominated Hayes, the Democrats, Tilden.*

> Honest Money!
> Honest Government!
> Honest Hayes!

> Tilden! Tilden! Tilden! And Reform!

Mine eyes behold the banner of the soldier patriot Hayes;
With the flashing stars of Liberty its field is all ablaze,
As it marshals us to battle in the cool November days;
>   Its light is shining on.
Glory, Glory, Hayes and Wheeler.
Glory, Glory, Hayes and Wheeler.
Glory, Glory, Hayes and Wheeler.
>   As we go marching on.

I hear the tramp of Negroes marching onward to the polls.
The thunder of their cheering over all the nation rolls;
God bless the burning ardor of their patriotic souls,
>   As they go voting on.
Glory, Glory, Hayes and Wheeler.
Glory, Glory, Hayes and Wheeler.
Glory, Glory, Hayes and Wheeler.
>   As we go voting on.

● *Tilden had the popular majority but Hayes won in the famous "steal of '76," when a Republican-dominated Senate* and House committee voted to seat the Hayes rather than the Tilden electors from several doubtful states. By 1880, after one term of Hayes, the cry for Sherman was louder than ever.

SHERMAN   It's simply absurd. I wouldn't think of it for the fortieth part of a second. I lead a peaceful life; and if I ran for President I'd wake up some morning and find all over the newspapers that I'd poisoned my grandmother. Now you know my mother's mother died before I was born. But the newspapers would say I killed her—and prove it.

• Because since the time of General Washington men have loudly insisted they didn't want the Presidency while actively campaigning for it, people had a tendency to disbelieve Sherman. Telegrams and letters urging him to run poured in. Sherman would storm: "Vox populi, vox humbug!"

Then the Republican convention officially begged him. The Republicans were worried. Grant wanted to make a political comeback and try for a third term. It was the pressure from this convention that caused Sherman to make his historic outburst: "Goddamn it! I would account myself a fool, a madman, an ass to embark now, at my age, in a political career. If nominated I will not accept; and if elected I will not serve."

Even desperate politicians had to believe that. So the Republicans settled on Garfield and Arthur and the nation got them. Arthur was a New York politician whom Hayes had removed as Inspector of Customs for New York because of crookedness.

• Garfield's campaign stressed his humble origins and Civil War service.

> From tow-path to the White House
> From canal boy to President
> Garfield!

Garfield and Arthur, a ticket to sing about!

We're the Radical Campaign Shouters
And we kick up lots of noise
We "woop-em-up" for our candidate,
And we sing to please the boys.
For Garfield and for Arthur
We will make the welkin ring,
And on the fourth of March next year,
In Washington we'll sing.
   Hurrah, hurrah, hurrah, hurrah!
   Bring out your banners gay,
   For Garfield is our President
   And we have won the day.
   We're the Radical Campaign Shouters,
   Just out upon a tare,
   And we mean to put Jim Garfield
   In the Presidential chair.

● *In Cleveland, Ohio, on a Saturday evening, Candidate Garfield delivered what the newspapers call "A major policy address."*

GARFIELD   Fellow Citizens, a word before I leave you on the eve of the holy day of God. A fit moment to consecrate ourselves to voting Republican next Tuesday. I see in this vast audience a great many young men who are about to cast their first vote. I want to give them a word of advice about in which political camp to pitch their tent. Pitch your tent among the living not among the dead! The Democratic party is a graveyard.

   Why look here! Here is a Democratic mound, a black tomb, and above it towers to the sky a monument of four million pairs of human fetters taken from the limbs of whipped slaves, and I read on its grim face: "Sacred to the memory of human slavery." For forty years of its infamous life the Democratic party taught that slavery was divine, God's institution. But here it lies dead by the hand of Abraham Lincoln, dead by the power of the Republican Party, dead by the justice of Almighty God. Don't camp there, young man.

But look, here is another, a little brimstone tomb, and I read across its yellow face in lurid lines of blood, these words: "Sacred to the Memory of Secession." Twelve millions of Democrats mustered around it to keep it alive. But here it lies, shot to death by the million guns of the Republic. Here it lies, its shrine burned to ashes under the blazing rafters of the burning confederacy.

I would not have you stay a moment, young man, even in this balmy night air, to look at such a place. Enter our camp young man; our camp of liberty, of order, of justice, of freedom, of all that is glorious, and more besides.

Is there any death in our Republican camp? Yes! Yes! Yes! Three hundred and fifty thousand soldiers, the noblest band of blessed martyrs that ever trod this sacred earth, died to make this the camp of glory and liberty forever. Twenty-five years ago the Republican party was married to liberty. And we are true to Liberty today and dearer to God than when we spoke our first word, which was—Liberty. Come into our camp where all is living and nothing is dead but the heroes that defended our starry banner of freedom, whose glorious folds, vindicated by our blood and truth, sweep all the earth and touch the immortal stars.—Good night.

• *Garfield won but was almost immediately assassinated—in keeping with the spirit of the times, not for ideological reasons but by a disappointed office-seeker. There was a genuine and enormous outpouring of grief over Garfield's death. The Presidency of the United States also draws power from its martyrs. At the next election, 1884, the cry was again for Sherman.*

SHERMAN   With universal suffrage and the organization of political parties no man of supreme ability can be President. King Log is as good as King Stork. Our President with only four years is a chip on the surface. Not a single person has been President in our time without having been the most abused, if not the most miserable, man in the whole community. It killed Harrison, Taylor, Lincoln and Garfield. It will kill Arthur. And meanwhile Queen Victoria has proved about the best executive any nation ever had.

● *The pressure built up.*

SHERMAN   Look—I would receive a sentence to be hung and damned with infinitely more composure than to be President. You cannot account for tastes, but I know mine. I would prefer a tent on the banks of some wilderness stream to the White House. . . .

Never fear that I will be infested with the poison of Presidential aspiration; on the contrary, the place has no temptations but quite the contrary. Let Blaine, Bristow, and Conkling, trained in that school of scandal and abuse have the office if they want it, each in turn.

● *Blaine was nominated by the Republicans in 1884 but was defeated by Cleveland. Next Harrison, a Republican, defeated Cleveland in 1888; Cleveland bounced back and defeated Harrison in 1892. Then in 1896 McKinley the Republican defeated Bryan, a Democrat. There is little need to remember any of this. By the election of 1888 Sherman was finally able to write: "I note with joy that my name is being gradually dropped and my sincerity recognized." In 1891 Sherman died, that rarity: a hero who, in a long life, had not worn his honors out.*

Two images stand out as the puppet play drew to a close. Harrison exclaiming when he learned he'd been elected: "Providence has given us the victory." Matthew Quay, Chairman of the Republican National Committee, hearing this, remarked: "Think of the man! He ought to know that Providence hadn't a damn thing to do with it." He added, "A number of men were compelled to approach the gates of the penitentiary to make him President."

The other is McKinley carefully putting his cigar away when he was photographed and saying: "We must not let the young men of this country see their President smoking."

Meanwhile off stage in McKinley's first term, during the Spanish–American war over Cuba, a new political force was building. That force's daughter, Alice Roosevelt, describes the beginning of the Teddy Roosevelt phenomenon:

ALICE ROOSEVELT   I was the "Colonel's daughter," and if I was in love with one of my father's Rough Riders, I was in love with twenty, even though I did have a pigtail and a short dress.

I don't suppose there was ever any group of men quite like the Rough Riders. There were men from the Western Plains, cowboys, Texas Rangers, Indian fighters, and a number of Indians. There were others whom father had known or who knew of "young Roosevelt" in ranching and big game hunting days; there were Southerners and Northerners, whose immediate forebears had been on opposite sides in the Civil War; there were several New York ex-policemen who had been on the force when father was Commissioner and a sprinkling of adventurers from other lands. A large number came from Harvard, Yale and Princeton.

• *At San Juan Hill, Teddy Roosevelt spoke the words that were to make him President.*

T.R.   Gentlemen, the Almighty God and the Just Cause are with you. Gentlemen! Charge!

Our candidate for President,
  McKinley in first place,
And Roosevelt for his running mate,
  Are sure to win the race.
McKinley brought prosperity,
  And Roosevelt won the day
At San Juan Hill, and Cuba freed
  From Spain's most cruel sway.

William McKinley gives our industries protection.
Roosevelt. Roosevelt. Roosevelt. Roosevelt.
William McKinley gives us dollars good as gold.
Roosevelt. Roosevelt. Roosevelt. Roosevelt.

Our candidates are true and tried,
   Our platform's up to date,
We'll vote for them election day,
   And seal Bill Bryan's fate.
Free Trade, Free Silver, and Free Soup,
   Free everything goodbye
Bryan will not do what Cleveland did;
   And rob us of our pie.
      William McKinley gives our industries protection.
      Roosevelt. Roosevelt. Roosevelt. Roosevelt.
      William McKinley gives us dollars good as gold.
      Roosevelt. Roosevelt. Roosevelt. Roosevelt.

• *Roosevelt had been given the Vice-Presidency because, as governor of New York, he had been reforming that state a little too energetically to suit the State's Republican leader, Boss Platt. The idea of Roosevelt on the ticket gave Mark Hanna, McKinley's campaign manager, fits.*

HANNA   You know a President sometimes dies. And where would we be if Roosevelt should come into the White House?

T.R.   That McKinley has no more backbone than a chocolate eclair.

HANNA   Don't any of you realize there's only one life between that madman and the Presidency?

T.R.   McKinley keeps his ear so close to the ground it's always full of grasshoppers.

• *McKinley was shot and Hanna delivered his classic line:* "Now that damn cowboy is President of the United States."
    "That damn cowboy" wrote to the English historian, George Trevelyan:

T.R.   Dear Sir George, I liked your son's book, England in the Age of Wycliffe, much. It gave me a much clearer idea of the times, a much more vivid picture of them, than I ever had before. . . .

Well, I have just been inaugurated and begun my second term. My first in my own right. Now watch me. I wish you could have been here, for I think that the ceremonies, if such they can be called, would have interested you. Of course I greatly enjoyed inauguration day, indeed I have thoroughly enjoyed being President. Others have lived longer in the White House, but none have ever really had more fun out of it than I have. This morning I shook hands with six thousand people at the reception. This afternoon I took a two hours' good hard ride with four of my children and a dozen of their cousins and friends; jumping fences, scrambling over the wooded hills, galloping on the level; just the kind of fun to fit a public man for work. . . .

When I first got to be President I used to box with some of my aides, as well as play singlestick with General Wood. After a few years I had to abandon boxing as well as wrestling, for in one bout a young captain of artillery cross-countered me on the eye, and the blow smashed the little blood vessels. Fortunately it was the left eye, if it had been the right I should have been unable to shoot. But I thought it better to acknowledge that I had become elderly and would have to stop boxing. I then took up jiu-jitsu for a year or two. . . .

While President, I tell you, I have *been* President, emphatically. I have used every ounce of power there was in the office. And I have not cared a rap for criticism of my usurpation of power, for I knew that that talk was all nonsense. I believe the efficiency of this government depends on a strong central executive; and whenever I could establish a precedent for strength, I did. I believe in power. . . .

Take the voyage of our battle fleet round the world. I determined on that move without consulting the Cabinet or

Congress, just as I took Panama without consulting the Cabinet or Congress. The British and the Germans didn't believe their own fleets, much less the American could sail around the world. So I made up my mind to have a showdown.

There were some pretty funny moments. Most of the wealthy people and leaders of opinion in the East were panic stricken at the idea to take the fleet away from the Atlantic. The head of the Senate naval committee, he was from the Eastern seaboard, announced the fleet could not go because Congress would not appropriate the money. I told them I had enough money to take the fleet as far as the Philippines; and if Congress didn't choose to appropriate the money to get the fleet back why it could stay in the Pacific. I sent the fleet off. There was no difficulty about the money. . . .

You know what I wish about the Senate. I wish I had sixteen or twenty lions to turn loose on the Senate floor. (A friend asked the President if the lions might not eat the wrong Senators?)

Not if they stayed long enough. . . .

You know what I have to deal with in the Senate, frank enemies like Gorman; and in addition with the entire tribe of fat witted people, headed by a voluble pin-headed creature named Bacon from Georgia. There's a horrid example of the mischief that can be done by a man of very slender capacity, if only he possesses great loquacity, effrontery, and an entire indifference to the national welfare. Yet, on the whole, I'm making progress. . . .

Panama?—There's a bully example—If I had followed traditional, conservative methods I should have submitted a State Paper of probably 200 pages to Congress and the debate would be going on yet. But I took the Canal Zone and then let Congress debate. And the Canal was going on while they were debating. —I was accused of being unconstitutional. I was only that if Jefferson was unconstitutional when he took Louisiana. . . .

After a sufficient period of wrangling the Senate ratified the treaty with Panama. Congress insisted the Canal should be built by a commission of several men. I tried faithfully to get good work out of their Commission and found it quite impossible. When the Senate still refused to make the Commission single headed, I solved the difficulty by executive order. I put in Colonel Goethals as head of the Commission, enlarged the powers of the Chairman and made the other members dependent on him. I handled domestic affairs, disciplined the coal trust, the oil trust, and the railroad monopolies just the same way. I didn't flinch, didn't foul, and I hit the line hard; and I got substantial justice done.

(Mr. President, queried a reporter, how do you know substantial justice was done?)

Because I did it. I was doing my best.

(You mean to say that when you do a thing, substantial justice is automatically done?)

I do. When I do a thing I do it that way. I mean just that.

—Look if your soul does not rise up against corruption in politics and business. If you will tolerate the vileness, the unspeakable degradation and baseness of "leaders" like Rockefeller, Harriman, and Black and the New York Sun, then naturally you're out of sympathy with me. If you have that fervor for righteousness and decency without which mere goodness becomes an empty sham, why then you support me. . . .

No other President ever enjoyed the Presidency as I do. Not just the form and show. I don't care a rap for form and show; but I care immensely for what use can be made of power.

• *Though he realized how much he liked power, Roosevelt made the fatal public statement he was later to so bitterly regret.*

T.R.   Many of my supporters are insisting that as I have served only three and a half years of my first term, coming in

from the Vice Presidency when McKinley was killed, I really
have had only one elective term, so that the third term custom does not apply to me. I wish to repudiate this idea. The
wise custom which limits the President to two terms regards
the substance and not the form; and under no circumstances
will I be a candidate for or accept another nomination. . . .

• *He set about to find a candidate who would carry on the
Roosevelt tradition.*

T.R.   Now Will Taft, he's a blessed old trump. He is not
only absolutely fearless, absolutely disinterested and upright;
but he has the widest acquaintance with the nation's needs.
Taft would be as emphatically President of the plain people
as Lincoln. He would rank with any other man who has ever
been in the White House.

Taft   It's good of you, Theodore; but I'd rather be a judge.

T.R.   The most lovable personality I've ever come in con-
tact with.

Taft   No. There could hardly be a weaker candidate than I
would be.

T.R.   Hit them hard, old man. You big, generous, high-
minded fellow. Let them see you smile. Another Lincoln.

Taft   Politics when I am in it makes me sick.

T.R.   He'll make the greatest President.

• *At the Republican nominating convention the delegates
from the state of Texas paraded round the floor with a banner
bearing the following strange device: "As pants the hart for
cooling streams so Texas pants for Taft.—Taft, Taft, Taft,
Taft." Roosevelt was overjoyed at the way things were moving
for Taft. "Bully! Bully!" he told him. Taft replied: "I owe
a great deal to you, Theodore."*

T.R.   Dear Will, I do not want this letter seen by anyone but you and Mrs. Taft. It seems absurd but I'm convinced that the prominence given your golf playing has not been wise. From now on I hope your people will do everything they can to prevent word about either your fishing or your golf. . . .

When I get through the Presidency I'm going for a year to Africa to see the great beasts and get a few lions.

● *This news caused joy in Congress. At parties in Washington Senators rose to their feet and toasted: "The lions!" J. P. Morgan got off his notorious aside: "Let every lion do his duty."*

T.R.   Ha, ha, Will. You are making up your Cabinet. I, in a light hearted way am testing rifles for my African trip. Life has compensations. Ever yours.

TAFT   Whenever I hear someone say, "Mr. President," I look around expecting to see Roosevelt. And when I read in the morning papers that the President and Senator Aldrich and speaker Cannon have had a conference, my first thought is, I wonder what they talked about.

T.R.   For a year after Taft took office I would not let myself think ill of anything he did. I went out of the country to give him the fullest possible chance to work out his own salvation. I finally had to admit that he had gone wrong on certain points. I then had to admit to myself that deep, down underneath I had all along known he was wrong, but had tried to deceive myself by loudly proclaiming to myself that he was right. . . .

I dread getting back to America and having to plunge into this cauldron of politics. I do not attach any real importance to the seeming popularity which I for the moment enjoy. I don't see how it can work out for permanent good.

TAFT   Dear Theodore, It's now a year and three months since I assumed office and I have had a hard time. I do not know that I have had harder luck than other Presidents, but I do know that thus far I have succeeded far less than others. I have been conscientiously trying to carry out your policies, but my method of doing so has not worked smoothly. The fight, especially with the Senate, has been a hard one.

T.R.   I share very keenly people's disappointment in Taft, in a way perhaps feel it even more deeply than they; because it was I who made him President. Yet it behooves us to realize that it is not only possible but probable, that two years hence circumstances will be such as to make it necessary to renominate Taft and reelect him. All of us have had to support Presidents, Governors, and other candidates, not because they were the best men for the positions, or anywhere near that, but because they were the only men who could be nominated.

TAFT   I'm not criticizing the President, I mean Roosevelt, but simply saying our ways are different. There's no use trying to be William Howard Taft with Roosevelt's ways. I get rather tired hearing from his friends that I am not carrying out his policies; and when I ask them for one instance they cannot name one. I don't see that I'm open to the charge that I am anti-Roosevelt.

T.R.   Things are getting worse rather than better. Taft, who is such an admirable fellow, has shown himself such an utterly commonplace leader, good-natured, feebly well meaning, but with plenty of small motive; and totally unable to grasp or put into execution any great policy. As you know, I am a genuine radical. My view is that every executive officer in high position is a steward of the people, bound to do all he can actively for the people; and not to content himself with keeping his talents undamaged in a napkin.

I believe it not only the President's right but his duty to do anything that the needs of the nation demand unless such action is specifically forbidden by the Constitution or by its laws. I did many things not previously done by Presidents.

TAFT   Roosevelt's view of ascribing an undefined residuum of power to the President is an unsafe doctrine and it might lead under emergencies to irremediable injustice. The mainspring of such a view is that the Executive is charged with the responsibility for the welfare of all the people, that he is to play the part of a Universal Providence.

Real progress in Government must come by slow stages. Congress must be educated up to the value of new reform legislation and become convinced of its wisdom over many successive sessions. Radical and revolutionary changes, arbitrarily put into operation are not likely to accomplish the good prophesied.

T.R.   The course I followed of regarding the President as bound to serve the people affirmatively was substantially the course followed by both Andrew Jackson and Abraham Lincoln. Other honorable and well meaning Presidents such as James Buchanan, took the opposite view that the President is the servant of Congress rather than the people, and can do nothing unless the Constitution explicitly commands action. Most able lawyers who are past middle age take this view; and so does my successor. It's a question of temperament.

TAFT   Mr. Roosevelt by way of illustrating his meaning as to the differing usefulness of Presidents, divides the Presidents into two classes: the Lincoln Presidents and the Buchanan Presidents. He places himself in the Lincoln class and me in the Buchanan class.

The identification of Mr. Roosevelt with Mr. Lincoln might otherwise have escaped notice, because there are many differences between the two, presumably superficial, which would give the impartial student of history a different impression. It suggests a story which a friend of mine told me of his little daughter, Mary, who ran out of the house to greet him one afternoon all aglow with importance. She said:

"Papa, I am the best scholar in the class." The father's heart throbbed with pleasure as he inquired.

"Why Mary, you surprise me. When did the teacher tell you?"

'Oh,' Mary replied, "the teacher didn't tell me—I just noticed it myself."

T.R.   Taft means well; but he means well feebly.

TAFT   It's hard to take all the slaps Roosevelt is handing me. In his latest attack he practically calls me a hypocrite. I don't understand him. I don't understand what he's driving at except to make my way more difficult. I can't ask his advice on all questions. I cannot subordinate my administration to him and retain my self respect. But it's hard, hard to see a devoted friendship going to pieces like a rope of sand.

• *The pressure on Roosevelt to run again, largely from reformers and liberals in the Republican party, began to build. Others of his friends urged him not to run. Several newspapers were for him.*

T.R.   I'm not in the running and I'm not going to be dragged into it. Taft created the mess and let Taft take his spanking for it. . . .

If I wanted four more years in the White House I would say so and go after it. But I don't want it. I've had enough. . . .

Why should I be asked to take command of a sinking ship? Why should I be asked to imperil the satisfactory record of my first seven years by undertaking another term in which I might not do as well?

TAFT   I have not played with much luck during this adminstration. But if Roosevelt wanted to understand he could understand. But a falling out is just what he wants.

T.R.   Taft has been disloyal to our past friendship and disloyal to every canon of human decency. He has bowed to the political bosses with the grossest and outstanding hypocrisy.

• *Roosevelt began to shift his position. He was now saying: "I'm not sure I could live with myself if I did not go in." The* more interested he seemed in the nomination, the more his rivals, Democratic and Republican, hurled at him his former statement of withdrawal: "Under no circumstances will I be a candidate for or accept another nomination."

T.R.   I would cut off my hand right here if I could recall that statement. . . .

Look, when I said that I would not accept a nomination for a third term under any circumstances, what I meant of course was a third consecutive term. Now it's different. See, it's as if at breakfast this morning, I'd said I don't want a third cup of coffee. That doesn't mean I was never going to take another cup of coffee. I didn't say that at no time in my life would I accept another nomination.

• *The pressure on Roosevelt mounted. It wasn't all from outside himself.*

T.R.   My hat's in the ring!
The fight is on and I'm stripped to the buff!

TAFT   This wrenches my soul. I am here to reply to an old and true friend who has made many charges. I deny those charges. I deny all of them.

The truth with respect to me is the same as with respect to Mr. Roosevelt. When I am running for the Presidency I gratefully accept such support as comes to me. Mr. Roosevelt has done the same in the past and is doing it now. To attack me because men he characterizes as bosses are supporting me is audacious effrontery.

T.R.   Let us find out whether the Republican Party is the party of the plain people; or whether it is the party of the bosses and the sinister interests of special privilege.

• *Those for him adopted a rallying cry which was later to become a political party.*

I want to be a Bull Moose
And with the Bull Moose stand
With Antlers on my forehead
And a Big Stick in my hand.

T.R.   We are going to win.

TAFT   Condemn me if you will; but condemn me by other witnesses than Theodore Roosevelt. I have been a man of straw long enough. Every man who has blood in his body and has been as misrepresented as I have is forced to fight. I don't want to fight. But when I do fight I want to hit hard. Even a rat in a corner will fight.

T.R.   He called himself a rat in a corner. He is right.

• *The Taft slogan was: "Washington wouldn't! Grant couldn't! Roosevelt shan't. No third term!"*

TAFT   Death alone can take me out now. I'll fight to the finish. Whether I win is not the important thing. I am in this fight to perform a public duty—to keep Theodore Roosevelt out of the White House.

T.R.   Mr. Taft's policy is flabby indecision and helpless acquiescence in the wrongdoing of the crooked boss and the crooked financier. He has nothing back of him in his campaign but the support of the great sinister special interests.

TAFT   Four years ago Theodore Roosevelt painted me in such glowing language that I blushed. Now he is using about me language equally strenuous and equally inapplicable. Has he changed, or have I?

• *They ended yelling:*

T.R.   Barefaced fraud!

TAFT   Wild unconstitutional flatterer!

T.R.   Fathead!

TAFT   Demagogue!

T.R.   Apostate!

TAFT   Jacobin!

T.R.   Puzzlewit!

• *That was the charge that angered Taft most.*

TAFT   Honeyfugler!

• *That was the blow that got to Roosevelt.*

T.R.   Weakling!

TAFT   Brawler!

• *Though Roosevelt won all the open primaries he had been too much of a reformer for the bosses and the big money in the Republican party. They gave the nomination to Taft. In anger Roosevelt formed his own party, the Bull Moose, and went on to run as an independent. This guaranteed the election of Woodrow Wilson.*

T.R.   What happens to me is not of the slightest consequence. I went before the people and I won. Now I am denied the nomination. But the victory shall still be ours; and we shall gain it by honest fighting for the loftiest of causes. We fight for the good of mankind, unheeding of our individual fates; with unflinching hearts and undimmed eyes.

We stand at Armageddon; and we battle for the Lord.

• *What was Teddy Roosevelt? History has pushed him around a great deal. He seems in retrospect to have been neither a cowboy, nor a shallow braggart, nor a consistent crusader; but an almost perfect embodiment of Victorian Man, with all the strengths and weaknesses of that awakening but self-satisfied age. Like all politicians, and he was a master politician; his success and power came in large part because he lived the philosophy of his time. England had the glorious reign of Queen Victoria. The United States had the exciting term of Theodore Roosevelt.*

VII .. Breaking the Heart of the World

• • WOODROW WILSON
1913–1921

Woodrow Wilson's public life had three phases: President of Princeton, Governor of New Jersey, and President of the United States. In all three he started out magnificently, then slipped. What happened?

First, as President of Princeton, Wilson raised the endowment, improved the quality of education, bettered faculty-student relationships and moved to break the power of Princeton's fraternities. Then he got into a crippling battle over the nature of the new graduate school. Wilson's inflexibility in that battle caused faculty and trustees to turn from him and penalized graduate education at Princeton for a long while.

Disgusted with Princeton and in danger of being fired, Wilson was nominated for Governor by the old line Democratic bosses of New Jersey. He was elected in 1910, carrying a normally Republican state by 49,000 votes. Wilson served for little more than a year as Governor, so he did not have the time to leave New Jersey's Democrats in the shambles he left the Princeton faculty. He broke with the conservatives who had nominated him and joined the reform wing of his party to give New Jersey such outstanding legislation as a direct primary law, a Public Utilities Commission, and an Employers Liability Act. Yet by 1911 he had so thoroughly riled many of his fellow Democrats that the Republicans captured the legislature.

Elected President of the United States in large part because of the Taft-Roosevelt split, Wilson began his Presidency by skillfully and vitally maneuvering through Congress tariff reduction, currency reform, laws to regulate industry and other progressive measures. But even in this period the skillful politician and the inflexible prophet prowled together inside him. His gunboat diplomacy in the Dominican Republic, Nicaragua, Haiti and Mexico combined crude force with a high moral cant that went beyond the worst of Teddy Roosevelt. Born and raised in the South, he acquiesced in the resegregation of the Navy.

The nature of the First World War he grasped slowly and partially. He failed to convince his own country to accept the great objective for which he took America into war, his beloved League of Nations. Did this pattern of fine start and final failure stem from Wilson himself? Or did the times in which he lived not permit him to achieve his potential?

Historians have been kind to Wilson. He is one of them, an historian who became President. They often cover for him as policemen do for policemen who go wrong. When they write about him they sometimes sound as if they saw themselves in the Presidential chair. Only recently has the stature of Wilson's historical image begun to be questioned.

When Wilson went to Paris in December of 1918 to negotiate a treaty to end all wars, he was at the zenith of his fame. America's power had turned the tide in the Allies' favor and Wilson was the man who had led America in. His fourteen points for a just peace had fired the imagination of the world. Yet, hating dissent, he had not included any powerful Republicans in the treaty-making delegation. And many Republicans were wholeheartedly for his proposals, including ex-President

William Howard Taft. At the peace conference itself, Britain's Lloyd George and France's Clemenceau negotiated circles around him. But perhaps this was inevitable. Wilson was an idealist with few cards to play in a bitter, divided world; and France and Britain had borne the full cost and horror of war.

Strong Presidents from Andrew Jackson to John Kennedy have trended toward confidential advisers and kitchen cabinets. President Wilson's confidant at the Paris peace conference was Colonel Edward M. House, a dapper and urbane Texan who had been the President's virtual second-in-command during the long negotiations. Colonel House described both the great hour and his concern over Woodrow Wilson.

HOUSE   June 28, 1919: This is the great day! I left the Crillon about 2:15. The approach to Versailles was an imposing sight, as was the entrance to the palace. Thousands of people lined the roadway from Paris to Versailles, increasing in number as we drew near the palace. There was a great display of cavalry with pennants flying and upon the Grand Stairway, which witnessed the last stand of the bodyguards during the French Revolution, chasseurs in gorgeous uniforms lined both sides up to the very entrance of the Hall of Mirrors, where the signing of the peace treaty took place. Arthur Balfour and I went in together and presently were joined by Lloyd George and Baron Sonnino.

The ceremonies lasted nearly an hour. When the Germans had signed and the great allied powers had done so the cannons began to boom. The fountains played for the first time since the war began. Aeroplanes were in the air, guns were being fired, and the thousands surrounding Versailles made a brilliant and memorable scene.

Afterwards we went to the station to see the President and his party off for the boat and home. There was a large crowd of notables and the whole affair was brilliant and successful. However, my last conversation with the President yesterday was not reassuring. I urged him to meet the Senate in a conciliatory spirit; if he treated them with the same consideration he had used with his foreign colleagues here, all would be well.

WILSON   House, I have found one can never get anything in this life that is worth while without fighting for it.

HOUSE   I combatted this and reminded him that the Anglo-Saxon civilization was built up on compromise. That to the ordinary man the distance between the Treaty and the reservations of some Senators was slight.

WILSON   We are the servants of mankind, and if we do not heed the mandates of mankind we shall make ourselves the most conspicuous and deserved failures in the history of the world. My prediction is that after the light has shone on this treaty it will not be necessary to do anything. Moral light is the most wholesome and rectifying thing in the world.

• *Historian that he was, Wilson should have realized that neither President John Adams nor his son John Quincy had gotten many votes from moral light. A great many persons had doubts about this or that section of the treaty creating the League. But only a few "irreconcilable" Senators like Borah, Johnson and LaFollette totally rejected the League. Most legislators were of the so-called "mild reservationists" who wanted a few changes here and there. What was needed was a little give and take, a little politics.*

Alice Roosevelt, the young girl who had described the Rough Riders, was now married to a conservative Ohio Congressman. She watched Wilson return to Washington.

ALICE ROOSEVELT   On Tuesday, July 8th, President Wilson got back from Paris. I wanted to see how many people turned out to greet him as he entered the White House grounds. It was a sparse crowd, not more than two or three hundred, of the sort to whom any man who happens to be

President is a spectacle; a hot summer night, women in light dresses, most of the men coatless. There was very little cheering—such as there was had a treble quality as women predominated.

I got out of my motor and stood an the curbstone to see the Presidential party pass, fingers crossed, making the sign of the evil eye, and saying: "A murrain on him, a murrain on him, a murrain on him!"

Two days later he laid before the Senate the Versailles Treaty which contained the League of Nations as an integral part. The presence of Lodge and Borah among the Senators delegated to escort him to the chamber raised a laugh.

WILSON   The Americans who went to Europe to die are a unique breed. Never before have men crossed the seas to a foreign land to fight for a cause which they did not pretend was peculiarly their own, which they knew was the cause of humanity and mankind. These Americans gave the greatest of all gifts, the gift of life and the gift of spirit.

It is our duty to take and maintain the safeguards which will see to it that the mothers of America and the mothers of all the other suffering nations shall never be called upon for this sacrifice again. This can be done. It must be done. And it will be done through the great instrument erected at Versailles, the League of Nations.

Now, if I may speak a personal word. I beg you to realize the compulsion that I, myself, feel I am under. By the Constitution of our great country I was the commander in chief. I sent those lads over there to die. Shall I—can I—ever speak a word of counsel that is inconsistent with the assurances I gave them when they went over? It is inconceivable.

Gentlemen of the Senate: the statesmen of Europe saw the League of Nations as not merely an instrument to adjust old wrongs under a new treaty of peace. They saw it was the only hope of mankind. They saw it as the hope of the world and that hope they did not dare disappoint. Shall we or any other free people hesitate to accept this great duty? Dare we reject the League and break the heart of the world?

• *One of Wilson's staunchest admirers was David Houston, a poor boy from South Carolina who became President of the University of Texas and whom Wilson appointed Secretary of Agriculture. During the crisis to come Houston was to remain totally loyal to Wilson; but he also used his eyes.*

HOUSTON   The President was overconfident. He's likely to be when a question involving a moral issue is before the people. Seeing the issue very clearly himself, he trusts the masses of the people to see it clearly; and see it his way. Also I don't think the President had sensed the change in the minds of people since the Armistice; and the headway his opponents had made with their skillful arguments.

WILSON   I never went into battle; I was never under fire; but I fancy that there are things just as hard to do as go under fire. I fancy that it is just as hard to do your duty when men are sneering at you as when they are shooting at you. When they shoot at you they can only take your natural life; when they sneer at you they can wound your living heart. Men who are brave enough to go about their duty whether there are hisses or cheers, they are men for a nation to be proud of.

• *Woodrow Wilson's second wife, his first had died while he was in the White House, was a corpulent, powerful widow. He proposed to her shortly after they first met. They were inseparable. In the evening with his head on her lap he would pour out to her the troubles governing gave him.*

MRS. WILSON   Anyone who knows the heat of Washington in July and August can picture the way energy is sapped with no strain needed to add to that of the weather. The increasing demands on my husband's brain and body exacted a toll which pyramided, while I looked on with anxious heart.

WILSON   I have been talking to more Senators about the League. They are endeavoring to humiliate me. They know and I realize that I am everywhere regarded as the foremost leader of liberal thought in the world.

MRS. WILSON   We learned today that Dudley Malone had espoused the cause of those detestable suffragette pickets. If anyone had told us that Dudley Malone could be such a traitor we would not have believed it. But Dudley came to see Woodrow who said he could do nothing with him. I hope he will resign and we will never see or hear of him again. My precious one did not come home from the office until six-thirty and was so weary it broke my heart to look at him.

WILSON   To Herbert Hoover, Personal. I have noticed that on one or two posters of the Food Administration are the words "Our Allies." I would be much obliged if you would issue instructions that "Our Associates in the Late War" is to be substituted. I have been very careful about this myself because we have no allies and I think I am right in believing that the people of this country are very jealous of any intimation that there are formal alliances; and I also think it important that we should all use the same language. . . .

It's no compliment to me to have it said that I am a great intellectual machine. Good Heavens, is there no more in me than that? I want people to love me—but I suppose they never will.

MRS. WILSON   My poor precious is working so hard for the League. He looked so tired again.—Oh, that stinker Senator Lodge is a snake in the grass, or rather not in the grass. He is a snake in the open.

WILSON   Senators are bungalow men, no upper story, ha, ha. They don't know what the people are thinking. They are as far from the people, the great mass of our people, as I am from Mars.

ALICE ROOSEVELT How we did cherish and nourish our hatreds in those days.

WILSON I know that in certain quarters of the country there is a popular demand for the pardon of Eugene V. Debs; but I shall never consent. Were I to consent to it, I should never to able to look into the faces of the mothers of this country who sent their boys to the other side. While the flower of American youth was pouring out its blood to vindicate the cause of civilization, this man, Debs, stood behind the lines, sniping, attacking and denouncing them.

They will say I am cold blooded and indifferent, but it will make no impression on me. . . .

The League will be ratified. There is a great wind of moral force moving and every man who opposes himself to that wind will go down to disgrace.

MRS. WILSON Towards the last of August, when there was apparently no more my precious could do alone to get the League ratified by the Senate, he said that as a last resort he must go to the country and explain to the people.

WILSON I will not be a slacker and unable to look our boys who went overseas in the eye. The League of Nations is the covenant that our lads shall not have died in vain.

MRS. WILSON This proposed trip was stoutly opposed by Dr. Grayson, who did not think the President could draw further on his strength without risking disaster.

• Dr. Grayson was a navy doctor who had been an assistant White House physician under Teddy Roosevelt. Wilson liked him and made him his personal doctor. The two were constantly together. Wilson was something of a hypochondriac and his health was never good. By the time of the Paris peace conference Grayson had emerged as a major backstage power *totally loyal to the President. One of the great unanswered questions of Wilson's reign is did the President have a mild stroke in Paris that Grayson failed to diagnose? There is a good deal of evidence that this happened.*

GRAYSON   I persuaded him once to cancel plans for the journey. But opposition to the League was increasing in the Senate and he felt he must rally the moral opinion of the country. Going into his study one morning I found the President seated at his desk, writing. I looked up.

WILSON   I do not want to do anything foolhardy, Doctor. But in the crucial test in the trenches our soldiers did not turn back. I cannot turn back now. I must go.

GRAYSON   I had played my last card and lost. There was nothing I could do except to go with him and take such care of him as I could.

MRS. WILSON   The tour had not progressed far when serious headaches began to afflict my husband. He paid little attention to them, though I could see that each day, each meeting, each appearance was calling more and more on his depleted reserve of nervous energy.

• *Everywhere the President goes the Secret Service unobstrusively follows. Colonel Starling was the Deputy-Chief of the White House detail.*

STARLING   At the Pueblo Colorado auditorium I walked beside the President from the car to the entrance. There was a single step. He stumbled on it and I caught him. I kept my hand on his arm, and almost lifted him up the steps to the platform. He made no objection, though in the past he had refused any suggestion of physical assistance from me. When he spoke I stood close behind him.

WILSON   We are dealing with a document simon pure, this League of Nations, and we have got to do one or the other of two things;—we have got to adopt it or reject it. There is no middle course. If we draw ourselves apart with dangerous pride, that means we shall have to maintain great standing armies and an irresistible navy; and that means we shall have the organization of a military nation; and that means we shall have a general staff with the kind of power the general staff of Germany. . . .

• *This speech which Wilson was delivering at Pueblo was the standard speech he had given all across the nation. Now suddenly he lost the thread. He made a try at continuing. He lost the thread again. Close to tears, he looked about bewildered. Starling, Mrs. Wilson and his confidential secretary, Joe Tumulty, started toward him. Wilson drew himself together and tried to find words.*

WILSON   Which must never be allowed. . . .
A lesson must be taught Germany. . . .
The world will not allow Germany to have. . . .

• *Then he grasped a theme.*

WILSON   Again and again my fellow citizens, mothers who lost their sons in France have come to me and, taking my hand, have shed tears upon it not only, but they have added, "God bless you, Mr. President."

Why, my fellow citizens, should they pray God to bless me? I ordered their sons overseas. They blessed me because they believed that their boys died for something that vastly transcends any of the immediate and palpable objects of the war. That they were crusaders. There seems to me to stand between us and rejection or qualification of the League the serried ranks of those boys in khaki, not only those boys who came home, but those dear ghosts that still deploy upon the fields of France.

Now that the mists about this great question have cleared away, I believe that men will see the truth, eye to eye and face to face. We are going out into the pastures of quietness and peace.

MRS. WILSON   On the train that evening about 11:30 I was surprised when my poor precious knocked at the intervening compartment door and asked would I come in as he was very sick. He said he had tried to sleep but that the pain had grown unbearable and thought I had better call Doctor Grayson.

That night was the longest and most heartbreaking in my life. Nothing the doctor could do gave relief. About five in the morning a blessed release came and sitting upright in the stiff train seat my husband fell asleep. The dear face opposite me was drawn and lined; and as I sat there, watching the dawn break slowly, I felt that from that hour I would have to wear a mask. Not only to the public but to the one I loved best, for he must never know how ill he was.

WILSON   I must keep on, little girl. I must keep on.

• On the Presidential train, which as usual was carrying the reporters covering the President, the cover-up began.

GRAYSON   The President has exerted himself so constantly and has been under such a strain the last year and has so spent himself on this trip that it has produced a serious reaction in his digestive organs.

The President is suffering from nervous exhaustion. It is altogether against his will that he give up this speech making tour. He was insistent he would be able to go on. But my judgment as a doctor, and the judgment of Mrs. Wilson, and of his executive assistant Mr. Tumulty is that we must get him as soon as possible into the restful atmosphere of the White House.

• Joe Tumulty, the President's confidential secretary, was one of the great figures in the Wilson era. He loved Wilson and had been with him since Wilson was governor of New Jersey. A warm, humorous man and an astute politician he had been invaluable. Yet now though he did not know it he was on the way out. Mrs. Wilson did not like him.

TUMULTY   We are not going to Wichita. The President is
ill with a nervous reaction. It will be necessary for us to start
back for Washington as soon as the railroad arrangements
are completed; and we'll go through with no stops but those
that are imperative.

MRS. WILSON   Tracks were cleared and with a pilot engine
running ahead of us we left Wichita for Washington. People
gathered at every station to see the train roar through. At
the stops they crowded round so that we pulled down the
shades. The car seemed like a funeral.

• *Back at the White House, Ike Hoover was waiting for
them. Ike Hoover, no relation to the future President, was
more or less the general manager of the White House from
President Harrison through Franklin D. Roosevelt.*

IKE HOOVER   Upon his return President Wilson looked no
worse than when he had left, except a little peaked. Then
four days later on Thursday, October 2nd, 1919, the crash
came. At exactly ten minutes before nine my telephone on the
ushers' desk in the White House rang and Mrs. Wilson's
voice said, "Please get Dr. Grayson. The President is very
sick."

Mrs. Wilson had come all the way out to the end of the
upper hall to use this particular phone that did not go through
the general switchboard instead of the regular one in their
bedroom. I reasoned this was because of the talk that the
switchboard operators listened in and told what they picked
up. I immediately called Dr. Grayson and then went upstairs
to see if there was anything I could do; but was helpless because all the doors were locked.

I waited up there until Dr. Grayson came. The whole
truth about the President's lasting illness can only be told
by Mrs. Woodrow Wilson; and I doubt whether she ever will.

MRS. WILSON   Dr. Grayson and I lifted the President into

his bed. He had suffered a stroke, paralyzing the left side of his body. An arm and one leg were useless but, thank God, the brain was clear and untouched. Nurses came and the house was organized as a hospital.

IKE HOOVER   There were all kinds of medical apparatus and more doctors and more nurses. All his natural functions had to be artificially assisted and he appeared just as helpless as one could possibly be and live. It was perhaps three weeks or more before any change came over things.

GRAYSON   Memorandum to the Press: The President is a very sick man. His condition is less favorable today and he has remained in bed throughout the day. After consultation in which all agreed as to his condition, it was determined that absolute rest is essential for some time.

MRS. WILSON   I asked the doctors to be frank with me. They all said that the brain was as clear as ever and that with the progress made in the past few days there was every reason to think recovery possible if the President were released from every disturbing problem.

The physicians said that if I could convey the messages of Cabinet members and others to the President he would escape the nervous drain. Even little courteous personal conversations would consume the President's strength. So began my stewardship.

HOUSTON   On Friday October 3rd I saw Secretary of War Baker at the Shoreham. He said, "I am literally scared to death." He looked it. Saturday I saw Tumulty. He gave me the first direct word I had concerning the President. He said he was paralyzed in one leg and one arm. We agreed it would be a tragedy if the President were to become incapacitated.

• One of the factors in the tragedy was the stature of Thomas R. Marshall, the Vice-President. He has gone down in history as the man who said: "What America needs is a good five cent cigar." There seems little other reason to put him down, or up, in history. He spent a great deal of his time outside of Washington supplementing his Vice-President's income by lecturing on what the government was doing.

HOUSTON   Sunday I saw Vice-President Marshall. Marshall was much disturbed and expressed regret that he was being kept in the dark about the President's condition. He asked me if I had any real facts. I could not even repeat what had been told me because it was said in confidence.

Finally several Cabinet members got to Doctor Grayson. He told us that the President's mind was very clear, but that he was suffering from a nervous breakdown, from indigestion and a depleted system. Dr. Grayson was asked if he could tell us more exactly what was the trouble. He replied he could add nothing to what he had already said.

GRAYSON   For more than a year while the President remained in office an invalid, Mrs. Wilson had to stand between him and the public. As she herself said, it seemed cruelty to disturb him with public affairs. If the business was too vital to be kept from his attention Mrs. Wilson had to listen to the Cabinet officers or delegations from the hill, take the matter to her husband and report back his decisions.

She was a great reporter and user of precise language. She said she was trained to accuracy when she was a child because her mother would tell her to be sure to observe closely anything she saw or heard in the town of Wytheville, Virginia, and repeat it to one of her grandparents who was an invalid.

• Secretary of State Lansing, talked to Tumulty about this situation.

LANSING   I send up memoranda to the President in the simplest form which anyone could understand; and get answers back from Mrs. Wilson so confused that no one can interpret them.

• Tumulty had his own problems, as he told a friend: "Mrs. Wilson keeps me from the President." In desperation he drew up a list.

TUMULTY   Dear Mrs. Wilson, Please don't think that I am trying to crowd you or to urge immediate action by the President, but I thought it would help you if you could have before you a list of matters that at intervals the President might wish to have presented to him for discussion and settlement. I might submit such a list as follows:

Return of the railways to private ownership, Costa Rica recognition, the mining strike, appointments for Secretary of the Treasury and the Interior and the Assistant Secretary of Agriculture; vacancies in the Civil Service Commission, Federal Trade Commission, and Interstate Commerce Commission.

There also are quite a few diplomatic appointments, such as Bulgaria, China, and Italy.

Also when you get a chance to talk to the President will you please tell him that Senator Hitchcock, the Democratic Majority Leader, sent for me yesterday and wanted to know whether the President would look with favor upon any effort on his part to make an adjustment with the mild reservationists to soften the Lodge reservations and thus avoid splitting the Democratic Party.

• There is no evidence Mrs. Wilson ever took any of this up with the President.

MRS. WILSON   At eleven o'clock a glass of milk and a cracker or cookie were brought to the President. If by chance this was late he would sit patiently for a while and then ask in a whisper: "Didn't anybody bring a tookie for me?" We so loved to hear him joke like this.

WILSON   Too many doctors, too many doctors. You know what too many cooks do.

TUMULTY   Dear Mrs. Wilson: I suggest you might read to the President the attached friendly editorial from the Oregon Journal on the need for compromise to save the League. If you could find the time.

MRS. WILSON   I would not be willing.

TUMULTY   Dear Mrs. Wilson: I do not know how the President feels about making an announcement with reference toward a third term. And I wonder whether in view of the League situation this is not the time to consider making a final statement. The Republicans circulate the story that the President is attempting to create out of the League an issue upon which he will soon base a reason for demanding a third term. I think a dignified statement of withdrawal now would greatly help all along the line and be made a ten strike for the League of Nations.

• *Mrs. Wilson never told the President. And the business of Government limped on.*

HOUSTON   I awoke Sunday morning, January 25th with the grippe. I was aching and chilly and had a temperature of 101. At 11:30 I was called up by the White House and was told that Mrs. Wilson wished me to call at 4:30 that afternoon. I hesitated for a moment on account of my slight illness, but finally said that I would be glad to call as requested. She greeted me very graciously and discussed various matters until the servants had finished serving tea. Then she said,

"You are wondering why I sent for you this afternoon. Of course, you know that I did not ask you to take the trouble to come merely to drink tea. The President asked me to tell you that he is very anxious for you to accept the Secretaryship of the Treasury. He is reluctant to have you give up Agriculture, but still he thinks he now needs you more in Treasury."

When she finished I said: "Please give my greetings to the President and tell him I am in harness until March 4th, 1921, if he wishes it; and that as long as I am with him I will dig stumps, or act as Secretary of the Treasury, or assume any other task he assigns me."

• *Colonel Starling, the Secret Service Agent, described life at the White House as Wilson slowly improved.*

STARLING   We conspired in every way to give the President comfort and solace. We built a platform in the driveway at the South Entrance so that his wheel chair could be pushed up to a position level with the floor of the car. Then we would lift the President into the car and place him in the right hand corner, arranging his cape and adjusting his cap so that when he appeared on the streets there was no indication that anything was wrong with him.

When he was to go for a ride some of us organized a group to stand at the gate of the White House as he returned; and we told them to cheer as he passed through. The first time it happened, when we went to lift him from the car after driving around to the back, there were tears in his eyes.

WILSON   You see little girl, they still love me! They still love me!

How long in this nuclear age will the United States government continue to duck the problem of determining when a Chief Executive is physically fit to rule?

Now occurred one of the strangest parts of the power drama. In the early stages of Wilson's incapacitation Secretary of State Lansing had twice called the Cabinet together to aid in running the government. These meetings had been stopped partly by political pressure from Tumulty but largely because Grayson said the President knew of the meetings and they disturbed him. Yet Wilson now wrote:

WILSON   My dear Secretary Lansing: Is it true as I have been told, that during my illness you have frequently called the heads of departments of the Government into conference?

If it is, I feel it my duty to call your attention to considerations which I do not care to dwell upon until I learn from you yourself that this is a fact.

No one but the President has a right to summon the heads of executive departments into conference. I take this matter up with you because in the development of every constitutional system, custom and precedent are of the most serious consequences. I have therefore taken the liberty of writing you to ask this question. And I am sure you will be glad to answer.

I am happy to learn from your recent note to Mrs. Wilson that your strength is returning. Cordially and sincerely yours.

• *Lansing had had a slight cold.*

TUMULTY   When I received from the President's stenographer this letter to Mr. Lansing, I at once conferred with the President and argued with him that in the present state of public opinion, it was the wrong time to do the right thing. The President was seated in his invalid chair.

WILSON   Tumulty, it is never the wrong time to spike disloyalty. When Lansing sought to oust me I was on my back. I'm on my feet now and I will not have disloyalty about me.

MRS. WILSON   I hate Lansing.

• *Mrs. Wilson had quite a few hatreds. Among the more violent were Colonel House, the British Ambassador, and the young Assistant Secretary of the Navy, Franklin D. Roosevelt.*

WILSON   Dear Secretary Lansing: I need not tell you with what reluctance I take advantage of your suggestion that you retire, or that I do so with the kindliest feeling. In matters of transcendent importance like this the only wise course is the course of perfect candor, where personal feeling is as much as possible left out of the reckoning.

• *Courageously Tumulty kept on bringing to the President's attention the need for compromise of some sort to save the League of Nations.*

WILSON   You can't fight God. We're right. We're right. That's enough. Don't fear the outcome. We're winning. We're right.

• Tumulty finally arranged a meeting between the Senate Democratic Majority Leader, Senator Hitchcock, and the President. The meeting took place in the President's bedroom with Wilson in bed.

HITCHCOCK   Mr. President, it might be wise to compromise with Lodge on a few points.

WILSON   Let Lodge compromise.

HITCHCOCK   Well, of course, he must compromise also. But we might well hold out the olive branch.

WILSON   Let Lodge hold out the olive branch.

HITCHCOCK   That ended it. For he was too sick a man to argue with in the presence of his doctor and his more anxious wife.

WILSON   These evil men intend to destroy the League. I shall consent to nothing. The Senate must take its own medicine.

• Even Mrs. Wilson finally urged compromise.

MRS. WILSON   For my sake accept these reservations and get this awful thing settled.

WILSON   Little girl, don't you desert me; that I cannot stand. Can't you see that I have no moral right to accept any change in a paper I have signed. It's not that I will not accept —it is the Nation's honor that is at stake.

• A moral issue. At times before in his life when Wilson had been able to convince himself he was God's instrument he had refused any compromise. During the war he had suspended civil liberties more brutally than either Lincoln or Franklin Roosevelt ever felt necessary. Before the final vote *he wrote the Senate Democratic Majority Leader his instructions.*

WILSON   Dear Senator Hitchcock: A word of counsel for Democratic Senators. I hear of reservationists and mild reservationists, but I cannot understand the differences between a nullifier and a mild nullifier. Our responsibility as a nation at this turning point in history is an overwhelming one. Either we should enter the League fearlessly, accepting the responsibility and not fearing the role of leadership which we now enjoy, or we should retire as gracefully as possible from the great concert of powers by which the world was saved.

I trust that all true friends of the League will refuse to support a treaty that has any reservations.

GRAYSON   The Senate rejected the Treaty of Versailles containing the League of Nations by a vote of 49 to 35 on March 19th.

• *Though a majority of Senators, 49, had voted for the treaty, it failed to get the necessary two-thirds vote. With a few compromises it is almost certain the treaty would have passed. The United States would have joined the League of Nations. What had happened? Certainly the majority of the opposition to the treaty came from Republicans. Mrs. Wilson rendered the verdict with which most historians agree.*

MRS. WILSON   My conviction is that Mr. Lodge put the world back fifty years and that at his door lies the wreckage of human hopes.

• *No doubt Lodge helped; but Senator Hitchcock disagreed with Mrs. Wilson's verdict.*

HITCHCOCK   Well, you know, as Democratic Majority Leader, I am the man who really defeated the ratification of the Treaty of Versailles with the reservations proposed by the Republicans. I did this not only at the request but virtually at the command of President Wilson. It was the mistake of my life.

GRAYSON   The President had never believed rejection possible.

WILSON   Doctor, the devil is a busy man. I feel like going to bed and staying there. If I were not a Christian I think I should go mad, but God is in some way working out his own plans through human perversities and mistakes.

GRAYSON   The President on April 14th, six months after his attack, held his first Cabinet meeting since his illness. He enjoyed meeting with the various members of his Cabinet and talking to them.

I suggested beforehand that it only last an hour to prevent him from overtaxing himself; and that I come in at the end of an hour. This would be the signal for adjournment. When I entered the room he shook his head at me, meaning I should not interrupt them. A little later I returned with Mrs. Wilson and then he reluctantly adjourned the meeting. He showed very plainly that it had done him a lot of good.

HOUSTON   It was the first Cabinet meeting since the President's attack and I arrived several minutes late. The President was already seated. I noted that I was announced to the President by a White House aide; and I wondered why this was done.

It was enough to make one weep to look at him. One of his arms was useless. When he tried to speak, his jaw tended to drop to one side. His voice was very weak and strained. He put up a brave front and spent several minutes cracking jokes. Then there was a brief silence. It appeared he would not take the initiative.

Someone brought up the railroad situation. The President seemed at first to have some difficulty fixing his mind on what we were discussing. Doctor Grayson looked in the door several times as if to warn us not to weary the President. The discussion dragged on for more than an hour. Finally Mrs. Wilson came in, looking rather disturbed, and suggested we had better go.

• *Houston and Grayson are talking about the same meeting!*

Life in the White House was looking up for Wilson. He told his wife over and over, "Little girl, when you are beside me work seems like play."

One of Tumulty's letters finally got through and the President talked it over with his doctor.

WILSON Tumulty has sent me a letter asking that I come out and say that I will not run again for the Presidency. I do not see anything to be gained at this time by so doing. I feel that it would be presumptuous and in bad taste for me to decline something that has not been offered to me.

GRAYSON One night he summoned me to his room and asking the nurse to leave us, said that he believed he had the strength to administer the office of President capably. He did not ask me if I thought he could stand another Presidential campaign; and for medical reasons I preferred not to volunteer that it would be impossible for him to take part in a campaign, as I was fearful it might have a depressing effect.

• *Wilson's presence in the race for the nomination was handicapping the Democratic party in its search for a strong candidate. Tumulty tried again.*

TUMULTY Dear Mrs. Wilson: In my opinion this is the time to act on a definite statement of withdrawal.

MRS. WILSON There will be no comment on a third term.

TUMULTY She should go straight to hell.

WILSON I think it would be entirely out of place for me to say now that I would not run. The Democratic convention may get into a hopeless tie-up. And with the League of Nations as the dominant issue there may be a practically universal demand for the selection of someone to lead them out of the wilderness. The members of the convention may feel that I am the logical one to lead—perhaps the only one to champion this cause. In such circumstances I would feel obliged to accept the nomination even if I thought it would cost me my life. I see nothing to be gained by making a declaration that I will not run.

STARLING   On our drives around Washington he got the idea that no automobiles should pass us, despite the fact that we proceeded at a very moderate rate of speed, frequently going at only fifteen or twenty miles an hour so he could enjoy the scenery. Whenever a car passed us he would order the Secret Service car to pursue it and bring the driver back for questioning. We always told him the car was going too fast to be overhauled.

Then he wanted to be a Justice of the Peace so he could arrest these drivers on the spot. We told him it would not suit the dignity of the President.

Yet sick as he was, he was plotting to get the Democratic nomination for a third term. He sent the new Secretary of State, Bainbridge Colby out to the convention in San Francisco with instructions to have his picture thrown on a screen at a psychological moment to stampede the delegates in his favor.

• *One of Wilson's close friends was Carter Glass of Virginia. Glass was to remain a power in the Senate through the time of Franklin Roosevelt. He recorded in his diary:*

GLASS   June 10, 1920. Grayson told me the President seriously contemplates permitting himself to be named for a third term and said it would kill him. Later in the day saw Postmaster General Burleson who told me he believed President wanted third term. Tumulty at the Executive Offices also expressed to me concern about this third term manifestation.

June 19: Took noonday tea with the President and Mrs. Wilson on south portico of White House. We talked about the convention. President concerned nomination of Bainbridge Colby for Chairman of Convention was being opposed. President asked me what I thought of Cox. "As for Cox," I started, when the President broke in saying Cox's nomination would be a joke, to which I fervently assented.

Grayson and Tumulty met me at the treasury entrance to the White House and accompanied me to the Union Station. (Glass was leaving for San Francisco to be Chairman of the Resolutions Committee at the Democratic Convention.) They were particularly anxious whether the President had charged me with any mission on a third term. I told them he had said no single word about it; also told them in confidence what he had said against Cox and several other of the candidates.

Grayson accompanied me to my sleeper and remained talking until the train moved, saying at the last: "Save the life of this man from false friends."

• *Seated in his special wheel chair that prevented his falling out, Wilson learned that the ticket was James Cox and Franklin D. Roosevelt. Though he was a man who never uttered more than a faint "damn" and that seldom, eye witnesses report that as he was wheeled off to bed he was swearing horribly.*

Comic fiction, and some not so comic, now and then chooses as a subject the man who would rather die than learn the truth. Was Wilson such a character? Did he come to suspect at the Paris peace table that his simplistic, idealized picture of the world was not true? That his fourteen points were impossible of realization; and even if they had all flowered would not lead to the millennium? To live in the real world is hard. Did Wilson deliberately choose overwork? Choose to die a martyr with his League of Nations unused but intact? Would this adoring son of a Presbyterian divine go to such lengths to escape the knowledge that he, his father and his father's God had been wrong? Moral force did not rule the world? Did the shock of power treat him to unbearable visions?

VIII .. Between Two Wars

- • WARREN HARDING
  1921–1923
- • CALVIN COOLIDGE
  1923–1929
- • HERBERT HOOVER
  1929–1933

After Wilson and the First World War the country ricocheted away from Federal power as it had after Lincoln and the Civil War. The post Civil War jamboree had almost ended in disaster with Congress in control. Now unfettered business speculation was to bring the nation close to the brink. But before the piper had to be paid, two figures of high farce, or perhaps political tragedy, Presidents Harding and Coolidge, briefly hoofed it across the stage. As a matter of fact President Hoover might have been pretty funny too; but it was harder to laugh with all those people starving. (During the Truman Administration the late Senator Taft used to introduce ex-President Hoover as "the world's greatest living expert on depressions," and no one would even smile.)

Harding, Coolidge and Hoover, all of whom recoiled from power as if they were being offered tainted oysters, could be left out completely. But then it would seem that the country leapt directly from Woodrow Wilson to Franklin D. Roosevelt. This would be a wrong impression. By the time the Second World War loomed, it wasn't a question of beginning where Wilson had left off; but of trying to get back to where Theodore Roosevelt had started. Power is hard to gain; but easy to loose.

It is important not to forget these three men. They set the stage for what was to follow. The first performer is introduced by the great jazz singer, Al Jolson, warbling a little ditty. The headliner's name is Warren Harding. He is playing his most improbable role, President of the United States.

> We think the country's ready
> For another man like Teddy.
> We need another Lincoln
> To do the nation's thinkin'.
>
> Mis-ter Hard-ding
> Mis-ter Hard-ding
> You're the man for us!

HARDING   No people in eighteen-dollar shoes is equipped for the march of civilization. . . .

My wife says cigars are all right; but it's undignified to chew.

> We think the country's ready
> For another man like Teddy.
> We need another Lincoln
> To do the nation's thinkin'.
>
> Mis-ter Hard-ding
> Mis-ter Hard-ding
> You're the man for us!

HARDING Why can't I ever get sauerkraut and wiener-wurst in the White House. . . .

I should be proud indeed if my Administration were marked by the final passing of the twelve hour working day. . . .

I'm a man of limited talents from a small town. I don't seem to grasp that I am president.

• *Other things he had less trouble grasping.*

NAN BRITTON My dear Mr. Harding, I wonder if you will remember me. My father was Dr. Britton of Marion, Ohio. I have been away from Marion for about two years; and shall finish a secretarial course in less than three weeks. I have been reading of the imperative demand for stenographers and typists and it has occurred to me that you are in a position to help me along if there is an opening. Any suggestions you might give me would be greatly appreciated; and I assure you it would please me so to hear from you. Sincerely, Nan Britton.

HARDING Why sure. We're just a couple of small-towners together, aren't we, Nan?

> Nannie and Warren were lovers.
> Oh my God how they could love!
> They swore to be true to each other,
> Just as true as the stars above.
>   He was her man,
>   And he done her wrong.

HARDING I can't make a damn thing out of this tax problem. I listen to one side and they seem right; and then—God —I talk to the other side and they seem just as right, and I'm where I started. I know somewhere there's a book that will give me the truth, but, hell, I couldn't read the book. God! What a job!

> Nannie was so young and unable
> She didn't know nothing before.

Warren had to tell her what her navel
By God had been created for.
He was her man
And he done her wrong.

HARDING The United States should adopt a protective
tariff as will help the struggling industries of Europe.

• *One of the reporters covering the President could not
believe he had heard this correctly and asked Harding to repeat
it. Harding did.*

HARDING The United States should adopt a protective
tariff as will help the struggling industries of Europe.

One night in New York City
At a hotel they got pinched
The house detectives hadn't no pity,
But twenty dollars made it a cinch.
He was her man,
And he done her wrong.

HARDING It is my conviction that the fundamental trouble
with the people of the United States is that they have gotten
too far away from Almighty God. We need common everyday
honesty everywhere.

One time in a friend's apartment
Somebody came in too soon.
Says she, "Why go hide in the closet,
When your clothes is all over the room?"
He was her man
And he done her wrong.

NAN BRITTON There were windows along one side of his
office which looked out upon the White House lawn. Outside,
stalking up and down, face rigidly to the front, moved the
President's guard. Mr. Harding said to me that those people
seemed to have eyes in the sides of their heads.

Whereupon he introduced me to the one place where he said we might share kisses in safety. This was a small closet in the anteroom. We repaired to this dark space, not more than five feet square, many times in the course of my visits to the White House and there the President and his adoring sweetheart made love.

> Nannie went down to the White House
> To see her Warren again.
> And they had to hide in the cloak room
> From those Secret Service men.
>> He was her man
>> And he done her wrong.

HARDING   Eugene Debs. I've heard so damn much about him. Let the poor feller out in time to eat Christmas dinner with his wife.

> Then they went over to the Senate,
> Where all them great lovers love.
> But they didn't have nothin' to prevent it,
> That will of God above
>> He was her man,
>> And he done her wrong!

HARDING   I guess there's going to be hell to pay over this Teapot Dome business; but those fellows seem to know what they're doing.

> So in spite of all he'd taught her,
> So in spite of all they'd done
> She had the President's daughter
> And that was the end of the fun.
>> He was her man
>> And he done her wrong.

● With scandals breaking all around him and his close personal friends charged with graft, Harding became a physically and emotionally beaten man.

HARDING   In this job I'm not worried about my enemies. It's my friends that are keeping me awake nights. . . .

How did I ever get here? I'm so very tired. Oh so very, very tired.

• *Worn down, Harding died. In a small farm in Plymouth Vermont, Coolidge, asleep in bed, heard his father coming up the stairs and calling: "Calvin, wake up. You're President of the United States."*

Coolidge was a quieter kind of comic. He had a solo act where he just sort of stood stage center and threw away his lines dead pan. And lo and behold, at election time in 1924 the act wound up with 54 percent of the popular vote.

COOLIDGE   My father had been the first to address me as President. The culmination of a life long desire of a father for the success of his son. . . .

Nine-tenths of the visitors who come to the White House want something they shouldn't have. If you keep dead still they will run down in three to four minutes. If you even cough or smile they start up all over again. . . .

The business of America is business. . . .

I don't work at night. If a man can't finish his job in the daytime, he's not smart. . . .

If you ever get married don't let your wife go into a store with a big window. My wife went into a store with a big window once and it cost me a lot of money. . . .

If you see ten troubles coming down the road you can be sure that nine will run into a ditch before they reach you. . . .

I have never been hurt by what I have not said. . . .

If you see a woman in a Ford be careful. One of them struck me in Northampton and bruised my hip. . . .

I don't see why we have to have six hams for one state dinner. It seems an awful lot of ham to me. . . .

When a great many people are unable to find work, unemployment results. . . .

I got free passage to picture shows while I was Mayor of Northampton. . . .

Many people don't understand why I'm President; least of all my father. . . .

I do not choose to run for President in 1928.

● *Many people felt that in making the last statement Coolidge meant he didn't choose to run but sure wanted to be drafted. In any event his "I do not choose to run" was used as an excuse to hustle him off stage before the next act billed as "Herbert Hoover and His Full Dinner Pail."*

HOOVER   There is no question in my opinion that prohibition is making America more productive. . . .

One of the oldest and perhaps the noblest of human aspirations has been the abolition of poverty. We in America today are nearer to the final triumph over poverty than ever before in the history of any land. We have not reached the goal, but given a chance to go forward with the policies of Harding and Coolidge we shall soon, with the help of God, be in sight of the day when poverty can be banished from this nation.

There is no guarantee against poverty equal to a job for every man. This is the primary purpose of the policies we advocate. . . .

Now I want to tell you, some water falls are in the wrong place where few people can see them. Moreover, in many waterfalls the same effect could be secured by a smaller expenditure of water. Scientifically as well as industrially we can be better off through civilizing our rivers. We could save water and have water falls at better locations. . . .

It is vital to the welfare of the United States that the Republican Party should continue to administer the government. If elected my fellow countrymen I shall give the best within me to uphold the traditions of the Republican party so effectively exemplified by Calvin Coolidge. . . .

I'll tell you what our trouble is. We are opposed by 6,000,000 unemployed; 10,000 bonus marchers; and ten-cent corn. Is it any wonder that the prospects are dark. . . .

We cannot squander ourselves into prosperity. Neither legislative or executive action can cure this depression. Economic wounds must be healed by the producers and consumers themselves.

The Government must correct abuses without entry into business. If it cannot then democracy shall have failed. . . .

The most essential factor to economic recovery today is the restoration of confidence. . . .

We are at the end of our string. There is nothing more we can do.

• *The Hoover act closed the house and the voice of Franklin D. Roosevelt was heard in the land over the blossoming invention, radio.*

FDR   I am certain that my fellow Americans expect that on my induction into the Presidency I will address them with a candor and a decision which the present situation of our Nation impels. We need not shrink from honestly facing conditions in our country today. This great nation will endure as it has endured, will revive and prosper. So, first of all, let me assert my firm belief that the only thing we have to fear is fear itself. In such a spirit on my part and on yours we face our common difficulties. Only a foolish optimist can deny the dark realities of the moment.

The money changers have fled from their high seats in the temple of our civilization. We may now restore that temple to the ancient truths. The measure of the restoration lies in the extent to which we apply social values more noble than mere monetary profit.

This nation calls for action and action now. Our greatest primary task is to put people to work. This is no unsolvable problem if we face it wisely and courageously. Hand in hand with this we must endeavor to provide a better use of the land for those best fitted for the land. Finally there must be a strict supervision of all banking and credits and investments, so that there will be an end to speculation with other people's money.

It is to be hoped that the normal balance of Executive and Legislative authority may be wholly adequate to meet the unprecedented task before us. But in the event that Congress shall fail to act; and in the event the national emergency is still critical, I shall not evade the clear course of duty that will then confront me. I shall ask Congress for broad Executive power to wage a war against the emergency. As great a power as if we were in fact invaded.

For the trust imposed in me I will return the courage and devotion that befit the time. I can do no less.

IX .. How Much to Tell?

• • FRANKLIN D. ROOSEVELT
1933–1945

With Franklin D. Roosevelt the scene evokes the ohs and ahs of recognition. He is contemporary. We bring emotion and bias to the background and the man. There are several possible ways to approach Roosevelt's use of power. For example the modern shape of the Presidency took its general form in the social legislation and governmental reorganization of the early New Deal. It was then Roosevelt sent the message to Congress that "The President needs help; he cannot adequately handle his responsibilities." Unfortunately many important acts of this time were technical changes in the structure of government, abstractions of power. They had to wait for future political and bureaucratic leaders to flesh them out with human characteristics before they achieved their full meaning.

There is also Roosevelt the war leader, "Doctor-Win-the-War" as he called himself. However, here the canvas is so broad, there are so many characters and so many scenes that the personal nature of power is diffused. Also though Roosevelt took an active part in running the war he was not involved with war in the same intimate way as Lincoln or even Churchill. The dark hours, the agony, the possibility of defeat were not there for him. Instead of being across the Potomac or in the skies over Britain, the ultimate reality of dying was oceans away.

This leaves a third period. The transition time when America edged toward war protesting bitterly at every grudging step. During this period Roosevelt sometimes led, sometimes pushed, sometimes followed. At all times his political antennae were highly active and his zest for power glittered. This period offers an intimate view of Roosevelt's use of power at a critical moment in history.

Roosevelt's serious concern in the possibility of war coming to America seems to have begun toward the end of 1937, the year before Munich. Until then he appears to have thought about any future war in conventional post World War One stereotypes. Early in his first term he supported the Nye investigation, a three ring circus run by Senator Gerald Nye of Nevada that was bent on proving the sole cause of American participation in World War I was the thirst of American bankers and munitions makers for profits. This investigation helped set the Congressional tone for passage of the Neutrality Act of 1935. Roosevelt was vaguely unhappy about the act but signed it when he had the votes to veto the Act and make the veto stick. The Neutrality Act forbade the United States to export military supplies to either side in any war.

In 1936 Roosevelt shattered the Republicans under Alf Landon with his historic plurality of 523 electoral votes to 8, a record that still stands. Landon, in a nostalgic throwback to simpler times, had been billed as: "The Kansas Coolidge." The political power of this great majority Roosevelt then proceeded to dissipate in his futile and losing battle to pack the Supreme Court. In 1936 he spoke on the possibility of war as follows.

ROOSEVELT   We are not isolationists except insofar as we

seek to isolate ourselves completely from war. I have seen war. I have seen blood running from the wounded. I have seen men coughing out their gassed lungs. I have seen the dead in the mud. I have seen cities destroyed. I have seen children starving. I hate war. I have passed unnumbered hours, I shall pass unnumbered hours, thinking and planning how war may be kept from this nation.

If war should break out on another continent, we would find in this country thousands of Americans who seeking immediate riches would attempt to break down our neutrality. To resist the clamor of those greedy men, if war should come, would require the unswerving support of all Americans who love peace. If we face the choice of profits or peace, the Nation will answer—must answer—"We choose peace."

● *Later that year Hitler invaded the Rhineland and forged the Rome-Berlin-Tokyo Axis. Next the Spanish civil war began. Americans remained deeply divided over the course of action to follow. Just how deep was the division and how powerful were the isolationists is a fascinating political question since it leads to an intensely personal question about Roosevelt. Was he a forceful executive at this time? Could he have led the country earlier out of isolationism and into the necessity of war? There are as many degrees of answer to this question as there are historians of the period.*

Certainly Congress held many vocal isolationists from both political parties. In the Senate opposition to "foreign entanglements" was represented by such men as Borah, Clark, Lundeen, Nye, Reynolds, Taft, Vandenberg and Wheeler.

In October of 1937, in a speech at Chicago, Roosevelt sent up this trial balloon against isolationism.

FDR   It seems unfortunately true that the epidemic of world lawlessness is spreading. When an epidemic of physical disease starts to spread the community joins in a quarantine of the patients in order to protect the health of the community. We are determined to keep out of war. We are adopting such measures as will minimize our risk of involvement; but surely the ninety percent of the population of the world who want to live in peace under law can and must find some way to make their will prevail.

America hates war.

America hopes for peace.

Therefore America actively engages in the search for peace.

• *The speech was too forceful for the times. Roosevelt immediately began to duck. Reporters questioned him about the speech next day. (The reporters' questions are enclosed in parentheses.)*

(About that speech of yesterday, Mr. President, I had two things in mind. What type of measure did you have in mind with reference to quarantining? And how do you reconcile that speech with the policy of neutrality laid down by act of Congress?)

Read the last line of the speech.

(The Herald Tribune didn't carry it.)

"America actively engages in the search for peace."

(But you also said the peace loving nations must find a way to make their wills prevail?)

Yes.

(Is anything contemplated?)

Just the speech itself.

(Do you accept the fact that that's a repudiation of neutrality?)

It may be an expansion.

(What?)

(How about economic sanctions?)

Sanctions is a terrible word. They are right out the window.

(It's an attitude without a program?)

It's an attitude. It does not outline a program. But it says we are looking for a program.

(Wouldn't it be almost inevitable if any program is reached that our neutrality act will have to be overhauled?)

Not necessarily. That is the interesting thing.

(That is very interesting.)

(What you outline and the Neutrality Act seem at opposite poles to me.)

Put your thinking cap on.

(To align yourself with one group of nations is no longer neutrality.)

On the contrary, it might be a stronger neutrality.

(Is a quarantine a sanction?)

No. I said don't talk about sanctions.

(Better then to keep it in the moral sphere?)

No, it can be in a very practical sphere.

(Thank you, Mr. President.)

• *As a result of the hostile reaction it was to be a long time before Roosevelt was publicly so forceful again. The domestic opposition remained isolationist. But Hitler kept chipping away at them. On March 13th, 1938, he invaded Austria.*

HITLER   Germans! Deeply grieved, we have for years watched the fate of our German brothers in Austria. Sorrow inflicted on them we feel is our own suffering. Germans! For the last few years I have tried to warn the rulers of Austria of the consequences of oppressing the German population.

Yesterday the German people in Austria arose. I have decided to put the power of the Reich at their disposal. Since this morning there are marching across all the frontiers of German-Austria the soldiers of the Third Reich. I myself as Führer of the German people shall be happy to enter again that country that is also my homeland.

Long live the German Reich! Long live German-Austria!

• *Then, in September came Munich and the handwriting was on the wall—though written for many in invisible ink. Since there was no war yet, the Neutrality Act was not in force. The French, desperate for airplanes, tried to secretly buy some* from the United States. *Isolationists in the Cabinet led by Secretary of War Woodring, who had the support of the myopic Air Corps staff, turned thumbs down. It took the personal intervention of Roosevelt to get General Arnold, the Air Corps Chief of Staff, to send the following telegram.*

GEN. ARNOLD   From General Arnold to Major Wolf, Army Air Corps representative at Douglas Aircraft Plant, Los Angeles. Confidential, in code. Arrange demonstration of attack bomber Sunday to three members of French mission. They are to inspect, fly in it, and negotiate for purchase. Keep this information confidential; and keep me informed.

• *Then fate stepped in and General Arnold found himself before the Senate.*

SENATOR   All right, General, let me read you this story from the Washington post. "America's most modern light bomber crashed in flames in a parking lot near Los Angeles today. Its pilot was killed. A passenger identified as Paul Chemidlin, a representative of the French Air Ministry, was dragged from the rear of the plane." Now what was this Frenchman doing in that plane?

GEN. ARNOLD   He was out there under the direction of the Treasury Department.

SENATOR   The War Department did not authorize this Frenchman to be in that plane?

GEN. ARNOLD   The War Department knew that French officer was going out there.

SENATOR   According to the newspapers, the Douglas people and the Air Corps denied they knew who the man was. They said he was a mechanic called Smithson. They did a great deal of lying.

• *General Arnold, an isolationist himself, hadn't wanted the French to look at the plane, and twisted and turned trying*

to throw the full blame, if blame there was, on the Treasury
Department.

SENATOR   General, what I'd like to know is have we already
picked our enemies and our friends without the Senate knowing? I think Congress should have something to say about what
enemies we are going to have.

• *Faced with this sort of insubordination in the ranks, Roosevelt was blunt.*

FDR   General, if some members of the Air Corps don't
get on the team when testifying before Congress, they may
find themselves in Guam.

• *In an effort to place squarely on the President the blame
for having a French military mission secretly in the United
States, the Senate next roasted Secretary of the Treasury
Morgenthau.*

SENATOR   Now Secretary Morgenthau, could you tell me, if
you know, how the Treasury Department came to be in this
military plane deal?

MORGENTHAU   We did it at the request of the President.

SENATOR   The President himself requested it?

MORGENTHAU   The President himself.

SENATOR Mr. Secretary, we are being committed to war
through secret diplomacy.

• *Secret diplomacy! The Republican members of the Foreign Affairs Committee rose as one man against that. "We
the minority members of the Committee on Foreign Affairs
deplore and protest the unneutral actions and secret methods
of the President which would not have become known except
through the accidental injury of a French officer."*

SENATOR NYE   That crash revealed the existence in this
country of a secret foreign mission, witnessing secret demon-
strations over the protests of our own military experts.

FDR   I can only move as fast as the people will let me.

• *At the time of Calvin Coolidge the President used to get about 100 letters a month. By Roosevelt's second term the letters were running at several thousand a week. One of these letters was to change history.*

Dear Mr. President:

In the course of the last four months it has been made probable through the work of Joliot in France as well as Fermi and Szilard in America—that it may become possible to set up a nuclear chain reaction in a large mass of uranium, by which vast amounts of power and large quantities of new radium-like elements would be generated. Now it appears almost certain that this could be achieved in the immediate future.

This new phenomenon would also lead to the construction of bombs, and it is conceivable—though much less certain—that extremely powerful bombs of a new type may thus be constructed. A single bomb of this type, carried by boat and exploded in a port, might very well destroy the whole port together with some of the surrounding territory. However, such bombs might very well prove to be too heavy for transportation by air.

I understand that Germany has actually stopped the sale of uranium from the Czechoslovakian mines which she has taken over.

Yours very truly,
Albert Einstein.

• Then on August 23rd, 1939, two governments that had declared their implacable hostility to each other joined hands. The first two paragraphs of their treaty read: "The Governments of the German Reich and the Union of Soviet Socialist Republics directed by the wish to strengthen the cause of peace, have reached the following agreement. Article one. The two contracting parties agree to refrain from any act or *attack against one another. Article two. In case one of the contracting powers should become the object of warlike acts on the part of a third power, the other contracting power will not support the third power in any form."*

After the war the archives of the German Foreign Office revealed there had been secret protocols to this agreement. "Secret Protocol Two: In the event of a territorial rearrangement of Poland the spheres of influence of Germany and the USSR will be bounded by the line of the rivers Narew, Vistula and San. Signed—Ribbentrop and Molotov."

On September 1st Hitler invaded Poland; Britain and France declared war on Germany. U. S. Communists and their sympathizers joined the isolationists in opposing American involvement. Roosevelt was asked by a reporter if he had any comment on the declaration of war.

FDR   Only this. I not only sincerely hope we can stay out, but I believe we can. And every effort will be made by this Administration to do so.

• With war declared, the provisions of the Neutrality Act went into effect. The United States could not supply materiels of war to any of the belligerents, even to neighboring Canada. Roosevelt asked for the Act's repeal.

FDR   I have asked the Congress to reassemble in extraordinary session in order that it may consider and act on the amendment of certain legislation. The legislation is the so-called Neutrality Act of 1935, continued in force by the joint resolution of May 1937. I regret that Congress passed that Act. I regret equally that I signed that Act. In July of this year I asked Congress in the cause of peace and in the interests of real American neutrality to change that Act. I now ask again.

• Instead of repeal he got amendment. America could supply the allies with two big "buts." All sales must be for cash. No cargoes could be carried in United States ships. Congress *still believed that World War I and World War II were the same and that America had been drawn into World War I by torpedoing of U.S. ships and the desire of business-men to collect their debts.*

Then on May 10, 1940, the German foreign office issued the following announcement: The Führer has issued orders to safeguard the neutrality of Belgium and Holland with all the military means of the Reich." The blitzkreig began. France fell. Dunkirk was evacuated. Roosevelt maneuvered the pas-sage of the draft act and signed an historic letter.

From the President of the United States—Greetings. Having submitted yourself to a local board for the purpose of determining your availability for training and service in the armed forces of the United States, you are hereby notified that you have been selected.

• *Also in 1940 there was an election. Roosevelt was running against Wendell Wilkie for a precedent-shattering third term. That he was plotting to take the country into war was a major issue.*

FDR   In all these plans for national defense only those who seek to play upon the fears of the American people dis-cover an attempt to lead us into war. I hate war now more than ever. I stand with my party, and outside of my party as President of all the people, on the Democratic Party platform which says: "We will not participate in foreign wars and we will not send our forces to fight in foreign lands outside of the Americas, except in case of attack."

Let me give you mothers and fathers one more reassur-ance. I have said this before, but I shall say it again and again. Your boys are not going to be sent into any foreign wars. They are going into training to form a force so strong that it will keep the threat of war away from our shores. The purpose of our defense is defense.

• *Did Roosevelt have to be so emphatic, so careful; and*

handicap himself in his future efforts to help Great Britain? Just before the campaign he had successfully engineered the swap of 50 over-age destroyers for several British bases in the Western Hemisphere such as Bermuda. The Gallop poll showed 62% of the American people willing to aid the allies. He beat Wilkie by a shattering 5 million votes. Still the first duty of a politician is to get elected.

Almost right after the election, Roosevelt sent Congress his Lend-Lease proposals. These were vital because British cash, necessary under the Neutrality Act, was running out.

FDR   What I am trying to do is get rid of the silly, foolish old dollar sign. Let me give you an illustration. Suppose my neighbor's home catches fire and I have a length of garden hose. If he can take my hose I may be able to help him put out his fire.

Now what do I do? I don't say to him, "Neighbor, that hose cost me fifteen dollars. You have to pay me fifteen dollars for it." I don't want fifteen dollars. I want my hose back after the fire is over. If it goes through the fire all right, he gives it back to me and thanks me for the use of it. But if it gets holes in it during the fire I say to him: "I can't use that hose any more—it's all smashed up." He says: "All right, I will replace it." I get a nice garden hose back and I'm in pretty good shape. That's what I mean by lend-lease.

SENATOR TAFT   With this Act, the administration is trying to gradually edge us into a convoy policy which will mean war for the United States. Lend-lease is designed to take the power to declare war from the Congress.

FDR   I have never considered using American naval vessels to convoy ships bearing supplies to Great Britain.

SENATOR WHEELER   If it is our war, how can we justify lending them the stuff and then asking them to pay us back? If it is our war, we ought to go over and fight it. But it is not our war.

SENATOR TAFT   If the members of the Senate intend to keep their pledges to their constituents and themselves, they can only vote "no" on this measure.

• *Congress passed the Lend-Lease Act with an important provision: "March 11, 1941. Be it enacted by the Senate and House of Representatives that notwithstanding the provisions of any other law the President may from time to time sell, transfer, exchange, lease, lend, or otherwise dispose of defense articles. But nothing in this Act shall be construed to permit convoying by naval vessels of the United States."*

FDR   Dear Prime Minister Churchill—4 April—Secret— I want to tell you of the steps we propose to take to affect your shipping. We will extend our patrol zone east and north from Newfoundland, Greenland, Nova Scotia, the West Indies and Bermuda. We will want to be notified by you in great secrecy about your convoys so that our patrol units can seek out the ships of an aggressor nation operating our side of the new line.

• *Admiral Stark, Chief of Naval Operations, moved in secrecy to put Roosevelt's ideas into effect.*

ADM. STARK   Navy Hemisphere Defense Plan 2, April 21, 1941. Secret. Entrance into the Western Hemisphere by German and Italian naval vessels will be viewed as of unfriendly intent. Naval operating forces will trail vessels and aircraft of hostile powers and broadcast in plain language their movements at four hour intervals or oftener if necessary. Prevent interference with United States shipping by hostile powers. The execution of this plan should give the appearance of a routine exercise.

• *At his press conference of April 25th, 1941, Roosevelt was asked (Reporters' questions again enclosed in parentheses):*

(Mr. President, has the Government any idea of escorting convoys?)

No. No. None at all. That, I'm afraid, will be bad news to some of you.

(Well, how far will these patrols go?)

As far as necessary for the defense of the American Hemisphere.

(Will there be any extension of the patrol's functions?)

No. No.

(What is the patrol's function?)

Protection of the American Hemisphere.

(Does that include protection of shipping?)

Protection of the American Hemisphere.

(Doesn't that include. . . .)

We will not convoy.

• At his club Admiral Stark made some remarks he thought were off the record.

ADM. STARK   I wish I could talk about convoys. I would like to tell you about the Navy's patrols and where they are 2000 miles out from the high latitudes to the equator. But if I did so somebody would say, "I wonder if old Admiral Betty Stark's gone crazy giving all that secret information out."

• More and more Roosevelt was publicly toughening his position.

FDR   The Axis powers can never achieve their objective of world domination unless they first obtain control of the seas. That is their supreme purpose today; and to achieve it they must capture Great Britain.

Our patrols are now helping to insure delivery of needed supplies to Britain. I say that the delivery of needed supplies to Britain is imperative. I say that this can be done. It must be done and it will be done.

There are some timid ones among us who say that we must preserve peace at any price. To them I say this: "The only thing we have to fear is fear itself." With profound con-

sciousness of my responsibilities, I have tonight issued a proclamation that an unlimited national emergency exists.

● *Reporters kept asking questions.*

(Mr. President, can you just explain to us the difference
between a patrol and a convoy?)

Do you know what a horse looks like?

(Yes.)

I think you also know what a cow looks like. You can
call a horse a cow all you want, but it's still a cow. Now this is
a patrol. It's always been a patrol. It's not a convoy.

(Why not?)

You know the difference between a cow and a horse?

(I know the difference.)

All right. There's just as much difference, just as much
difference between a patrol and a convoy.

ADM. STARK   To the active naval forces, Atlantic. Top Secret. Effective immediately you will protect United States and
Iceland shipping by escorting and covering as required and
by destroying hostile forces which threaten such shipping. You
will escort convoys of United States and Iceland shipping including the shipping of any nationality which may join such
convoys.

FDR   There will be no convoys. Convoys means shooting,
and shooting means war.

● *The draft act was scheduled to expire in September of
1942. Congress, which had originally passed the law for just
one year, showed great hesitation about renewal—especially
the House of Representatives.*

FDR   Last year the Congress of the United States, recogniz-
ing the gravity of the world situation, passed the Selective
Service Act. In the absence of further action now by Congress,
all of the 900,000 men inducted into the Army must be released from active service on the expiration of twelve months.

This means that beginning this autumn about two-thirds of the Army of the United States will begin demobilization.

I do believe, I know, that the danger today is infinitely greater than a year ago. I do believe, I know, that in all truth in this year 1941 we are in the midst of a national emergency. I hope the Congress will acknowledge this national emergency and authorize the continuance in service of the selectees and other components of the Army.

One final word. Time counts. Within two months disintegration, which would follow failure to take Congressional action, will commence in the armies of the United States. Time counts.

SENATOR VANDENBERG   I am imputing nothing to anyone, but if one wished to create a permanent military dictatorship in the United States would he require much more than what we have just been asked to do?

SENATOR TAFT   This measure authorizes the President of the United States to retain indefinitely in the army anyone he wants. Further, the President may draft new men for any number of years.

SENATOR NYE   We borrow the ways of dictators when we have peacetime conscription. I insist that in spite of efforts to prove the contrary, if Congress holds these boys for more than twelve months, Congress breaks faith with the finest youth upon the face of the earth.

• *By one vote the draft extension passed the House of Representatives.*

SENATOR WHEELER   That the House kept selective service in force by only one vote is notice to this administration that they could not get a resolution through Congress for a declaration of war.

And it also proves the Congress does not take seriously the cry of the Administration that the so-called emergency is greater now than it was a year ago.

SENATOR TAFT   The War Department and the Administration will note that this law specifically excludes the sending of U.S. forces anywhere outside this Western Hemisphere.

FDR   I have an announcement. Our Army and Navy have temporarily landed in Iceland for the defense of the Western Hemisphere.

• *Iceland! Senators and Congressmen cried betrayal. But Roosevelt had found a National Geographic map that placed Iceland in the Western Hemisphere. Then the tempo of events began to race.*

FDR   The Navy has reported to me, that on the morning of September 4th the United States destroyer Greer proceeding in full daylight towards Iceland, was attacked by a submarine southeast of Greenland. The Greer was carrying American mail to Iceland. It was full daylight. She was flying the American flag. Her identity as American was unmistakable. Germany admits it was a German submarine.

In spite of what Hitler's propaganda bureau has invented, I tell you the blunt fact that the German submarine fired first upon this American destroyer without warning. This was piracy.

• *That is what the President had told Congress and the people. But it is difficult to keep secrets in a democracy at peace. A sailor on the Greer wrote the isolationist Senator Wheeler.*

Dear Senator Wheeler. The truth about the Greer was not told by the President. Me and my shipmates read the papers when we got them and see how the President said that the sub attacked us first, when, honestly, we and the outfit we was with done the attacking first. We had to because that was our orders.

• *Admiral Stark got out a further statement for Congress on the Greer.*

ADM. STARK   At 0840 the USS Greer while en route to Iceland was informed by a British plane of a submerged submarine
about ten miles ahead. Acting on this information, the Greer
proceeded to search for the submarine and at 1920 she located
the submarine by her underwater sound equipment.

The Greer proceeded to trail the submarine and broadcast the submarine's position to the plane. This action of the
Greer was not in accordance with her orders to give out information but not to attack. At 1032 the British plane dropped
four depth charges on the submarine and then departed.

The Greer continued to trail the submarine. At 1240 the
submarine changed course and closed on the Greer. At 1249
a torpedo track was sighted crossing the wake of the ship about
100 yards astern. The Greer then attacked the submarine with
a pattern of eight depth-charges. The results are believed nega-
tive.

• A reporter questioned the President: "Mr. President, are
we any closer to entering the war actually?"

FDR   I should say, no.

ADM. STARK   To Admiral Hart, Commander in Chief, Asi-
atic Fleet. Dear Tommy, as far as the Atlantic is concerned
we are all but, if not actually, in it. In a nutshell we are escorting convoys from the United States to the Iceland area where
these convoys are picked up by the British and escorted to the
British Isles. . . .

October 11th, to the Atlantic Fleet. Top Secret. At the
direction of the President, Western Hemisphere Defense Plan
Five to be put into effect immediately. Operations to be conducted under this plan are conceived to form a preparatory
phase for the operations of Navy Basic War Plan Rainbow
Five for open and declared war.

FDR   We don't want a war with Germany. We are acting
in defense, self-defense, every action.

Publicly this was the line. Privately the concern of the President and his Cabinet was not when war would come, but how. The new Secretary of War, Henry Stimson, a powerful Republican who had been Secretary of State in the early days of Hoover, recorded the days before Pearl Harbor in his diary.

STIMSON   November 7th. Cabinet meeting this afternoon. The President opened with the story of Lincoln and his Cabinet, how he polled his Cabinet and they all polled "no." And then he said: "I vote aye, the ayes have it."

With that the President started to have what he said was the first general poll of his Cabinet—and it was on the question of the Far East—whether the American people would back us up in case we struck at Japan and what the tactics should be. It was the best Cabinet meeting I think we have ever had. He went round the table. First Secretary of State Hull and then myself, and then around the whole number and we were unanimous in feeling that the country would support us. He said that this time the vote is unanimous, as he felt the same way.

The reporters kept throwing questions and Roosevelt fielded them as best he could.

(Can you tell us anything, sir, about these Japanese negotiations?)

I think I'd better not.

(Can you say, Mr. President, whether these negotiations have broken down temporarily?)

No. They have not.

(When will the next meeting be held with the Japanese?)

I don't know. We are waiting.

Having broken the Japanese code, the United States was aware a crisis was approaching.

STIMSON   November 25th. At twelve o'clock General Marshall and I went to the White House. At the meeting were Hull, Secretary of the Navy Knox, Marshall, Stark and myself.

The President brought up our relations with the Japanese. He brought up the event that we were likely to be attacked perhaps as soon as next Monday for the Japanese are notorious for making an attack without warning. The question for us was how we should maneuver the Japanese into the position of firing the first shot without allowing too much danger to ourselves. It was a difficult proposition.

● *To the U.S. Military commanders in Hawaii went an urgent telegram on Nov. 27.*

From the War and Navy Departments: To General Short and Admiral Kimmel, Pearl Harbor. Negotiations with Japanese appear to be terminated to all practical purposes. Japanese future action unpredictable but hostile action possible at any moment.

If hostilities cannot, repeat cannot be avoided, the U. S. desires that Japan commit the first overt act.

This policy should not, repeat not, be construed as restricting you to a course of action that might jeopardize your defense. Prior to Japanese hostile action you are directed to undertake such reconaissance and other measures as you may deem necessary but these measures should be carried out so as not, repeat not, to alarm the civil population or disclose intent.

● *Press conference, December 2nd.*

(Mr. President, we were told at the State Department that you had asked that certain inquiries be made of the Japanese representatives—)

That is correct.

(Could you indicate the nature of these inquiries?)

Well, let me put it this way: the other day we got word from various sources that there were large additional bodies of Japanese forces, various kinds of forces, naval, air and land, on the way to Indo China. And the question was asked this morning of the Japanese Government, at my request, very politely, as to what the purpose of these forces was. And we hope to get a reply to that very simple question shortly.

(Was there any time limit put on it?)

No. No. That's a silly question. The United States is at peace with Japan and perfectly friendly too.

STIMSON   December 7th. Today is the day the Japanese are going to bring their answer. Everything we intercept and decode indicates that they have been keeping the time back until now in order to accomplish something hanging in the air.

Knox and I arranged a conference with Hull at 10:30 and we talked the whole matter over. Hull is very certain that the Japs are planning some deviltry and we are all wondering where the blow will strike. We three stayed in conference till lunch time, going over the plans for what should be said or done.

I returned home to lunch and just about two o'clock, while I was sitting at lunch, the President called me on the telephone and in a rather excited voice asked me:

"Have you heard the news?"

I said, "Well, I've heard the telegrams coming in about the Japanese advances in the Gulf of Siam."

He said, "Oh, I don't mean that. They've attacked Hawaii. They are now bombing Hawaii."

Well, that was an excitement indeed. Now the Japs have solved the whole thing by attacking us directly in Hawaii.

• *The rest is well-known history. The next day Roosevelt asked the Congress to declare war against Japan; but only against Japan. Still backing America into battle, he waited for Germany and Italy to declare war on the United States three days later. Then the Senate made the war against them, too, official.*

At the end of December, Prime Minister Churchill visited the United States to coordinate the war effort of the two countries. At an official dinner Roosevelt raised his glass.

FDR   Dear Prime Minister Churchill, I have a toast to offer. It has been in my head and on my heart for a long time. Now it is on the tip of my tongue.—"To the common cause!"

X .. The New World

• • *HARRY S TRUMAN*

1945–1953

While the United States fought, battles, defeats, victories, pro-
duction and politics occupied the national view. But out of
sight in a secret empire the chains of Leviathan had been
loosed and a new world was being born. The birth was highly
secret. Most of the documents that chronicle that birth still
are. Here is one, recently "declassified."

Dr. J. R. Oppenheimer, University of California. Dear Dr.
Oppenheimer:

We are addressing this letter to you as the Scientific Director of the special laboratory in New Mexico in order to
confirm our many conversations on the matters of organization and responsibility. You are at liberty to show this letter
to those with whom you are discussing the desirability of their
joining the project with you; they of course realizing their
responsibility as to secrecy, including the details of organization and personnel.

The laboratory will be concerned with the development
and final manufacture of an instrument of war, which we may
designate as Projectile S-1-T. To this end the laboratory will
be concerned with:

A. Certain experimental studies in science, engineering and ordnance; and

B. At a later date large scale experiments involving difficult ordnance procedures and the handling of highly dangerous material.

The laboratory is part of a large project which has been placed in a special category and assigned the highest priority by the President of the United States. By his order the Secretary of War and certain other high officials have arranged that the control of this project shall be in the hands of a Military Policy Committee. Brigadier General L. R. Groves has been given overall executive responsibility for this project. He works in close cooperation with Dr. Conant, who is Chairman of the group of scientists who were in charge of the earlier phases of some aspects of the investigation.

Signed: James B. Conant and L. R. Groves.
February 25th, 1943.

• On April 12, 1945, the man who was destined to order the use of the new "instrument of war" became President totally unaware of the plans for the weapon's existence.

TRUMAN   Say, I don't know whether you fellows ever had a load of hay or a bull fall on you, but yesterday the stars and all the planets fell on me.

I was called to the White House and got there about 5:25 P.M. and was immediately taken in the elevator to the second floor and ushered into Mrs. Roosevelt's study. Mrs. Roosevelt, together with Colonel John Roosevelt and Mrs. Anna Roosevelt Boettinger, and Steve Early were in the room as I entered; and I knew at once that something unusual had taken place.

Mrs. Roosevelt stepped forward and placed her arm gently about my shoulder. "Harry," she said quietly, "the President is dead."

For a moment I could not bring myself to speak. "Is there anything I can do for you?" I asked at last. She replied:

"Is there anything we can do for you? For you are the one in trouble now."

• *Perhaps the new President's mother most accurately summarized the mood of the nation.*

MRS. TRUMAN   I cannot really be glad my son is President because I am sorry that President Roosevelt is dead. If he had been voted in I would be out waving a flag; but it does not seem right to be very happy or wave any flags now. Harry will get along. He is sincere and will do what is best.

TRUMAN   My first meeting of the Cabinet was short; and when it adjourned the members rose silently and made their way from the room—except for Secretary Stimson. He asked to speak to me about a most urgent matter. Stimson told me that he wanted me to know about an immense project that was under way—a project looking to the development of a new explosive of almost unbelievable destructive power. That was all he felt free to say at the time and his statement left me puzzled.

STIMSON   Dear Mr. President. I think it very important that I should have a talk with you as soon as possible on a highly secret matter. I mentioned it to you shortly after you took office; but have not urged it since on account of the pressure you have been under. It, however, has such a bearing on our present foreign relations that I think you ought to know about it without much further delay.

TRUMAN   It was then that I was told enough to give me some understanding of the awful power that might soon be placed in our hands.

• *As usual the President received conflicting advice. Vannevar Bush, who was head of the Office of Scientific Research and Development, reported for the President's information.*

BUSH   This is the biggest fool thing that we have ever done. The bomb will never go off and I speak as an expert on explosives.

TRUMAN   Had dinner by myself tonight. Worked until dinner time. A butler came in very formally and said: "Mr. President, dinner is served."

I walked into the dining room. Barnett in tails and white tie pulls out my chair, pushes me up to the table. John in tails and white tie brings me a fruit cup. Barnett takes away the empty cup. John brings me a plate, Barnett brings me a tenderloin, John brings me asparagus, Barnett brings me carrots and beets.

I have to eat alone and in silence in a candlelit room. I ring. Barnett takes the plate and the butter plates. John comes in with a napkin and a silver crumb tray—there are no crumbs, but John has to brush them off the table anyway. Barnett brings me a plate with a finger bowl and doily on it. I remove the finger bowl and doily and John puts a glass saucer and a little bowl on the plate. Barnett brings me some chocolate custard. John brings me a demi-tasse—about two good gulps of coffee.

My dinner is over. I take a hand bath in the finger bowl and go back to work. What a life! . . .

You know there are probably a million people in this country who could do the Presidential job better than I. But I've got the job and I'm doing the best I can.

STIMSON   Mr. President, within four months we shall in all probability have completed the most terrible weapon ever known in human history, one bomb of which could destroy a whole city.

Although we shared its development with the United Kingdom, the United States is at present in the position of controlling the resources with which to construct and use it and no other nation could reach this position for some years.

Nevertheless it is practically certain that we could not remain in this position indefinitely. The future may see a time when such a weapon may be constructed in secret and used with devastating power by a wilful nation.

The world in the present state of moral advancement compared with its technical development would be eventually at the mercy of such a weapon. In other words, modern civilization might be completely destroyed. The development of this weapon has placed a certain moral responsibility upon us which we cannot shirk without very serious responsibility for any disaster to civilization.

• *On Stimson's advice President Truman appointed The Interim Committee to consider the proper use of the atomic bomb. Stimson opened their first meeting, on May 9th, 1945, two months before the first successful test of the new weapon.*

STIMSON   Gentlemen, it is our responsibility in this committee to recommend action that may turn the course of civilization. In our hands we expect soon to have a weapon of wholly unprecedented destructive power.

Today's prime fact is war. Our great task is to bring this war to a prompt and successful conclusion. We may assume that our new weapon puts in our hands overwhelming power. It is our obligation to use this power with the best wisdom we can command. To us now, the matter of first importance is how our use of this new weapon will appear in the long view of history.

• *Secretary of War Stimson himself chaired the Interim Committee. Also on the Committee were such men as Karl T. Compton, President of M.I.T., and James B. Conant, President of Harvard. The Committee was backed by a scientific panel among whose members were such figures as Enrico Fermi, Ernest O. Lawrence, Arthur H. Compton, and J. Robert Oppenheimer. The latter calculated for the members the number of casualties dropping an atomic bomb would produce.*

The Committee investigated both dropping or not drop-

ping the bomb and such alternative methods of use as a demonstration over neutral territory. The conclusion of both the Committee and its scientific advisers was that the bomb should be used against a military target. The degree of warning to be given the Japanese remained somewhat an open question.

It is sometimes alleged that the United States dropped the atomic bomb on Japan without thinking of the consequences. Nothing could be further from the facts. Nor would it be easy to find anywhere in history among men in power, four of the moral stature of Franklin Roosevelt, Harry Truman, George Marshall, and Henry Stimson, who made the ultimate recommendations and faced the final responsibility.*

TRUMAN   News of the first successful test reached me at Potsdam the day after I arrived for the conference of the Big Three. Stimson's staff had prepared a list of cities in Japan that might serve as targets. Kyoto though favored by General Arnold as a center of military activity was eliminated when Secretary Stimson pointed out that it was a cultural and religious shrine of the Japanese. But the final decision of when and where to use the bomb was upon me. Let there be no mistake about it.

• By the command of the President of the United States, the order went out. In the dull prose of military language, the new power was made ready.

To General Carl Spaatz, Commanding General, U.S. Army Strategic Air Forces.

ONE: The 509th Composite Group, 20th Air Force will deliver its first special bomb as soon as weather will permit visual bombing after about 3 August 1945 on one of the targets: Hiroshima, Kokura, Niigata, and Nagasaki.

Two: Additional bombs will be delivered on the above targets as soon as made ready by the project staff. Further in-

---

* The detailed mechanics of the decision to use the A-bomb are brilliantly explored, together with their moral implications, in Robert C. Batchelder's "The Irreversible Decision," Houghton Mifflin, 1962

structions will be issued concerning targets other than those listed above.

THREE: Dissemination of any and all information concerning the use of the weapon against Japan is reserved to the Secretary of War and the President of the United States.

FOUR: The foregoing order is issued to you by direction and with the approval of the Secretary of War and of the Chief of Staff. It is desired that you personally deliver one copy of this order to General MacArthur and one copy to Admiral Nimitz for their information.

• *The flight log of Navy Captain William Parsons, Weaponeer on the Enola Gay, the plane that carried the first atomic bomb:*

6 August 1945
0245 take-off
0300 started final loading of gun
0315 finished loading
0605 headed for Empire from Iwo
0730 red plugs in bomb armed
0741 started climb. Weather report received that weather over primary and tertiary targets was good but not over secondary target
0838 leveled off at 32,700 feet
0847 electronic fuses were tested and found to be O.K.
0904 course west
0909 target Hiroshima in sight
0915 ½—drop bomb.

• *Parsons described what happened to the Senate.*

SENATOR You released the first bomb personally, Captain Parsons, did you not?

PARSONS No Senator; I didn't pull the lever. I was there and the identification of the target was confirmed with me.

SENATOR You prepared the bomb didn't you, Captain, without going into detail?

PARSONS   You mean in the airplane? Yes, I had an assistant who made the electrical tests on the bomb in flight. I went into the bomb bay and performed an assembly operation on the bomb after the take-off. And then also supervised the final preparations which took place just before we climbed to delivery altitude.

We were about 20 minutes before the final climb which would put us at delivery altitude over Japan and decided to make it a final bomb then and there—of course we could have gone into reverse if we had to go back—but we made it a bomb about 20 minutes before we climbed to delivery altitude; and made final tests about ten minutes before we reached the target.

I did not see the bomb on Hiroshima actually function because we had just completed a maneuver to get a lot of distance between us and the bomb. The only one who could see it clearly was the tail gunner.

• *Some had a more immediate view than the tail gunner.*
School children who survived Hiroshima have recorded their
reactions.

On the 6th of August in Hiroshima I wasn't going to school yet. I was only five so I don't remember all the things that happened very well. However, Grandfather has told me various things so I will write those together with the things I remember myself. Since that time six years have already passed and now I'm a big girl of eleven.

I was playing in front of the public bath near home. Then Sei-chan said, "Please go to the garden and pick some flowers." So I was on my way to get them. All of a sudden there was a big flash and I was scared and tried to go back to the house.

And all of a sudden a lot of needles got in my eyes. I couldn't tell where anything was. When I tried to go toward the house I bumped into the front door. When I opened my eyes everything was darkish. Then Grandma rushed out with

Keika-chan on her back. I followed Grandma. We went toward our bomb shelter.

My younger big sister was already inside the shelter so the four of us huddled together. Then my older big sister came running in and we huddled together again. That older big sister was old enough so that she had already gone to work at a bakery; our mother had already died.

Father, who had been working with the Volunteer Labor Group, came back and was looking to find where we were. When she heard him, my big sister went out and took Father's hand and led him to the shelter. Father was burned all over above his hips. When Sister and the other people saw it they were all scared. A stranger spread some oil on his body for him.

In my heart I thought, "Thank you."

After that we went away to Fuchu in the hills. In a broken temple we put up a mosquito net and we lay down there. We stayed here for a long time. After a while other people began to go back to their homes so we went home too. When we got back we found that the glass was all broken, the chests were all toppled over, the family altar was tipped over, the shoji were torn, the roof tiles were broken and the plaster had fallen off the walls. We all helped to clear it away and laid Father there.

After about sixty days, in the middle of the night, Father called to Grandma and said he wanted to eat a sweet potato. Grandma said, "All right," and cooked the sweet potato.

"Father, the potato is ready," she said and looked at him, but he didn't answer. I touched his body and it was cold, and he was already dead.

Dear Father, dear Mother, good-bye.

TRUMAN   I do not know of an easy way to be President.

At the start of my research for this book Howard R. Lamar, Professor of History at Yale University, Harold C. Syrett, President of Queens College, New York, and General George A. "Abe" Lincoln, Chairman of the Department of Social Sciences, United States Military Academy, gave me of their time and helped me on my path. I am most grateful. Constance Hellyer Corning, my research assistant, possessed uncanny ability at finding what I wanted even when I wasn't quite sure what it was. She is as fine at tracing facts as she is at cooking; there is no higher praise. Kathleen A. Medernach skillfully aided in the final preparation of the notes.

NOTES AND BIBLIOGRAPHY

Sources for the quotations used in this book are given in the following pages. The complete bibliography for each chapter appears first. Then come the source references arranged by page and line.

To aid the reader in grasping the process I have followed to put together the book's quotations, these notes begin with the complete texts of the material used to produce the first five paragraphs of the Lincoln speech appearing on page 81. The speech as it appears on page 206 is given first. Next come the three documents from which it was culled. These are: Lincoln's Special Session Message of July 4th, 1861; Lincoln's Letter to Erastus Corning of June 13, 1863; and Lincoln's Executive Order No. 1 of Feb. 14, 1862. Selections from these three documents were chosen because in my opinion, and in that of leading historians, they best reflect Lincoln's thoughts on the need for executive action and the limits of Presidential power in meeting the emergency of rebellion.

Those portions of the original documents used in the quotation on page 81 appear in bold face.

LINCOLN   Fellow Citizens of the Senate and House of Representatives. Having been convened on an extraordinary occasion your attention is not called to any ordinary subject of legislation. The assailants of the Government have forced upon the country the issue: "Immediate dissolution or blood." Congress had not anticipated and so had not provided for the emergency. In this emergency the President felt it his duty to employ with energy the extraordinary powers which the Constitution confides to him in cases of insurrection. He called into the field such military and naval forces, unauthorized by the existing laws, as seemed necessary. He instituted a blockade, and suspended the writ of habeas corpus in various places, and caused persons engaged in treasonable practices to be detained in military custody.

This last authority has purposely been exercised but very sparingly. Nevertheless the legality of what has been done under it is questioned. The attention of the country has been called to the proposition that I who am sworn to "take care that the laws be faithfully executed" should not myself violate them. Are all the laws but one to go unexecuted and the Government itself to go to pieces lest that one be violated? But I do not believe that any law was violated. The Constitution itself states "the privilege of habeas corpus shall not be suspended unless in cases of rebellion the public safety may require it." Some insist that Congress and not the executive has this power. The Constitution is silent on this. Must I shoot a simple minded soldier boy who deserts, while I must not touch a hair of the wily agitator who induces him to desert? I think in such a case to silence the agitator and save the boy is not only constitutional, but withal a great mercy. The President in full view of his grave responsibility has so far done what he deemed his duty. You will now according to your own judgment, perform yours.

SPECIAL SESSION MESSAGE

July 4, 1861

Fellow-Citizens of the Senate and House of Representatives:

Having been convened on an extraordinary occasion, as authorized by the Constitution, your attention is not called to any ordinary subject of legislation.

At the beginning of the present Presidential term, four months ago, the functions of the Federal Government were found to be generally suspended within the several States of South Carolina, Georgia, Alabama, Mississippi, Louisiana, and Florida, excepting only those of the Post-Office Department.

Within these States all the forts, arsenals, dockyards, custom-houses, and the like, including the movable and stationary property in and about them, had been seized and were held in open hostility to this Government, excepting only Forts Pickens, Taylor, and Jefferson, on and near the Florida coast, and Fort Sumter, in Charleston Harbor, South Carolina. The forts thus seized had been put in improved condition, new ones had been built, and armed forces had been organized and were organizing, all avowedly with the same hostile purpose.

The forts remaining in the possession of the Federal Government in and near these States were either besieged or menaced by warlike preparations, and especially Fort Sumter was nearly surrounded by well-protected hostile batteries, with guns equal in quality to the best of its own and outnumbering the latter as perhaps ten to one. A disproportionate share of the Federal muskets and rifles had somehow found their way into these States, and had been seized to be used against the Government. Accumulations of the public revenue lying within them had been seized for the same object. The Navy was scattered in distant seas, leaving but a very small part of it within the immediate reach of the Government. Officers of the Federal Army and Navy had resigned in great numbers, and of those resigning a large proportion had taken up arms against the Government. Simultaneously and in connection with all this the purpose to sever the Federal Union was openly avowed. In accordance with this purpose, an ordinance had been adopted in each of these States declaring the States respectively to be separated from the National Union. A formula for instituting a combined government of these States had been promulgated, and this illegal organization, in the character of Confederate States, was already invoking recognition, aid, and intervention from foreign powers.

Finding this condition of things and believing it to be an imperative duty upon the incoming Executive to prevent, if possible, the consummation of such attempt to destroy the Federal Union, a choice of means to that end became indispensable. This choice was made, and was declared in the inaugural address. The policy chosen looked to the exhaustion of all peaceful measures before a resort to any stronger ones. It sought only to hold the public places and property not already wrested from the Government and to collect the revenue, relying for the rest on time, discussion, and the ballot box. It promised a continuance of the mails at Government expense to the very people who were resisting the Government, and it gave repeated pledges against any disturbance to any of the people or any of their rights. Of all that which a President might constitutionally and justifiably do in such a case, everything was forborne without which it was believed possible to keep the Government on foot.

On the 5th of March, the present incumbent's first full day in office, a letter of Major Anderson, commanding at Fort Sumter, written on the 28th of February and received at the War Department on the 4th of March, was by that Department placed in his hands. This letter expressed the professional opinion of the writer that reenforcements could not be thrown into that fort within the time for his relief rendered necessary by the limited supply of provisions, and with a view of holding possession of the same, with a force of less than 20,000 good and well-disciplined men. This opinion was concurred in by all the officers of his command, and their memoranda on the subject were made inclosures of Major Anderson's letter. The whole was immediately laid before Lieutenant-General Scott, who at once concurred with Major Anderson in opinion. On reflection, however, he took full time, consulting with other officers, both of the Army and the Navy, and at the end of four days came reluctantly, but decidedly, to the same conclusion as before. He also stated at the same time that no such sufficient force was then at the control of the Government or could be raised and brought to the ground within the time when the provisions in the fort would be exhausted. In a purely military point of view this reduced the duty of the Administration in the case to the mere matter of getting the garrison safely out of the fort.

It was believed, however, that to so abandon that position under the circumstances would be utterly ruinous; that the *necessity* under which it was to be done would not be fully understood; that by many it would be construed as a part of a *voluntary* policy; that at home it would discourage the friends of the Union, embolden its adversaries, and go far to insure to the latter a recognition abroad; that, in fact, it would be our national destruction consummated. This could not be allowed. Starvation was not yet upon the garrison, and ere it would be reached *Fort Pickens* might be reenforced. This last would be a clear indication of *policy*, and would better enable the country to accept the evacuation of Fort Sumter as a military *necessity*. An order was at once directed to be sent for the landing of the troops from the steamship *Brooklyn* into Fort Pickens. This order could not go by land, but must take the longer and slower route by sea. The first return news from the order was received just one week before the fall of Fort Sumter. The news itself was that the officer commanding the *Sabine*, to which vessel the troops had been transferred from the *Brooklyn*, acting upon some *quasi* armistice of the late Administration (and of the existence of which the present Administration, up to the time the order was dispatched, had only too vague and uncertain rumors to fix attention), had refused to land the troops. To now reenforce Fort Pickens before a crisis would be reached at Fort Sumter was impossible, rendered so by the near exhaustion of provisions in the latter-named fort. In precaution against such a conjuncture the Government had a few days before commenced preparing an expedition, as well adapted as might be, to relieve Fort Sumter, which expedition was intended to be ultimately used or not, according to circumstances. The strongest anticipated case for using it was now presented, and it was resolved to send it forward. As had been intended in this contingency, it was also resolved to notify the governor of South Carolina that he might expect an attempt would be made to provision the fort, and that if the attempt should not be resisted there would be no effort to throw in men, arms, or ammunition without further notice, or in case of an attack upon the fort. This notice was accordingly given, whereupon the fort was attacked and bombarded to its fall, without even awaiting the arrival of the provisioning expedition.

It is thus seen that the assault upon and reduction of Fort Sumter was in no sense a matter of self-defense on the part of the assailants. They well knew that the garrison in the fort could by no possibility commit aggression upon them. They knew—they were expressly notified—that the giving of bread to the few brave and hungry men of the garrison was all which would on that occasion be attempted, unless themselves, by resisting so much, should provoke more. They knew that this Government desired to keep the garrison in the fort, not to assail them, but merely to maintain visible possession, and thus to preserve the Union from actual and immediate dissolution, trusting, as hereinbefore stated, to time, discussion, and the ballot box for final adjustment; and they assailed and reduced the fort for precisely the reverse object—to drive out the visible authority of the Federal Union, and thus force it to immediate dissolution. That this was their object the Executive well understood; and having said to them in the inaugural address, "You can have no conflict without being yourselves the aggressors," he took pains not only to keep this declaration good, but also to keep the case so free from the power of ingenious sophistry as that the world should not be able to misunderstand it. By the affair at Fort Sumter, with its surrounding circumstances, that point was reached. Then and thereby the assailants of the Government began the conflict of arms, without a gun in sight or in expectancy to return their fire, save only the few in the fort, sent to that harbor years before for their own protection, and still ready to give that protection in whatever was lawful. In this act, discarding all else, they have forced upon the country the distinct issue, "Immediate dissolution or blood."

And this issue embraces more than the fate of these United States. It presents to the whole family of man the question whether a constitutional republic, or democracy—a government of the people by the same people— can or can not maintain its territorial integrity against its own domestic foes. It presents the question whether discontented individuals, too few in numbers to control administration according to organic law in any case, can always, upon the pretenses made in this case, or on any other pretenses, or arbitrarily without any pretense, break up their government, and thus practically put an end to free government upon the earth. It forces us to ask, Is there in all republics this inherent and fatal weakness? Must a government of necessity be too *strong* for the liberties of its own people, or too *weak* to maintain its own existence?

So viewing the issue, no choice was left but to call out the war power of the Government and so to resist force employed for its destruction by force for its preservation.

The call was made, and the response of the country was most gratifying, surpassing in unanimity and spirit the most sanguine expectation. Yet none of the States commonly called slave States, except Delaware, gave a regiment through regular State organization. A few regiments have been organized within some others of those States by individual enterprise and received into the Government service. Of course the seceded States, so called (and to which Texas had been joined about the time of the inauguration), gave no troops to the cause of the Union. The border States, so called, were not uniform in their action, some of them being almost *for* the Union, while in others, as Virginia, North Carolina, Tennessee, and Arkansas, the Union sentiment was nearly repressed and silenced. The course taken in Virginia was the most remarkable, perhaps the most important. A convention elected by the people of that State to consider this very question of disrupting the Federal Union was in session at the capital of Virginia when Fort Sumter fell. To this body the people had chosen a large majority of *professed* Union men. Almost immediately after the fall of Sumter many members of that majority went over to the original disunion minority, and with them adopted an ordinance for withdrawing the State from the Union. Whether this change was wrought by their great approval of the assault upon Sumter or their great resentment at the Government's resistance to that assault is not definitely known. Although they submitted the ordinance for ratification to a vote of the people, to be taken on a day then somewhat more than a month distant, the convention and the legislature (which was also in session at the same time and place), with leading men of the State not members of either, immediately commenced acting as if the State were already out of the Union. They pushed military preparations vigorously forward all over the State. They seized the United States armory at Harpers Ferry and the navy-yard at Gosport, near Norfolk. They received—perhaps invited—into their State large bodies of troops, with their warlike appointments, from the so-called seceded States. They formally entered into a treaty of temporary alliance and cooperation with the so-called "Confederate States," and sent members to their Congress at Montgomery; and, finally, they permitted the insurrectionary government to be transferred to their capital at Richmond.

The people of Virginia have thus allowed this giant insurrection to make its nest within her borders, and this Government has no choice left but to deal with it *where* it finds it; and it has the less regret, as the loyal citizens have in due form claimed its protection. Those loyal citizens this Government is bound to recognize and protect, as being Virginia.

In the border States, so called—in fact, the Middle States—there are those who favor a policy which they call "armed neutrality;" that is, an arming of those States to prevent the Union forces passing one way or the disunion the other over their soil. This would be disunion completed. Figuratively speaking, it would be the building of an impassable wall along the line of separation, and yet not quite an impassable one, for, under the guise of neutrality, it would tie the hands of the Union men and freely pass supplies from among them to the insurrectionists, which it could not do as an open enemy. At a stroke it would take all the trouble off the hands of secession, except only what proceeds from the external blockade. It would do for the disunionists that which of all things they most desire—feed them well and give them disunion without a struggle of their own. It recognizes no fidelity to the Constitution, no obligation to maintain the Union; and while very many who have favored it are doubtless loyal citizens, it is, nevertheless, very injurious in effect.

Recurring to the action of the Government, it may be stated that at first a call was made for 75,000 militia, and rapidly following this a proclamation was issued for closing the ports of the insurrectionary districts by proceedings in the nature of blockade. So far all was believed to be strictly legal. At this point the insurrectionists announced their purpose to enter upon the practice of privateering.

Other calls were made for volunteers to serve three years unless sooner discharged, and also for large additions to the Regular Army and Navy. These measures, whether strictly legal or not, were ventured upon under what appeared to be a popular demand and a public necessity, trusting then, as now, that Congress would readily ratify them. It is believed that nothing has been done beyond the constitutional competency of Congress.

Soon after the first call for militia it was considered a duty to authorize the Commanding General in proper cases, according to his discretion, to suspend the privilege of the writ of *habeas corpus*, or, in other words, to arrest and detain without resort to the ordinary processes and forms of law such individuals as he might deem dangerous to the public safety. This authority has purposely been exercised but very sparingly. Nevertheless, the legality and propriety of what has been done under it are questioned, and the attention of the country has been called to the proposition that one who is sworn to "take care that the laws be faithfully executed" should not himself violate them. Of course some consideration was given to the questions of power and propriety before this matter was acted upon. The whole of the laws which were required to be faithfully executed were being resisted and failing of execution in nearly one-third of the States. Must they be allowed to finally fail of execution, even had it been perfectly clear that by the use of the means necessary to their execution some single law, made in such extreme tenderness of the citizen's liberty that practically it relieves more of the guilty than of the innocent, should to a very limited extent be violated? To state the question more directly, Are all the laws *but one* to go unexecuted, and the Government itself go to pieces lest that one be violated? Even in such a case, would not the official oath be broken if the Government should be overthrown when it was believed that disregarding the single law would tend to preserve it? But it was not believed that this question was presented. It was not believed that any law was violated. The provision of the Constitution that "the privilege of the writ of *habeas corpus* shall not be suspended unless when, in cases of rebellion or invasion, the public safety may require it" is equivalent to a provision—is a provision—that such privilege may be suspended when, in cases of rebellion or invasion, the public safety *does* require it. It was decided that we have a case of rebellion and that the public safety does require the qualified suspension of the privilege of the writ which was authorized to be made. **Now it is insisted that Congress, and not the Executive, is vested with this power; but the Constitution itself is silent as to which** or who is to exercise the power; and as the provision was plainly made for a dangerous emergency, it can not be believed the framers of the instrument intended that in every case the danger should run its course until Congress could be called together, the very assembling of which might be prevented, as was intended in this case, by the rebellion.

No more extended argument is now offered, as an opinion at some length will probably be presented by the Attorney-General. Whether there shall be any legislation upon the subject, and, if any, what, is submitted entirely to the better judgment of Congress.

The forebearance of this Government had been so extraordinary and so long continued as to lead some foreign nations to shape their action as if they supposed the early destruction of our National Union was probable. While this on discovery gave the Executive some concern, he is now happy to say that the sovereignty and rights of the United States are now everywhere practically respected by foreign powers, and a general sympathy with the country is manifested throughout the world.

The reports of the Secretaries of the Treasury, War, and the Navy will give the information in detail deemed necessary and convenient for your deliberation and action, while the Executive and all the Departments will stand ready to supply omissions or to communicate new facts considered important for you to know.

It is now recommended that you give the legal means for making this contest a short and a decisive one; that you place at the control of the Government for the work at least 400,000 men and $400,000,000. That number of men is about one-tenth of those of proper ages within the regions where apparently *all* are willing to engage, and the sum is less than a twenty-third part of the money value owned by the men who seem ready to devote the whole. A debt of $600,000,000 *now* is a less sum per head than was the debt of our Revolution when we came out of that struggle, and the money value in the country now bears even a greater proportion to what it was *then* than does the population. Surely each man has as strong a motive *now* to *preserve* our liberties as each had *then* to *establish* them.

A right result at this time will be worth more to the world than ten times the men and ten times the money. The evidence reaching us from the country leaves no doubt that the material for the work is abundant, and that it needs only the hand of legislation to give it legal sanction and the hand of the Executive to give it practical shape and efficiency. One of the greatest perplexities of the Government is to avoid receiving troops faster than it can provide for them. In a word, the people will save their Government if the Government itself will do its part only indifferently well.

It might seem at first thought to be of little difference whether the present movement at the South be called "secession" or "rebellion." The movers, however, well understand the difference. At the beginning they knew they could never raise their treason to any respectable magnitude by any name which implies *violation* of law. They knew their people possessed as much of moral sense, as much of devotion to law and order, and as much pride in and reverence for the history and Government of their common country as any other civilized and patriotic people. They knew they could make no advancement directly in the teeth of these strong and noble sentiments. Accordingly, they commenced by an insidious debauching of the public mind. They invented an ingenious sophism, which, if conceded, was followed by perfectly logical steps through all the incidents to the complete destruction of the Union. The sophism itself is that any State of the Union may *consistently* with the National Constitution, and therefore *lawfully* and *peacefully*, withdraw from the Union without the consent of the Union or of any other State. The little disguise that the supposed right is to be exercised only for just cause, themselves to be the sole judge of its justice, is too thin to merit any notice.

With rebellion thus sugar coated they have been drugging the public mind of their section for more than thirty years, and until at length they have brought many good men to a willingness to take up arms against the Government the day *after* some assemblage of men have enacted the farcical pretense of taking their State out of the Union who could have been brought to no such thing the day *before*.

This sophism derives much, perhaps the whole, of its currency from the assumption that there is some omnipotent and sacred supremacy pertaining to a *State*—to each State of our Federal Union. Our States have neither more nor less power than that reserved to them in the Union by the Constitution, no one of them ever having been a State *out* of the Union. The original ones passed into the Union even *before* they cast off their British colonial dependence, and the new ones each came into the Union directly from a condition of dependence, excepting Texas; and even Texas, in its temporary independence, was never designated a State. The new ones only took the designation of States on coming into the Union, while that name was first adopted for the old ones in and by the Declaration of Independence. Therein the "United Colonies" were declared to be "free and independent States;" but even then the object plainly was not to declare their independence of one *another* or of the *Union*, but directly the contrary, as their mutual pledge and their mutual action before, at the time, and afterwards abundantly show. The express plighting of faith by each and all of the original thirteen in the Articles of Confederation, two years later, that the Union shall be perpetual is most conclusive. Having never been *States*, either in substance or in name, *outside* of the Union, whence this magical omnipotence of "State rights," asserting a claim of power to lawfully destroy the Union itself? Much is said about the "sovereignty" of the States, but the word even is not in the National Constitution, nor, as is believed, in any of the State constitutions. What is a "sovereignty" in the political sense of the term? Would it be far wrong to define it "a political community without a political superior"? Tested by this, no one of our States, except Texas, ever was a sovereignty; and even Texas gave up the character on coming into the Union, by which act she acknowledged the Constitution of the United States and the laws and treaties of the United States made in pursuance of the Constitution to be for her the supreme law of the land. The States have their status in the Union, and they have no other legal status. If they break from this, they can only do so against law and by revolution. The Union, and not themselves separately, procured their independence and their liberty. By conquest or purchase the Union gave each of them whatever of independence and liberty it has. The Union is older than any of the States, and, in fact, it created them as States. Originally some dependent colonies made the Union, and in turn the Union threw off their old dependence for them and made them States, such as they are. Not one of them ever had a State constitution independent of the Union. Of course it is not forgotten that all the new States framed their constitutions before they entered the Union, nevertheless dependent upon and preparatory to coming into the Union.

Unquestionably the States have the powers and rights reserved to them in and by the National Constitution; but among these surely are not included all conceivable powers, however mischievous or destructive, but at most such only as were known in the world at the time as governmental powers; and certainly a power to destroy the Government itself had never been known as a governmental—as a merely administrative power. This relative matter of national power and State rights, as a principle, is no other than the principle of *generality* and *locality*. Whatever concerns the whole should be confided to the whole—to the General Government—while whatever concerns *only* the State should be left exclusively to the State. This is all there is of original principle about it. Whether the National Constitution in defining boundaries between the two has applied the principle with exact accuracy is not to be questioned. We are all bound by that defining without question.

What is now combated is the position that secession is *consistent* with the Constitution—is *lawful* and *peaceful*. It is not contended that there is any express law for it, and nothing should ever be implied as law which leads to unjust or absurd consequences. The nation purchased with money the countries out of which several of these States were formed. Is it just that they shall go off without leave and without refunding? The nation paid very large sums (in the aggregate, I believe, nearly a hundred millions) to relieve Florida of the aboriginal tribes. Is it just that she shall now be off without consent or without making any return? The nation is now in debt for money applied to the benefit of these so-called seceding States in common with the rest. Is it just either that creditors shall go unpaid or the remaining States pay the whole? A part of the present national debt was contracted to pay the old debts of Texas. Is it just that she shall leave and pay no part of this herself?

Again: If one State may secede, so may another; and when all shall have seceded none is left to pay the debts. Is this quite just to creditors? Did we notify them of this sage view of ours when we borrowed their money? If we now recognize this doctrine by allowing the seceders to go in peace, it is difficult to see what we can do if others choose to go or to extort terms upon which they will promise to remain.

The seceders insist that our Constitution admits of secession. They have assumed to make a national constitution of their own, in which of necessity they have either *discarded* or *retained* the right of secession, as they insist it exists in ours. If they have discarded it, they thereby admit that on principle it ought not to be in ours. If they have retained it, by their own construction of ours they show that to be consistent they must secede from one another whenever they shall find it the easiest way of settling their debts or effecting any other selfish or unjust object. The principle itself is one of disintegration, and upon which no government can possibly endure.

If all the States save one should assert the power to *drive* that one out of the Union, it is presumed the whole class of seceder politicians would at once deny the power and denounce the act as the greatest outrage upon State rights. But suppose that precisely the same act, instead of being called "driving the one out," should be called "the seceding of the others from that one," it would be exactly what the seceders claim to do, unless, indeed, they make the point that the one, because it is a minority, may rightfully do what the others, because they are a majority, may not rightfully do. These politicians are subtle and profound on the rights of minorities. They are not partial to that power which made the Constitution and speaks from the preamble, calling itself "we, the people."

It may well be questioned whether there is to-day a majority of the legally qualified voters of any State, except, perhaps, South Carolina, in favor of disunion. There is much reason to believe that the Union men are the majority in many, if not in every other one, of the so-called seceded States. The contrary has not been demonstrated in any one of them. It is ventured to affirm this even of Virginia and Tennessee; for the result of an election held in military camps, where the bayonets are all on one side of the question voted upon, can scarcely be considered as demonstrating popular sentiment. At such an election all that large class who are at once *for* the Union and *against* coercion would be coerced to vote against the Union.

It may be affirmed without extravagance that the free institutions we enjoy have developed the powers and improved the condition of our whole people beyond any example in the world. Of this we now have a striking and an impressive illustration. So large an army as the Government has now on foot was never before known without a soldier in it but who had taken his place there of his own free choice. But more than this, there are many single regiments whose members, one and another, possess full practical knowledge of all the arts, sciences, professions, and whatever else, whether useful or elegant, is known in the world; and there is scarcely one from which there could not be selected a President, a Cabinet, a Congress, and perhaps a court, abundantly competent to administer the Government itself. Nor do I say this is not true also in the army of our late friends, now adversaries in this contest; but if it is, so much better the reason why the Government which has conferred such benefits on both them and us should not be broken up. Whoever in any section proposes to abandon such a government would do well to consider in deference to what principle it is that he does it; what better he is likely to get in its stead; whether the substitute will give, or be intended to give, so much of good to the people. There are some foreshadowings on this subject. Our adversaries have adopted some declarations of independence in which, unlike the good old one penned by Jefferson, they omit the words "all men are created equal." Why? They have adopted a temporary national constitution, in the preamble of which, unlike our good old one signed by Washington, they omit "We, the people," and substitute "We, the deputies of the sovereign and independent States." Why? Why this deliberate pressing out of view the rights of men and the authority of the people?

This is essentially a people's contest. On the side of the Union it is a struggle for maintaining in the world that form and substance of government whose leading object is to elevate the condition of men; to lift artificial weights from all shoulders; to clear the paths of laudable pursuit for all; to afford all an unfettered start and a fair chance in the race of life. Yielding to partial and temporary departures, from necessity, this is the leading object of the Government for whose existence we contend.

I am most happy to believe that the plain people understand and appreciate this. It is worthy of note that while in this the Government's hour of trial large numbers of those in the Army and Navy who have been favored with the offices have resigned and proved false to the hand which had pampered them, not one common soldier or common sailor is known to have deserted his flag.

Great honor is due to those officers who remained true despite the example of their treacherous associates; but the greatest honor and most important fact of all is the unanimous firmness of the common soldiers and common sailors. To the last man, so far as known, they have successfully resisted the traitorous efforts of those whose commands but an hour before they obeyed as absolute law. This is the patriotic instinct of plain people. They understand without an argument that the destroying the Government which was made by Washington means no good to them.

Our popular Government has often been called an experiment. Two points in it our people have already settled—the successful *establishing* and the successful *administering* of it. One still remains—its successful *maintenance* against a formidable internal attempt to overthrow it. It is now for them to demonstrate to the world that those who can fairly carry an election can also suppress a rebellion; that ballots are the rightful and peaceful successors of bullets, and that when ballots have fairly and constitutionally decided there can be no successful appeal back to bullets; that there can be no successful appeal except to ballots themselves at succeeding elections. Such will be a great lesson of peace, teaching men that what they can not take by an election neither can they take it by a war; teaching all the folly of being the beginners of a war.

Lest there be some uneasiness in the minds of candid men as to what is to be the course of the Government toward the Southern States *after* the rebellion shall have been suppressed, the Executive deems it proper to say it will be his purpose then, as ever, to be guided by the Constitution and the laws, and that he probably will have no different understanding of the powers and duties of the Federal Government relatively to the rights of the States and the people under the Constitution than that expressed in the inaugural address.

He desires to preserve the Government, that it may be administered for all as it was administered by the men who made it. Loyal citizens everywhere have the right to claim this of their government, and the government has no right to withhold or neglect it. It is not perceived that in giving it there is any coercion, any conquest, or any subjugation in any just sense of those terms.

The Constitution provides, and all the States have accepted the provision, that "the United States shall guarantee to every State in this Union a republican form of government." But if a State may lawfully go out of the Union, having done so it may also discard the republican form of government; so that to prevent its going out is an indispensable *means* to the *end* of maintaining the guaranty mentioned; and when an end is lawful and obligatory the indispensable means to it are also lawful and obligatory.

It was with the deepest regret that the Executive found the duty of employing the war power in defense of the Government forced upon him. He could but perform this duty or surrender the existence of the Government. No compromise by public servants could in this case be a cure; not that compromises are not often proper, but that no popular government can long survive a marked precedent that those who carry an election can only save the government from immediate destruction by giving up the main point upon which the people gave the election. The people themselves, and not their servants, can safely reverse their own deliberate decisions.

As a private citizen the Executive could not have consented that these institutions shall perish; much less could he in betrayal of so vast and so sacred a trust as these free people had confided to him. He felt that he had no moral right to shrink, nor even to count the chances of his own life, in what might follow. **In full view of his great responsibility he has so far done what he has deemed his duty. You will now, according to your own judgment, perform yours.** He sincerely hopes that your views and your action may so accord with his as to assure all faithful citizens who have been disturbed in their rights of a certain and speedy restoration to them under the Constitution and the laws.

And having thus chosen our course, without guile and with pure purpose, let us renew our trust in God and go forward without fear and with manly hearts.

EXECUTIVE MANSION, WASHINGTON, *June 13, 1863.*
HON. ERASTUS CORNING AND OTHERS:

Gentlemen:—Your letter of May 19, enclosing the resolutions of a public meeting held at Albany, N. Y., on the 16th of the same month, was received several days ago.

The resolutions, as I understand them, are resolvable into two propositions: first, the expression of a purpose to sustain the cause of the Union, to secure peace through victory, and to support the Administration in every constitutional and lawful measure to suppress the rebellion; and, secondly, a declaration of censure upon the Administration for supposed unconstitutional action, such as the making of military arrests. And from the two propositions a third is deduced, which is, that the gentlemen composing the meeting are resolved on doing their part to maintain our common Government and country, despite the folly or wickedness, as they may conceive, of any Administration. This position is eminently patriotic, and as such I thank the meeting and congratulate the nation for it. My own purpose is the same, so that the meeting and myself have a common object, and can have no difference, except in the choice of means or measures for effecting that object.

And here I ought to close this paper, and would close it, if there were no apprehension that more injurious consequences than any merely personal to myself might follow the censures systematically cast upon me for doing what, in my view of duty, I could not forbear. The resolutions promise to support me in every constitutional and lawful measure to suppress the rebellion, and I have not knowingly employed, nor shall knowingly employ any other. But the meeting, by their resolutions, assert and argue that certain military arrests, and proceedings following them, for which I am ultimately responsible, are unconstitutional. I think they are not. The resolutions quote from the Constitution the definition of treason, and also the limiting safeguards and guarantees therein provided for the citizen on trial for treason, and on his being held to answer for capital, or otherwise infamous crimes, and, in criminal prosecutions, his right to a speedy and public trial by an impartial jury. They proceed to resolve "that these safeguards of the rights of the citizen against the pretensions of arbitrary power were intended more *especially* for his protection in times of civil commotion."

And, apparently to demonstrate the proposition, the resolutions proceed: "They were secured substantially to the English people *after* years of protracted civil war, and were adopted into our Constitution at the *close* of the Revolution." Would not the demonstration have been better if it could have been truly said that these safeguards had been adopted and applied *during* the civil wars and *during* our Revolution, instead of *after* the one and at the *close* of the other? I, too, am devotedly for them *after* civil war, and *before* civil war, and at all times, "except when, in cases of rebellion or invasion, the public safety may require" their suspension. The resolutions proceed to tell us that these safeguards "have stood the test of seventy-six years of trial, under our republican system, under circumstances which show that, while they constitute the foundation of all free government, they are the elements of the enduring stability of the Republic." No one denies that they have so stood the test up to the beginning of the present rebellion, if we except a certain occurrence at New Orleans; nor does any one question that they will stand the same test much longer after the rebellion closes. But these provisions of the Constitution have no application to the case we have in hand, because the arrests complained of were not made for treason—that is, not for *the* treason defined in the Constitution, and upon conviction of which the punishment is death—nor yet were they made to hold persons to answer for any capital or otherwise infamous crimes; nor were the proceedings following, in any constitutional or legal sense, "criminal prosecutions." The arrests were made on totally different grounds, and the proceedings following accorded with the grounds of the arrest. Let us consider the real case with which we are dealing, and apply to it the parts of the Constitution plainly made for such cases.

Prior to my installation here, it had been inculcated that any State had a lawful right to secede from the National Union, and that it would be expedient to exercise the right whenever the devotees of the doctrine should fail to elect a President to their own liking. I was elected contrary to their liking, and accordingly, so far as it was legally possible, they had taken seven States out of the Union, had seized many of the United States forts, and had fired upon the United States flag, all before I was inaugurated, and, of course, before I had done any official act whatever. The rebellion thus began soon ran into the present civil war; and, in certain respects, it began on very unequal terms between the parties. The insurgents had been preparing for it more than thirty years, while the Government had taken no steps to resist them. The former had carefully considered all the means which could be turned to their account. It undoubtedly was a well-pondered reliance with them that, in their own unrestricted efforts to destroy Union, Constitution, and law altogether, the Government would, in great degree, be restrained by the same Constitution and law from arresting their progress. Their sympathizers pervaded all departments of the Government, and nearly all communities of the people. From this material, under cover of "liberty of speech," "liberty of the press," and "habeas corpus," they hoped to keep on foot among us a most efficient corps of spies, informers, suppliers, and aiders and abettors of their cause in a thousand ways. They knew that in times such as they were inaugurating, by the Constitution itself the "habeas corpus" might be suspended; but they also knew they had friends who would make a question as to *who* was to suspend it: meanwhile, their spies and others might remain at large to help on their cause. Or if, as has happened, the Executive should suspend the writ, without ruinous waste of time, instances of arresting innocent persons might occur, as are always likely to occur in such cases, and then a clamor could be raised in regard to this which might be, at least, of some service to the insurgent cause. It needed no very keen perception to discover this part of the enemy's programme, so soon as, by opening hostilities, their machinery was put fairly in motion. Yet, thoroughly imbued with a reverence for the guaranteed rights of individuals, I was slow to adopt the strong measures which by degrees I have been forced to regard as being within the exceptions of the Constitution, and as indispensable to the public safety. Nothing is better known to history than that courts of justice are utterly incompetent to such cases. Civil courts are organized chiefly for trials of individuals, or, at most, a few individuals acting in concert, and this in quiet times, and on charges of crimes well defined in the law. Even in times of peace, bands of horse-thieves and robbers frequently grow too numerous and powerful for the ordinary courts of justice. But what comparison, in numbers, have such bands ever borne to the insurgent sympathizers even in many of the loyal States? Again, a jury too frequently has at least one member more ready to hang the panel than to hang the traitor. And yet, again, he who dissuades one man from volunteering, or induces one soldier to desert, weakens the Union cause as much as he who kills a Union soldier in battle. Yet this dissuasion or inducement may be so conducted as to be no defined crime of which any civil court would take cognizance.

Ours is a case of rebellion—so called by the resolution before me—in fact, a clear, flagrant, and gigantic case of rebellion; and the provision of the Constitution that "the privilege of the writ of *habeus corpus* shall not be suspended unless when, in cases of rebellion or invasion, the public safety may require it," is *the* provision which specially applies to our present case. This provision plainly attests the understanding of those who made the Constitution, that ordinary courts of justice are inadequate to "cases of rebellion" —attests their purpose that, in such cases, men may be held in custody whom the courts, acting on ordinary rules, would discharge. *Habeas corpus* does not discharge men who are proved to be guilty of defined crime; and its suspension is allowed by the Constitution on purpose that men may be arrested and held who cannot be proved to be guilty of defined crime, "when, in cases of rebellion or invasion, the public safety may require it." This is precisely our present case—a case of rebellion, wherein the public saftey *does* require the suspension. Indeed, arrests by process of courts, and arrests in cases of rebellion, do not proceed altogether upon the same basis. The former is directed at the small percentage of ordinary and continuous perpetration of crime; while the latter is directed at sudden and extensive uprisings against the Government, which at most will succeed or fail in no great length of time. In the latter case arrests are made, not so much for what has been done as for what probably would be done. The latter is more for the preventive and less for the vindictive than the former. In such cases the purposes of men are much more easily understood than in cases of ordinary crime. The man who stands by and says nothing, when the peril of his Government is discussed, cannot be misunderstood. If not hindered, he is sure to help the enemy; much more, if he talks ambiguously—talks for his country with "buts," and "ifs," and "ands." Of how little value the constitutional provisions I have quoted will be rendered, if arrests shall never be made until defined crimes shall have been committed, may be illustrated by a few notable examples. General John C. Breckinridge, General Robert E. Lee, General Joseph E. Johnston, General John B. Magruder,

General William B. Preston, General Simon B. Buckner, and Commodore Franklin Buchanan, now occupying the very highest places in the rebel war service, were all within the power of the Government since the rebellion began, and were nearly as well known to be traitors then as now. Unquestionably, if we had seized and held them, the insurgent cause would be much weaker. But no one of them had then committed any crime defined in the law. Every one of them, if arrested, would have been discharged on *habeas corpus*, were the writ allowed to operate. In view of these and similar cases, I think the time not unlikely to come when I shall be blamed for having made too few arrests rather than too many.

By the third resolution, the meeting indicate their opinion that military arrests may be constitutional in localities where rebellion actually exists, but that such arrests are unconstitutional in localities where rebellion or insurrection does *not* actually exist. They insist that such arrests shall not be made "outside of the lines of necessary military occupation and the scenes of insurrection." Inasmuch, however, as the Constitution itself makes no such distinction, I am unable to believe that there *is* any such constitutional distinction. I concede that the class of arrests complained of can be constitutional only when, in cases of rebellion or invasion, the public safety may require them; and I insist that in such cases they are constitutional *wherever* the public safety does require them; as well in places to which they may prevent the rebellion extending as in those where it may be already prevailing; as well where they may restrain mischievous interference with the raising and supplying of armies to suppress the rebellion, as where the rebellion may actually be; as well where they may restrain the enticing men out of the army, as where they would prevent mutiny in the army; equally constitutional at all places where they will conduce to the public safety, as against the dangers of rebellion or invasion. Take the particular case mentioned by the meeting. It is asserted, in substance, that Mr. Vallandigham was, by a military commander, seized and tried "for no other reason than words addressed to a public meeting, in criticism of the course of the Administration, and in condemnation of the military orders of the general." Now, if there be no mistake about this; if this assertion is the truth and the whole truth; if there was no other reason for the arrest, then I concede that the arrest was wrong. But the arrest, as I understand, was made for a very different reason. Mr. Vallandigham avows his hostility to the war on the part of the Union; and his arrest was made because he was laboring, with some effect, to prevent the raising of troops; to encourage desertions from the army; and to leave the rebellion without an adequate military force to suppress it. He was not arrested because he was damaging the political prospects of the Administration, or the personal interests of the commanding general, but because he was damaging the army, upon the existence and vigor of which the life of the nation depends. He was warring upon the military, and this gave the military constitutional jurisdiction to lay hands upon him. If Mr. Vallandigham was not damaging the military power of the country, then this arrest was made on mistake of fact, which I would be glad to correct on reasonable satisfactory evidence.

I understand the meeting, whose resolutions I am considering, to be in favor of suppressing the rebellion by military force—by armies. Long experience has shown that armies cannot be maintained unless desertions shall be punished by the severe penalty of death. The case requires, and the law and the Constitution sanction, this punishment. **Must I shoot a simple-minded soldier boy** who deserts, while I must not touch a hair of a wily agitator who induces him to desert? This is none the less injurious when effected by getting a father, or brother, or friend, into a public meeting, and there working upon his feelings till he is persuaded to write the soldier boy that he is fighting in a bad cause, for a wicked Administration of a contemptible Government, too weak to arrest and punish him if he shall desert. **I think that in such a case to silence the agitator and save the boy is not only constitutional, but withal a great mercy.**

If I be wrong on this question of constitutional power, my error lies in believing that certain proceedings are constitutional when, in cases of rebellion or invasion, the public safety requires them, which would not be constitutional when, in the absence of rebellion or invasion, the public safety dos *not* require them; in other words, that the Constitution is not, in its application, in all respects the same, in cases of rebellion or invasion involving the public safety, as it is in time of profound peace and public security. The Constitution itself makes the distinction; and I can no more be persuaded that the Government can constitutionally take no strong measures in time of rebellion, because it can be shown that the same could not be lawfully taken in time of peace, than I can be persuaded that a particular drug is not good medicine for a sick man, because it can be shown not to be good food for a well one. Nor am I able to appreciate the danger apprehended by the meeting that the American people will, by means of military arrests during the rebellion, lose the right of public discussion, the liberty of speech and the press, the law of evidence, trial by jury, and *habeas corpus*, throughout the indefinite peaceful future, which I trust lies before them, any more than I am able to believe that a man could contract so strong an appetite for emetics during temporary illness as to persist in feeding upon them during the remainder of his healthful life.

In giving the resolutions that earnest consideration which you request of me, I cannot overlook the fact that the meeting speak as "Democrats." Nor can I, with full respect for their known intelligence, and the fairly presumed deliberation with which they prepared their resolutions, be permitted to suppose that this occurred by accident, or in any way other than that they preferred to designate themselves "Democrats" rather than "American citizens." In this time of national peril, I would have preferred to meet you on a level one step higher than any party platform; because I am sure that, from such more elevated position, we could do better battle for the country we all love than we possibly can from those lower ones where, from the force of habit, the prejudices of the past, and selfish hopes of the future, we are sure to expend much of our ingenuity and strength in finding fault with and aiming blows at each other. But, since you have denied me this, I will yet be thankful, for the country's sake, that not all Democrats have done so. He on whose discretionary judgment Mr. Vallandigham was arrested and tried is a Democrat, having no old party affinity with me; and the judge who rejected the constitutional view expressed in these resolutions, by refusing to discharge Mr. Vallandigham on *habeas corpus*, is a Democrat of better days than these, having received his judicial mantle at the hands of President Jackson. And still more, of all those Democrats who are nobly exposing their lives and shedding their blood on the battle-field, I have learned that many approve the course taken with Mr. Vallandigham, while I have not heard of a single one condemning it. I cannot assert that there are none such. And the name of Jackson recalls an incident of pertinent history: After the battle of New Orleans, and while the fact that the treaty of peace had been concluded was well known in the city, but before official knowledge of it had arrived, General Jackson still maintained martial or military law. Now that it could be said the war was over, the clamor against martial law, which had existed from the first, grew more furious. Among other things, a Mr. Louiallier published a denunciatory newspaper article. General Jackson arrested him. A lawyer by the name of Morrel procured the United States Judge Hall to issue a writ of *habeas corpus* to relieve Mr. Louiallier. General Jackson arrested both the lawyer and the judge. A Mr. Hollander ventured to say of some part of the matter that "it was a dirty trick." General Jackson arrested him. When the officer undertook to serve the writ of *habeas corpus*, General Jackson took it from him, and sent him away with a copy. Holding the judge in custody a few days, the General sent him beyond the limits of his encampment, and set him at liberty, with an order to remain till the ratification of peace should be regularly announced, or until the British should have left the Southern coast. A day or two more elapsed, the ratification of a treaty of peace was regularly announced, and the judge and others were fully liberated. A few days more, and the judge called General Jackson into court and fined him $1,000 for having arrested him and the others named. The General paid the fine, and there the matter rested for nearly thirty years, when Congress refunded principal and interest. The late Senator Douglas, then in the House of Representatives, took a leading part in the debates, in which the constitutional question was much discussed. I am not prepared to say whom the journals would show to have voted for the measure.

It may be remarked: First, that we had the same Constitution then as now; secondly, that we then had a case of invasion, and now we have a case of rebellion; and, thirdly, that the permanent right of the people to public discussion, the liberty of speech and of the press, the trial by jury, the law of evidence, and the *habeas corpus*, suffered no detriment whatever by that conduct of General Jackson, or its subsequent approval by the American Congress.

And yet, let me say that, in my own discretion, I do not know whether I would have ordered the arrest of Mr. Vallandigham. While I cannot shift the responsibility from myself, I hold that, as a general rule, the commander in the field is the better judge of the necessity in any particular case. Of course, I must practise a general directory and revisory power in the matter.

One of the resolutions expresses the opinion of the meeting that arbitrary arrests will have the effect to divide and distract those who should be united in suppressing the rebellion, and I am specifically called on to discharge Mr. Vallandigham. I regard this as, at least, a fair appeal to me on the expediency of exercising a constitutional power which I think exists. In response to such appeal, I have to say, it gave me pain when I learned that Mr. Vallandigham had been arrested—that is, I was pained that there should have seemed to be a necessity for arresting him—and that it will afford me great pleasure to discharge him so soon as I can, by any means, believe the public safety will not suffer by it. I further say that, as the war progresses, it appears to me, opinion and action, which were in great confusion at first, take shape and fall into more regular channels, so that the necessity for strong dealing with them gradually decreases. I have every reason to desire that it should cease altogether; and far from the least is my regard for the opinions and wishes of those who, like the meeting at Albany, declare their purpose to sustain the Government in every constitutional and lawful measure to suppress the rebellion. Still, I must continue to do so much as may seem to be required by the public safety.

A. LINCOLN

EXECUTIVE ORDER NO. 1, RELATING TO POLITICAL PRISONERS.
WAR DEPARTMENT, *Washington, February 14, 1862.*

The breaking out of a formidable insurrection based on a conflict of political ideas, being an event without precedent in the United States, was necessarily attended by great confusion and perplexity of the public mind. Disloyalty before unsuspected suddenly became bold, and treason astonished the world by bringing at once into the field military forces superior in number to the standing Army of the United States.

Every department of the Government was paralyzed by treason. Defection appeared in the Senate, in the House of Representatives, in the Cabinet, in the Federal courts; ministers and consuls returned from foreign countries to enter the insurrectionary councils or land or naval forces; commanding and other officers of the Army and in the Navy betrayed our councils or deserted their posts for commands in the insurgent forces. Treason was flagrant in the revenue and in the post-office service, as well as in the Territorial governments and in the Indian reserves.

Not only governors, judges, legislators, and ministerial officers in the States, but even whole States rushed one after another with apparent unanimity into rebellion. The capital was besieged and its connection with all the States cut off.

Even in the portions of the country which were most loyal political combinations and secret societies were formed furthering the work of disunion, while, from motives of disloyalty or cupidity or from excited passions or perverted sympathies, individuals were found furnishing men, money, and materials of war and supplies to the insurgents' military and naval forces. Armies, ships, fortifications, navy-yards, arsenals, military posts, and garrisons one after another were betrayed or abandoned to the insurgents.

Congress had not anticipated, and so had not provided for, the emergency. The municipal authorities were powerless and inactive. The judicial machinery seemed as if it had been designed, not to sustain the Government, but to embarrass and betray it.

Foreign intervention, openly invited and industriously instigated by the abettors of the insurrection, became imminent, and has only been prevented by the practice of strict and impartial justice, with the most perfect moderation, in our intercourse with nations.

The public mind was alarmed and apprehensive, though fortunately not distracted or disheartened. It seemed to be doubtful whether the Federal Government, which one year before had been thought a model worthy of universal acceptance, had indeed the ability to defend and maintain itself.

Some reverses, which, perhaps, were unavoidable, suffered by newly levied and inefficient forces, discouraged the loyal and gave new hopes to the insurgents. Voluntary enlistments seemed about to cease and desertions commenced. Parties speculated upon the question whether conscription had not become necessary to fill up the armies of the United States.

In this emergency the President felt it his duty to employ with energy the extraordinary powers which the Constitution confides to him in cases of

insurrection. He called into the field such military and naval forces, un-authorized by the existing laws, as seemed necessary. He directed measures to prevent the use of the post-office for treasonable correspondence. He sub-jected passengers to and from foreign countries to new passport regulations, and he instituted a blockade, suspended the writ of *habeas corpus* in various places, and caused persons who were represented to him as being or about to be engaged in disloyal and treasonable practices to be arrested by special civil as well as military agencies and detained in military custody when necessary to prevent them and deter others from such practices. Examinations of such cases were instituted, and some of the persons so arrested have been dis-charged from time to time under circumstances or upon conditions compatible, as was thought, with the public safety.

Meantime a favorable change of public opinion has occurred. The line between loyalty and disloyalty is plainly defined. The whole structure of the Government is firm and stable. Apprehension of public danger and facilities for treasonable practices have diminished with the passions which prompted heedless persons to adopt them. The insurrection is believed to have culminated and to be declining.

The President, in view of these facts, and anxious to favor a return to the normal course of the Administration as far as regard for the public welfare will allow, directs that all political prisoners or state prisoners now held in military custody be released on their subscribing to a parole engaging them to render no aid or comfort to the enemies in hostility to the United States.

The Secretary of War will, however, in his discretion, except from the effect of this order any persons detained as spies in the service of the insurgents, or others whose release at the present moment may be deemed incompatible with the public safety.

To all persons who shall be so released and who shall keep their parole the President grants an amnesty for any past offenses of treason or disloyalty which they may have committed.

Extraordinary arrests will hereafter be made under the direction of the military authorities alone.

By order of the President:

A Further Word of Explanation About the Notes

Because of the nature of this book, I have attempted to make the documentation as simple as possible. Individual bibliographies have been prepared for each chapter according to the style recommended by the Modern Language Association of America. A key phrase, using either the author's or editor's name, or even part of the book's title, has been given for each book in the bibliography. For example:

Jefferson, Thomas, *The Writings of Thomas Jefferson*, ed. P. L. Ford, 10 vols.
New York, Putnam and Sons, 1892-1899. (Ford)

In the above example *Ford* is the key phrase. In the notes
following each bibliography the page and line numbers refer to
the text of *Power's Human Face*. These are followed by the key
phrase and the location of the quoted material. For example:

page 21 line 9 Ford VIII, p. 67

A.T.H.

I . . Thomas Jefferson

BIBLIOGRAPHY

Adams, John, *The Adams-Jefferson Letters*, ed. Lester J. Cappon. 2 vols.
Williamsburg, Virginia, University of North Carolina Press, 1959. (Cappon)
Adams, John Quincy, *The Diary of John Q. Adams 1794-1845*, ed. Allan
Nevins. New York, C. Scribner's Sons, 1951. (Nevins)
————, *The Memoirs of John Quincy Adams*, ed. Charles Francis Adams.
12 vols. Philadelphia, J. B. Lippincott and Company, 1874-1877. (Adams
Memoirs)
Beveridge, Albert Jeremiah, *The Life of John Marshall*. 4 vols. Boston,
Houghton Mifflin Company, 1929. (Beveridge)
Corwin, Edward Samuel, *The President, Office and Powers*. New York, New
York University Press, 1948. (Corwin)
Foley, J. P., editor, *The Jeffersonian Cyclopedia: A Comprehensive Collection
of the Views of Thomas Jefferson*. New York, Funk and Wagnalls Company, 1900. (Foley)
Jefferson, Thomas, *The Writings of Thomas Jefferson*, ed. P. L. Ford. 10
vols. New York, Putnam and Sons, 1892-1899. (Ford)
Marshall, John, *The Life of George Washington*. 5 vols. London, 1840.
(Marshall)
Padover, Saul K., editor, *The Complete Jefferson*. New York, Duell, Sloan
and Pearce, Inc., 1943.
Parton, James, *The Life and Times of Aaron Burr*. New York, Mason Brothers,
1858. (Parton)
Richardson, James D., *A Compilation of the Messages and Papers of the
Presidents 1789-1897*. 10 vols. Washington, D.C., Government Printing
Office, 1897. (Richardson)

Smith, Mrs. Samuel Harrison, *The First Forty Years of Washington Society*, ed. Gaillard Hunt. New York, C. Scribner's Sons, 1906. (Smith)

I NOTES

Page	Line	Source
21	9	Ford VIII, p. 67.
	11	Marshall V, pp. 33 ff.
	16	Foley, p. 6916.
	17	Ford VII, p. 8.
	32	Ford VIII, pp. 4-5.
22	2	Ford IX, p. 126.
	6	Foley, p. 8547.
	22	Richardson I, p. 321.
23	1	Ford VIII, p. 252.
	6	Ibid., p. 47.
	9	Ibid., p. 67.
	11	Ibid., p. 50.
	14	Ibid., p. 87.
	14	Ibid., p. 317.
	17	Ibid., p. 53.
	22	Ibid., p. 69.
24	1	Cappon I, pp. 276-277.
	15	Ibid., pp. 278-280.
	35	Ibid., pp. 280-282.
25	11	Ford VII, pp. 149-150.
	24	Nevins, p. 28.
	32	Ibid., p. 25.
26	4	Ibid., pp. 408-409.
	17	Ford VIII, pp. 144-145.
27	1	Ibid., p. 192.
	11	Ibid., p. 203.
	32	Ibid., pp. 244-247.
28	23	Adams' Memoirs I, p. 266.
	25	Adams' Memoirs V, pp. 364-365.
	31	Nevins, p. 468.
	33	Ibid., pp. 408-409.
29	13	Ford VIII, p. 244.
	24	Ibid., pp. 220-221.
30	27	Richardson I, p. 400.
31	5	Beveridge, p. 274.
	10	Ford IX, p. 41.
	26	Beveridge, p. 405.
	32	Parton, p. 458.
32	9	Ford IX, p. 53.

Page	Line	Source
	15	*Ibid.*, pp. 52 ff.
	26	*Ibid.*, p. 68.
	32	*Ibid.*, p. 61.
33	7	*Ibid.*, p. 58.
	11	*Ibid.*, p. 142.
	17	Beveridge, p. 398.
	25	Smith, p. 77.
34	11	*Ibid.*, pp. 77 ff.
	21	Ford VIII, pp. 338-340.
35	3	Corwin, p. 332.
	12	Adams' Memoirs IV, pp. 492-493.
	21	Smith, pp. 65-66.

II . . Andrew Jackson

BIBLIOGRAPHY

Adams, John, *The Works of John Adams*, ed. Charles Francis Adams. 10 vols. Boston, Little, Brown and Company, 1851-1866. (Works of J. Adams)

Adams, John Quincy, *The Diary of John Q. Adams 1794-1845*, ed. Allan Nevins, New York, C. Scribner's Sons, 1951. (Nevins)

———, *The Memoirs of John Quincy Adams*. 12 vols. ed. Charles Francis Adams. Philadelphia, J. B. Lippincott and Company, 1874-1877. (Adams Memoirs)

Bancroft, Frederick, *Calhoun and the South Carolina Nullification Movement*. Baltimore, The Johns Hopkins Press, 1928. (Bancroft)

Bowers, Claude Gernade, *Party Battles of the Jackson Period*. Boston, Houghton Mifflin Company, 1922. (Bowers)

Buell, Augustus C., *History of Andrew Jackson; Pioneer, Patriot, Soldier, Politician, President*. 2 vols. London, Bickers and Sons, 1904. (Buell)

Calhoun, John C., "Letters to the People of the Southern States." (1850?) (Calhoun Letters)

Curtis, George T., *Life of James Buchanan*. 2 vols. New York, Harper & Brothers, 1883. (Curtis)

Eaton, Peggy, *The Autobiography of Peggy Eaton*. New York, C. Scribner's Sons, 1932. (Eaton)

Hamilton, James Alexander, *Reminiscences: Or, Men and Events, At Home and Abroad, During Three Quarters of a Century*. New York, C. Scribner's Sons, 1869. (Hamilton Reminiscences)

James, Marquis, *Andrew Jackson: Portrait of a President.* New York, Garden City Publishing Company, 1937. (James)

Jackson, Andrew, *Correspondence of Andrew Jackson,* ed. John Spencer Basset. 7 vols. Carnegie Institute of Washington Publication No. 371, 1926-1935. (Jackson Correspondence)

Jefferson, Thomas, *The Writings of Thomas Jefferson,* ed. P. L. Ford. 10 vols. New York, Putnam and Sons, 1892-1899. (Ford)

"John C. Calhoun and the Secession Movement of 1850," *American Antiquarian Society Proceedings,* XXVIII (1918), 19-50. (Calhoun and Secession Movement)

Kendall, Amos, *Life of Andrew Jackson.* New York, Harper and Brothers, 1843. (Kendall)

Parton, James, *The Life of Andrew Jackson.* 3 vols. Boston, Houghton Mifflin Company, 1860. (Life of Jackson)

Quincy, Josiah, *Figures of the Past From the Leaves of Old Journals.* Boston, Roberts Brothers, 1892. (Quincy)

Richardson, James D., *A Compilation of the Messages and Papers of the Presidents 1789-1897.* 10 vols. Washington, D.C., Government Printing Office, 1897. (Richardson)

Smith, Mrs. Samuel Harrison, *The First Forty Years of Washington Society,* ed. Gaillard Hunt. New York, C. Scribner's Sons, 1906. (Smith)

Van Buren, Martin, "Autobiography: Martin Van Buren," *Annual Report of the American Historical Society,* II (1920), 7-808. (Autobiography: Van Buren)

Webster, Daniel, *Private Correspondence of Daniel Webster,* ed. Fletcher Webster. 2 vols. Boston, Little, Brown and Company, 1857. (Webster)

II NOTES

Page	Line	Source
38	19	Works of J. Adams I, p. 643.
40	23	Webster I, p. 364.
41	3	Smith, pp. 252-253.
	13	Eaton, p. 14.
	17	Ibid., pp. 69-70
	32	Adams' Memoirs VIII, p. 101.
42	4	Smith, p. 259.
	16	James, p. 174.
	21	Nevins, p. 390.
	28	Smith, p. 290.
43	20	Nevins, p. 398.
	30	Adams' Memoirs VIII, p. 356.
44	6	Eaton, p. 83.
	9	Ibid., p. 65.

Page	Line	Source
	19	Jackson Correspondence IV, p. 14.
	21	*Ibid.*, p. 33.
	30	Nevins, p. 396.
45	3	Richardson II, p. 449.
	15	Life of Jackson III, p. 247.
	18	*Ibid.*, p. 248.
	32	Bancroft, p. 161.
46	14	Calhoun and Secession Movement, p. 28.
	27	Smith, pp. 287-289.
47	9	Nevins, p. 400.
	21	Jackson Correspondence IV, p. 123.
48	17	James, pp. 272-273.
	27	Kendall, pp. 396-397.
49	8	Calhoun Letters.
	18	Nevins, p. 437.
	27	Jackson Correspondence IV, pp. 30-31.
50	6	Eaton, pp. 146-147.
	29	*Ibid.*, pp. 133-142 ff.
51	22	Hamilton Reminiscences, pp. 146-147.
	32	Eaton, p. 145.
52	3	Hamilton Reminiscences, pp. 146-147.
	20	Autobiography: Van Buren, pp. 401 ff.
54	21	Jackson Correspondence IV, pp. 268-269.
55	1	Nevins, pp. 418-419.
	14	Jackson Correspondence IV, pp. 268-269
56	5	Smith, pp. 318-321.
	17	Jackson Correspondence IV, pp. 397-398.
57	5	Bancroft, p. 111.
	11	James, p. 306.
	12	Jackson Correspondence IV, p. 506.
	20	Bancroft, pp. 42-44.
	23	*Ibid.*, p. 47.
58	10	Life of Jackson, p. 283.
	21	Richardson II, pp. 640-656.
59	25	Buell II, p. 245.
	29	Jackson Correspondence IV, pp. 502-503.
60	14	Bowers, pp. 464-467 ff.
	19	Kendall, p. 631.
	30	Bowers, pp. 464-467 ff.
61	1	Curtis I, pp. 185-186.
	30	Quincy, pp. 360-361.
62	8	Nevins, p. 440.
	22	Quincy, p. 361.
	32	Nevins, p. 439.
63	15	Quincy, pp. 363-365.

III . . James Buchanan

BIBLIOGRAPHY

Allen, J. W., Gilder, R. W., Allen, W. F., eds., *The Leaflet*, nos. 1-16. Bordentown, New Jersey, July 23, 1860. (Leaflet I)

Americana VII, "Campaign Songs of a Century," *New York Evening Post*, March 16, 1912. (Americana VII)

Baker, Ray Stannard, *American Chronicle*. New York, C. Scribner's Sons, 1945. (Baker)

The Congressional Globe, Pt. 1, Appendix of vol. 22, February 20, 1850. (Congressional Globe)

Craven, Avery Odelle, *The Coming of the Civil War*. New York, C. Scribner's Sons, 1942. (Craven)

Davis, Jefferson, *The Rise and Fall of the Confederate Government*. 2 vols. New York, D. Appleton and Company, 1881.

"Declaration of the Immediate Causes Which Induce and Justify the Secession of South Carolina from the Federal Union; and the Ordinance of Secession." Charlestown, Evans and Cogswell, 1860. (Declaration of South Carolina Secession)

Hayes, Melvin L., *Mr. Lincoln Runs For President*. New York, Citadel Press, 1960. (Hayes)

Johnson, Allen, *Stephen A. Douglas: A Study in American Politics*. New York, Macmillan Company, 1908.

Lossing, Benson John, editor, *Harper's Encyclopedia of United States History*. 10 vols. New York, Harper and Brothers, 1905.

Klein, Philip Shriver, *President Buchanan, A Biography*. University Park, Penn State University Press, 1962. (Klein)

Lamon, Ward Hill *Recollections of Lincoln 1847-1865*, ed. Dorothy Lamon Teillard. Washington, 1911. (Lamon)

Lincoln, Abraham, *Lincoln's Own Stories*, ed. Anthony Gross, New York, Harper and Brothers, 1912. (Own Stories)

———, *The Writings of Abraham Lincoln*, ed. Arthur Brooks Lapsley. 8 vols. New York, Lamb Publishing Company, 1905. (Writings)

Nicolay, John G., and Hay, John, *Abraham Lincoln: A History*. 10 vols. New York, Century Company, 1890. (Nicolay and Hay)

Oldroyd, Osborn H., *Lincoln's Campaign or the Political Revolution of 1860*. Chicago, Laird and Lee, 1896. (Oldroyd)

Pryor, Sarah Agnes, *Reminiscences of Peace and War*. New York, Macmillan Company, 1904. (Pryor)

Richardson, James D., A Compilation of the Messages and Papers of the Presidents 1789-1897. 10 vols. Washington, D.C., Government Printing Office, 1897. (Richardson)

Roseboom, Eugene Halloway, A History of Presidential Elections. New York, Macmillan Company, 1959. (Roseboom)

Sanborn, Franklin Benjamin, Life and Letters of John Brown, Liberator of Kansas and Martyr of Virginia. Boston, Roberts Brothers, 1891. (Sanborn)

Shankle, George Earlie, American Mottoes and Slogans. New York, The H. W. Wilson Company, 1941. (Shankle)

Stevenson, Burton Egbert, editor, The Home Book of Quotations. Philadelphia, The Blakiston Company, 1949. (Home Book of Quotes)

Stillwell, Lucille, John Cabell Breckinridge. Caldwell, Indiana, The Caxton Printers Ltd., 1936. (Stillwell)

Welles, Gideon, Diary, ed. Howard K. Beale. 3 vols. New York, W. W. Norton, 1960. (Welles' Diary)

Williams, Kenneth Powers, Lincoln Finds a General. 3 vols. New York, Macmillan Company, 1949-1952. (Lincoln Finds a General)

III NOTES

Page	Line	Source
64	18	Richardson V, pp. 137-138.
65	7	Craven, pp. 247-248.
	18	Sanborn, p. 620.
	27	Congressional Globe, pp. 141-143.
66	8	Craven, p. 295.
	26	Pryor, pp. 109-112.
67	30	Declaration of South Carolina Secession, p. 10.
68	9	Richardson V, pp. 656-657.
69	5	Hayes, pp. 23 ff.
	6	Hayes, p. 144.
	7	Shankle, p. 30.
	9	Hayes, p. 23.
	11	Hayes, p. 90.
	11	Leaflet I, No. 16.
	13	Stillwell, p. 86.
	15	Hayes, p. 151.
	17	Hayes, p. 173.
	19	Americana VII, p. 556.
70	2	Home Book of Quotes, p. 1159.
	6	Oldroyd, pp. 151-153.

Page	Line	Source
	30	Klein, p. 386.
71	4	Ibid., p. 382.
	6	Richardson V, pp. 657-658.
	14	Nicolay and Hay II, pp. 394 ff.
	17	Richardson V, pp. 658 ff.
	22	Johnson, pp. 442-443.
	30	Nicolay and Hay II, pp. 397-398.
72	8	Richardson V, pp. 635 ff.
	9	Klein, pp. 391 ff.
	10	Ibid., p. 387.
	11	Hayes, p. 325.
	14	Klein, p. 402.
	17	Constitution of the United States of America, Art II; Sec. I; paragraph 8.
	23	Constitution of the Confederate States of America. Art. II; Sec. 1; paragraph 10.
73	8	Writings V, pp. 253-256.
74	3	Klein, pp. 405-406.
	5	Shankle, p. 12.
	12	Welles' Diary, p. 10.
	22	Baker VII, p. 543.
	24	Roseboom, p. 193.
	31	Welles' Diary, p. 10.
75	4	Lamon, p. 135.
	8	Own Stories, p. 78.
	19	Nicolay and Hay III, pp. 445-446.
76	15	Ibid., p. 448.
	17	Ibid., p. 433.
	19	Lincoln Finds a General I, pp. 40-43.
77	1	Richardson VI, pp. 13-14.

IV .. Abraham Lincoln

BIBLIOGRAPHY

Bartlett, John, editor, *Familiar Quotations*. Boston, Little Brown and Company, 1956. (Bartlett)

Beale, Howard K., *The Critical Year*. New York, Frederick Ungar Publishing Company, 1958. (Beale)

Brooks, Noah, *Washington In Lincoln's Time*. New York, Century Company, 1896. (Brooks)

Carpenter, Francis B., *The Inner Life of Abraham Lincoln*. New York, Hurd and Houghton, 1868. (Carpenter)

Commager, Henry Steele, editor, *Documents of American History*. 2 vols. New York, F. S. Crofts, 1935. (Commager)

——, and Nevins, Allan, editors, *Heritage of America*. Boston, Little, Brown and Company, 1939. (Heritage of America)

The Congressional Globe, Pt. 1, 38 Congress, 1st Session, January 22, 1864. (Congressional Globe)

The Congressional Globe, Pt. 1, 38 Congress, 1st Session, July 1, 1864. (Congressional Globe)

Grant, Ulysses S., *Personal Memoirs*. 2 vols. New York, C. L. Webster and Company, 1894. (Grant's Memoirs)

Gray, Tom S. Jr., "The March to the Sea," *Georgia Historical Quarterly*, XIV (1930), 111-138. (Gray)

Herndon, William Henry, and Weik, Jesse W., *Abraham Lincoln, the True Story of a Great Life*. 2 vols. New York, D. Appleton and Company, 1902. (Herndon and Weik)

Hesseltine, William Best, *Lincoln's Plan of Reconstruction*. Tuscaloosa, Alabama, Confederate Centennial Studies no. 13, 1960. (Hesseltine)

Keckley, Elizabeth, *Behind the Scenes*. New York, 1868. (Keckley)

Lincoln, Abraham, *Conversations With Lincoln*, ed. Charles M. Segal. New York, Putnam, 1961. (Segal)

——, *The Living Lincoln*, eds. Paul M. Angle and Earl Schenck Miers. New Brunswick, New Jersey, Rutgers University Press, 1955. (Angle and Miers)

——, *The Writings of Abraham Lincoln*, ed. Arthur Brooks Lapsley. 8 vols. New York, Lamb Publishing Company, 1905. (Writings)

Morison, Samuel Eliot, and Commager, Henry Steele, editors, *The Growth of the American Republic*. 2 vols. New York, Oxford University Press, 1940. (Growth of America)

Nevins, Allan, *Statesmanship of the Civil War*. Virginia University, Barbour Page Foundation, 1951. (Statesmanship)

Nicolay, John G., and Hay, John, *Abraham Lincoln: A History*. 10 vols. New York, Century Company, 1890. (Nicolay and Hay)

Randall, Ruth Painter, *Mary Lincoln: Biography of a Marriage*. Boston, Little, Brown and Company, 1953. (Randall)

Raymond, Henry J., *Life and Public Services of Abraham Lincoln*. New York, Derby and Miller, 1865. (Raymond)

Richardson, James D., *A Compilation of the Messages and Papers of the Presidents 1789-1897*. 10 vols. Washington, D.C., Government Printing Office, 1897. (Richardson)

Roseboom, Eugene Halloway, *A History of Presidential Elections*. New York, Macmillan Company, 1959. (Roseboom)

Scott, Eben Greenough, *Reconstruction During the Civil War*. Boston, 1895. (Scott)

Shaw, Archer W., editor, *The Lincoln Encyclopedia*. New York, Macmillan Company, 1950. (Lincoln Encyclopedia)

Sherman, William T., *From Atlanta to the Sea*, ed. B. H. Liddell Hart. London, London Folio Society, 1961. (From Atlanta to the Sea)

————, *Home Letters of General Sherman*, ed. M. A. DeWolfe Howe. New York, C. Scribner's Sons, 1909. (Home Letters)

————, *The Sherman Letters*, ed. R. S. Thorndike. New York, C. Scribner's Sons, 1894. (Sherman Letters)

Silber, Irwin, *Songs of the Civil War*. New York, Columbia University Press, 1960. (Silber)

Sumner, Charles, "Our Domestic Relations: Or, How to Treat the Rebel States," *Atlantic Monthly*, (October, 1863), 507-529. (Sumner Pamphlet)

————, *Charles Sumner, His Complete Works*. 20 vols. Boston, Lee and Shepard, 1910. (Sumner's Works)

Tarbell, Ida Minerva, *Life of Abraham Lincoln*. 2 vols. New York, Macmillan Company, 1928. (Tarbell)

Thomas, B. P., *Abraham Lincoln, A Biography*. New York, A. A. Knopf, 1952. (Thomas)

Welles, Gideon, *Diary*, ed. Howard K. Beale. 3 vols. New York, W. W. Norton, 1960. (Welles' Diary)

Whitman, Walt, *Complete Writings of Walt Whitman*, eds. Richard Maurice Bucke, Thomas B. Harned, and Horace L. Traubel. 12 vols. New York, G. P. Putnam's Sons, 1902. (Whitman)

Williams, Kenneth Powers, *Lincoln Finds a General*. 3 vols. New York, Macmillan Company, 1949-1952. (Lincoln Finds a General)

Williams, T. Harry, *Lincoln and His Generals*. New York, A. A. Knopf, 1952. (Lincoln and His Generals)

————, *McClellan, Sherman, and Grant*. New Brunswick, New Jersey, Rutgers University Press, 1962. (McClellan, Sherman, and Grant)

IV NOTES

Page	Line	Source
78	18	Whitman IV, pp. 31-34.
79	19	Thomas, pp. 273-274.
	23	Nicolay and Hay IV, pp. 368-369.
	33	Nicolay and Hay IX, pp. 376-377.
80	11	Grant's Memoirs I, pp. 143-144.
81	6	Richardson VI, pp. 20-31.

Page	Line	Source
	11	Raymond, pp. 386-393.
	15	Richardson V, pp. 102-104.
83	1	Grant's Memoirs I, pp. 148-149.
	14	Writings VII, pp. 123-124.
	29	Writings VI, p. 28.
	32	*Ibid.*, p. 29.
84	1	*Ibid.*, p. 388.
	7	*Ibid.*, p. 31-32.
	11	*Ibid.*, p. 31-32
	19	Grant's Memoirs I, pp. 183-184.
85	5	McClellan, Sherman, Grant, pp. 90-91.
	10	*Ibid.*, p. 97.
	17	Writings VII, p. 63.
	22	Writings VI, p. 389.
	25	*Ibid.*, p. 309.
	27	*Ibid.*, p. 129.
	30	*Ibid*, p. 286.
	32	*Ibid.*, pp. 154-155.
86	9	Nicolay and Hay V, p. 442.
	18	Tarbell II, p. 70.
	20	Nicolay and Hay V., p. 442.
	22	Writings VI, p. 57.
	26	Lincoln Encyclopedia, p. 16.
87	4	Writings VI, pp. 161-163.
	12	Lincoln Finds a General I, p. 136.
	18	Writings VI, p. 166.
	26	*Ibid.*, p. 223.
	33	Lincoln and His Generals, pp. 130-131.
88	3	Writings VI, pp. 254-255.
	19	Carpenter, pp. 273-274.
89	1	Randall, p. 180.
	3	Keckley, p. 101.
	17	Carpenter, pp. 109-110.
	30	*Ibid.*, pp. 173-174.
90	1	Heritage of America, pp. 660-661.
	25	*Ibid.*, pp. 664-665.
91	1	Roseboom, p. 190.
	7	Writings VI, pp. 392-395.
	14	Segal, p. 215.
	14	Carpenter, p. 264.
	17	Randall, p. 339.
	19	Grant's Memoirs I, pp. 210-211, 218.
	31	Growth of America I, p. 612.
92	1	Whitman II, p. 284.

Page	Line	Source
	11	Carpenter, p. 17.
	12	Randall, p. 318.
	14	Carpenter, p. 177.
	17	Writings VII, p. 188.
	18	Segal, p. 272.
	21	Lincoln and His Generals, pp. 280-281.
	23	Statesmanship, p. 57.
	25	Grant's Memoirs I, pp. 262-263.
93	3	McClellan, Sherman, Grant, p. 98.
	9	Writings VI, p. 394.
	11	Nicolay and Hay VII, p. 154.
	13	Bartlett, p. 613.
	14	From Atlanta to the Sea, pp. 122-123.
	17	Bartlett, p. 613.
	19	McClellan, Sherman, Grant, pp. 58-59.
	24	Ibid., p. 46.
	27	Ibid., pp. 58 ff.
94	7	Nicolay and Hay VII, pp. 280-281.
	10	Lincoln and His Generals, pp. 270-271.
	11	Ibid., pp. 280-281.
	18	Grant's Memoirs I, pp. 403-404.
	27	Herndon and Weik II, pp. 267-268.
95	7	Statesmanship, p. 58.
	17	Silber, pp. 17-19.
96	3	Nicolay and Hay IX, p. 251.
	22	From Atlanta to the Sea, pp. 162-163.
	28	Angle and Miers, p. 634.
	32	Gray, pp. 169-170.
98	4	Writings VII, p. 273.
	5	Ibid., pp. 273-274.
	11	From Atlanta to the Sea, pp. 154-155.
	15	Home Letters, pp. 318-319.
	26	Grant's Memoirs I, pp. 439-440.
99	23	Congressional Globe; January 22, 1864, pp. 317 ff.
	26	Sumner's Works IX, p. 94.
100	1	Segal, p. 382.
	8	Hesseltine, p. 100.
	15	Segal, p. 339.
	28	Randall, p. 320.
	29	Segal, p. 361.
101	1	Sumner pamphlet, p. 517.
	2	Congressional Globe; January 22, 1864, pp. 317 ff.
	7	Ibid., pp. 317 ff.
	13	Writings VII, pp. 28-30.

Page	Line	Source
	26	Sumner pamphlet, p. 507.
	28	Congressional Globe; July 1, 1864; p. 3450.
	31	Nicolay and Hay IX, pp. 117 ff.
102	1	Carpenter, p. 49.
	24	Brooks, p. 170.
	26	Carpenter, p. 189.
	32	Lincoln and His Generals, pp. 107-108.
103	1	Writings VII, p. 192.
	5	Bartlett, p. 623.
	12	Heritage of America, pp. 667-668.
104	8	Writings VII, pp. 349-350.
	14	Ibid., pp. 355-356.
	24	Welles' Diary II, pp. 280-281.
	31	Carpenter, p. 284.
105	13	Welles' Diary II, pp. 282-283.
	29	Randall, p. 329.
	33	Carpenter, p. 189.
106	3	Angle and Miers, p. 652.
	5	Welles' Diary II, pp. 283-288.
107	26	Whitman II, p. 106.

V . . Andrew Johnson

BIBLIOGRAPHY

Beale, Howard K., *The Critical Year*. New York, Frederick Ungar Publishing Company, 1958. (Beale)

Commager, Henry Steele, editor, *Documents of American History*. 2 vols. New York, F. S. Crofts, 1935. (Commager)

———, and Nevins, Allan, editors, *Heritage of America*. Boston, Little, Brown and Company, 1939. (Heritage of America)

Fessenden, William Pitt, *Impeachment*. (Opinion delivered in the U.S. Senate on May 11, 1868, by the Hon. W. P. Fessenden). Washington, D.C., Government Printing Office, 1868. (Fessenden)

The Grant Campaign Songster. New York, R. M. DeWitt, 1868. (Grant Campaign Songster)

The Great Impeachment and Trial of Andrew Johnson President of the United States. (Proceedings from impeachment and trial). Philadelphia, T. B. Peterson and Brothers, 1868. (Impeachment of A. Johnson)

Irelan, John Robert, M. D., *The Republic: Or a History of the United States of America in the Administrations From the Monarchic Colonial Days to the Present Times.* 18 vols. Chicago, Fairbanks and Palmer Publishing Company, 1888. (Irelan)

McKitrick, Eric L., *Andrew Johnson and Reconstruction,* Chicago, University of Chicago Press, 1960. (McKitrick)

Richardson, James D., *A Compilation of the Messages and Papers of the Presidents 1789-1897.* 10 vols. Washington, D.C., Government Printing Office, 1897. (Richardson)

Sumner, Charles, "The One Man Power vs. Congress!" (Address of Hon. Charles Sumner at the Music Hall, Boston, October 2, 1866). Boston, Wright and Potter, State Printers, 1866.

V NOTES

Page	Line	Source
108	10	Beale, p. 34.
109	27	Commager II, p. 12.
110	1	Beale, p. 213.
	8	Richardson VI, pp. 492-493.
	18	Commager II, p. 31.
	25	One Man Power vs. Congress, p. 1.
111	4	Commager II, p. 15.
	9	Beale, p. 213.
	11	Irelan XVIII, p. 507.
	12	*Ibid.,* p. 400.
	14	Beale, p. 371.
	19	Irelan XVIII, p. 506.
	20	McKitrick, p. 438.
112	1	Richardson VI, pp. 531, 534.
	6	Beale, p. 370.
	8	Richardson VI, p. 536-545.
	15	Beale, p. 314.
	22	*Ibid.,* p. 214.
	24	*Ibid.,* p. 355.
	27	McKitrick, p. 432.
	29	One Man Power vs. Congress, p. 18
113	9	McKitrick, p. 432.
	11	Beale, pp. 370-371 ff.
	15	McKitrick, p. 432.
	19	Beale, p. 361.
	21	Irelan XVIII, p. 491.
	28	*Ibid.,* p. 505.
114	14	Impeachment of A. Johnson, p. 284.

Page	Line	Source
115	1	Heritage of America, pp. 286-287.
	28	Fessenden, pp. 9, 17.
116	18	Grant Campaign Songster, p. 10.

VI . . Sherman, Roosevelt, Taft

BIBLIOGRAPHY

N.B.   Unless otherwise noted, the political slogans in the following chapters were taken from various newspapers of the times of the campaigns in question.

Adams, Henry, *The Education of Henry Adams; An Autobiography.* Boston, Houghton Mifflin Company, 1918? (Henry Adams)

Allen, Frederick Lewis, *The Big Change.* New York, Harper and Brothers, 1952. (Allen)

"As One President to the Next," *American Heritage,* XI, no. 5 (August 1960) 106. (American Heritage)

Bishop, Joseph B., *Theodore Roosevelt and His Time.* 2 vols. New York, C. Scribner's Sons, 1920. (Bishop)

Buchanan, Lamont, *Ballot For Americans.* New York, Dutton, 1956. (Ballot For Americans)

Butt, Archibald Willingham, *Taft and Roosevelt.* 2 vols. New York, Doubleday, Doran and Company, 1930. (Butt)

Corwin, Edward S., *The President, Office and Powers.* New York, New York University Press, 1948. (Corwin)

Denison, Charles Wheeler, and Herbert, G. B., *Hancock "The Superb."* Cincinnati, Ohio, Forshee and McMakin, 1880. (Denison and Herbert)

The Encyclopedia Britannica, ed. Walter Yust et. al. Chicago, William Benton, 1959. (Encyclopedia Britannica)

The "Farmer of Chappaqua" Songster. New York, R. M. DeWitt, 1872. (Farmer of Chappaqua Songster)

Garfield and Arthur Campaign Song Book. Republican Congressional Committee, 1880. (Garfield-Arthur Song Book)

Garfield, James A., "Don't Pitch Your Tent Among the Dead," Campaign speech delivered at Cleveland, Ohio. New York, Republican State Committee, 1879. (Garfield's Cleveland Speech)

Grant, Ulysses Simpson, *Speeches of General U. S. Grant.* Washington, D.C., Union Republican Congressional Executive Committee, 1868. (Grant Speeches)

Hart, Albert Bushnell, and Ferleger, Herbert Ronald, eds., *Theodore Roosevelt*

Cyclopedia. New York, Roosevelt Memorial Association, 1941. (Roosevelt Cyclopedia)

The Hayes Illustrated Campaign Song and Joke Book. New York, The American News Company, 1876? (Hayes Campaign Song and Joke Book)

Lewis, Lloyd, *Sherman, Fighting Prophet.* New York, Harcourt, Brace and Company, 1932. (Lewis)

Lidell Hart, Basil Henry, *Sherman, Soldier, Realist, American.* New York, Dodd, Meade and Company, 1929. (Lidell Hart)

Longworth, Alice Lee Roosevelt, *Crowded Hours; Reminiscences.* New York, C. Scribner's Sons, 1933. (Longworth)

Lorant, Stefan, *The Presidency.* New York, Macmillan Company, 1951. (Lorant)

Pringle, Henry Fowlers, *Life and Times of William Howard Taft.* 2 vols. New York, Farrar and Rinehart, 1939. (Pringle: Life of Taft)

————, *Theodore Roosevelt A Biography.* New York, Harcourt Brace and Company, 1931. (Pringle: T. Roosevelt)

Republican Campaign Melodist and Register, in The Grant Campaign Song-ster. New York, R. M. DeWitt, 1868. (Campaign Melodist)

Roosevelt, Theodore, *An Autobiography.* New York, C. Scribner's Sons, 1913. (Autobiography)

————, *The Letters of Theodore Roosevelt,* ed. Elting E. Morison. 8 vols. Cambridge, Massachusetts, Harvard University Press, 1951-1954. (Letters)

————, *The Rough Riders.* New York, C. Scribner's Sons, 1899. (Rough Riders)

————, *The Works of Theodore Roosevelt.* 8 vols. New York, P. F. Collier and Son, 1910? (Roosevelt: Works)

Roseboom, Eugene Halloway, *A History of Presidential Elections.* New York, Macmillan Company, 1959. (Roseboom)

Shankle, George Earlie, *American Mottoes and Slogans.* New York, The H. W. Wilson Company, 1941. (Shankle)

Sherman, William T., *Home Letters of General Sherman,* ed. M. A. De-Wolfe Howe. New York, C. Scribner's Sons, 1909. (Home Letters)

————, *The Sherman Letters,* ed. R. S. Thorndike. New York, C. Scribner's Sons, 1894. (Sherman Letters)

Stoddard, Henry L., *As I Knew Them: Presidents and Politics From Grant To Coolidge.* New York, Harper and Brothers, 1927. (Stoddard)

————, *Presidential Sweepstakes,* ed., Francis W. Leary. New York, G. P. Putnam's Sons, 1948. (Presidential Sweepstakes)

Taft, William Howard, *Our Chief Magistrate and His Powers.* New York, Columbia University Press, 1916. (Taft)

Thompson, Charles Willis, *Presidents I've Known and Two Near Presidents.* Indianapolis, Bobbs-Merrill Company, 1929. (Thompson)

The New York Times, 1912. April 9; April 30; May 6; May 14; May 16; May 19; June 20.

Van Deusen, Glyndon Garlock, *Horace Greeley, Nineteenth Century Crusader*. Philadelphia, University of Pennsylvania Press, 1953. (Van Deusen)

Warren, Sidney, "How to Pick a President," *Saturday Review*, XLVII, no. 27 (July 4, 1964), 10-13. (Saturday Review)

White, William Allen, *Masks In a Pageant*. New York, Macmillan Company, 1928. ("Masks")

VI NOTES

Page	Line	Source
119	3	Henry Adams, p. 355.
	9	Home Letters, p. 352.
	33	*Ibid.*, p. 287.
	34	*Ibid.*, p. 265.
120	7	Grant Speeches, p. 1.
	13	Shankle, p. 44.
	22	Campaign Melodist, p. 71.
121	1	*Ibid.*, p. 71.
	12	Stoddard, p. 74.
	32	Lewis, p. 411.
122	2	Sherman Letters, pp. 245-246.
	5	*Ibid.*, p. 227.
	9	Lorant, p. 298.
	18	Stoddard, pp. 74 ff.
	22	Farmer of Chappaqua Songster, p. 12.
	25	Van Deusen, p. 406.
	27	Lewis, p. 592.
	28	*Ibid.*, p. 629.
	29	*Ibid.*, p. 592.
	29	Lidell Hart, p. 414.
123	2	Sherman Letters, p. 358.
	4	Lidell Hart, pp. 414, 417.
	11	Lorant, pp. 332 ff.
	14	Shankle, pp. 176 ff.
	15	Hayes Campaign Song and Joke Book
124	4	Lewis, p. 631.
	14	Home Letters, p. 265.
	19	Lewis, p. 631.
	32	Ballot for Americans, p. 62.
125	1	Garfield-Arthur Song Book, No. 41.
	10	Garfield's Cleveland Speech.
126	31	Sherman Letters, p. 361.
	33	Lidell Hart, p. 421.

Page	Line	Source
	35	Lewis, p. 629.
127	7	Sherman Letters, p. 313.
	9	Home Letters, pp. 375, 392.
	12	*Ibid.*, p. 384.
	23	Sherman Letters, pp. 380-381.
	29	Lorant, p. 405.
	31	Roseboom, p. 284.
128	2	Allen, p. 75.
	8	Longworth, pp. 22-25.
	24	Rough Riders, pp. 129-130 ff.
129	5	Campaign Songs: 1900.
	22	Lorant, p. 457.
	24	Campaign Songs: 1900.
	26	Allen, pp. 76-77.
	28	"Masks," p. 156.
	31	Allen, p. 82.
130	1	Letters IV, pp. 1132-1133.
	5	Bishop I, p. 364.
	6	Letters IV, p. 1133.
	8	*Ibid.*, p. 1132.
	12	Letters VI, p. 883.
	18	Autobiography, p. 41.
	27	Letters VI, p. 1087.
	34	Autobiography, p. 548.
131	5	*Ibid.*, pp. 552-553.
	15	Corwin, p. 498.
	20	Letters IV, pp. 1133-1134.
	28	Pringle: T. Roosevelt, p. 330.
	31	Roosevelt Cyclopedia, p. 407.
	33	Autobiography, pp. 512, 525, 522, 527-528.
132	11	Allen, p. 87.
	12	Pringle: T. Roosevelt, p. 446.
	19	Letters VI, pp. 924-925.
	26	Letters VII, p. 29.
	27	Autobiography, pp. 357.
	34	*Ibid.*, pp. 387-388.
133	9	Letters VI, p. 1157.
	10	Pringle: T. Roosevelt, p. 502.
	14	Letters VI, p. 1085.
	19	Thompson, p. 233.
	20	Lorant, p. 486.
	22	Pringle: Life of Taft I, p. 218.
	24	Pringle: T. Roosevelt, p. 504.
	26	Saturday Review, July 4, 1964, p. 12.

Page	Line	Source
	27	Letters VI, p. 1157.
	30	Lorant, p. 486.
	33	Thompson, p. 225.
134	1	American Heritage, August, 1960, p. 106.
	6	Letters VI, p. 1089.
	11	Lorant, p. 498.
	14	Butt I, p. 9.
	19	Roosevelt Cyclopedia, p. 596.
	27	Letters VII, pp. 80-81.
	31	Pringle: T. Roosevelt, pp. 531-532.
135	5	Letters VII, pp. 95-96.
	15	Butt I, pp. 235-236.
	22	Letters VII, p. 112.
	27	Autobiography, p. 357.
136	1	Taft, p. 144.
	8	Ibid., pp. 12-13.
	13	Autobiography, pp. 362-363.
	22	Taft, pp. 143-144.
137	6	Butt II, p. 804.
	17	Stoddard, p. 391.
	22	Presidential Sweepstakes, p. 135.
	26	Butt II, pp. 813-814.
	29	Pringle: T. Roosevelt, pp. 560-561.
	33	Presidential Sweepstakes, p. 136.
138	1	Autobiography, p. 387.
	5	Lorant, p. 483.
	7	Corwin, pp. 44-45.
	16	New York Times, April 9, 1912.
	17	Presidential Sweepstakes, p. 136.
	18	Pringle: T. Roosevelt, pp. 560-561.
	27	Ibid., p. 565.
139	1	Stoddard, p. 410.
	6	Pringle: T. Roosevelt, pp. 560-561.
	15	Stoddard, pp. 388, 418.
	19	New York Times, April 30, 1912, p. 5.
	23	New York Times, May 16, 1912.
	28	New York Times, May 6, 1912.
	29	New York Times, May 14, 1912.
	30	Roseboom, p. 362.
140	1	Ibid., p. 362.
	4	New York Times, May 16, May 19, 1912.
	6	New York Times, May 14, 1912.
	7	Roseboom, p. 362.
	14	Roosevelt: Works XVII, pp. 204 ff.
	16	New York Times, June 20, 1912.

VII .. Woodrow Wilson

BIBLIOGRAPHY

Bailey, Thomas A., *Woodrow Wilson and the Great Betrayal*. New York, Macmillan Company, 1945. (Bailey)

Baker, Ray Stannard, *American Chronicle*. New York, C. Scribner's Sons, 1945. (Baker)

——, *Woodrow Wilson; Life and Letters*. 8 vols. Garden City, New York, Doubleday, Page and Company, 1927-1939. (W. W. Wilson: Life and Letters)

Blum, John Morton, *Joe Tumulty and the Wilson Era*. Boston, Houghton Mifflin Company, 1951. (Tumulty and the Wilson Era)

——, *Woodrow Wilson and the Politics of Morality*. Boston, Little, Brown and Company, 1956. (W. W. Wilson and Politics of Morality)

Bonsal, Stephen, *Unfinished Business*. New York, Doubleday-Doran Company, 1944. (Bonsal)

Butler, Nicholas M., *Across the Busy Years*. 2 vols. New York, C. Scribner's Sons, 1935. (Butler)

Daniels, Josephus, *The Cabinet Diaries of Josephus Daniels*, ed. E. David Cronin. Lincoln, Nebraska, University of Nebraska Press, 1963. (Daniels)

Grayson, Cary Travers, *Woodrow Wilson: An Intimate Memoir*. New York, Holt, Rinehart and Winston, 1960. (Grayson)

Hatch, Alden, *Edith Bolling Wilson First Lady Extraordinary*. New York, Dodd, Mead and Company, 1961. (Hatch)

Hoover, Irving Hood, *Forty-two Years in the White House*. Boston, Houghton Mifflin Company, 1934. (Forty-two Years in the White House)

House, Edward M., *The Intimate Papers of Colonel House*. 4 vols. Boston, Houghton Mifflin Company, 1928. (House)

Houston, David F., *Eight Years with Wilson's Cabinet, 1913 to 1920*. 2 vols. Garden City, New York, Doubleday, Page and Company, 1926. (Houston)

Kerney, James, *The Political Education of Woodrow Wilson*. New York, Century Company, 1926. (Kerney)

Longworth, Alice Lee Roosevelt, *Crowded Hours; Reminiscences*. New York, C. Scribner's Sons, 1933. (Longworth)

Starling, Edmund W., and Sugrue, Thomas, *Starling of the White House*. New York, Simon and Schuster, 1946. (Starling)

Stoddard, Henry L., *As I Knew Them*. New York, Harper and Brothers, 1927. (Stoddard)

Smith, Gene, *When the Cheering Stopped*. New York, William Morrow, 1964. (Gene Smith)

Smith, Rixey and Beasley, Norman, *Carter Glass*. New York, Longmans, Green and Company, 1939. (Smith and Beasley)

The New York Times, 1920. February 14, and March 9.

Tumulty, Joseph P., *Woodrow Wilson As I Knew Him*. Garden City, New York, Doubleday, Page and Company, 1921. (Tumulty)

White, William Allen, *Woodrow Wilson*. Boston, Houghton Mifflin Company, 1924. (White)

Wilson, Edith Bolling, *My Memoir*. Indianapolis, Bobbs-Merrill Company, 1939. (Edith Wilson: Memoirs)

Wilson, Woodrow, *The Public Papers of Woodrow Wilson*, ed. Ray Stannard Baker. 6 vols. New York, Harper and Brothers, 1927. (Public Papers)

VII   NOTES

Page	Line	Source
143	13	House IV, pp. 486-487.
144	8	*Ibid.*, p. 510.
	11	Public Papers I, Pt.3, p. 329.
	14	W. W. and Politics of Morality, p. 94.
	29	Longworth, pp. 285-286.
145	13	Hatch, pp. 185-186.
	31	Public Papers I, Pt. 3, p. 548.
146	10	Houston II, pp. 5-6.
	17	Grayson, p. 5.
	31	Edith Wilson: Memoirs, pp. 273-274.
147	4	Kerney, p. 469.
	7	Hatch, p. 80.
	15	W.W.: Life and Letters VII, p. 403.
	24	White, p. 282.
	27	Hatch, pp. 171-172.
	31	Daniels, p. 598.
	32	Bonsal, p. 48.
148	3	Bailey, p. 40.
	5	Tumulty, p. 505.
	15	Public Papers I, Pt. 3, p. 329.
	18	Edith Wilson: Memoirs, pp. 273-274.
	23	Hatch, pp. 185-186.
	25	Edith Wilson: Memoirs, pp. 273-274.
149	5	Grayson, pp. 94-95.
	16	Edith Wilson: Memoirs, p. 276.

Page	Line	Source
	24	Starling, pp. 151-152.
	31	Public Papers II, Pt. 3, pp. 413-416.
151	1	Edith Wilson: Memoirs, p. 282.
	14	*Ibid.*, p. 285.
	17	Gene Smith, pp. 89-91.
152	1	*Ibid.*, p. 89.
	6	Edith Wilson: Memoirs, pp. 282 ff.
	15	Forty-two Years in the White House, pp. 100-101.
	33	Edith Wilson: Memoirs, pp. 287-290.
153	5	Forty-two Years in the White House, pp. 102-103.
	10	Hatch, p. 220.
	15	Edith Wilson: Memoirs, pp. 287-290.
	25	Houston II, pp. 36-37.
	33	Gene Smith, p. 102.
154	5	Houston II, p. 37.
	10	*Ibid.*, pp. 37-39.
	15	Grayson, pp. 52-53.
	29	Gene Smith, p. 125.
155	4	*Ibid.*, pp. 127-28.
	27	Edith Wilson: Memoirs, pp. 303-304 ff.
	32	Grayson, pp. 52-53 ff.
156	1	Tumulty and the Wilson Era, pp. 236 ff.
	6	*Ibid.*, pp. 232-243.
	18	Houston II, pp. 60-61.
157	6	Starling, pp. 156-157.
	32	New York Times, February 14, 1920.
158	13	Tumulty, pp. 444-445.
	21	Daniels, p. 497.
	25	New York Times, February 14, 1920.
159	1	White, p. 458.
	8	Bailey, p. 178.
	17	Baker, p. 474.
	17	Bailey, p. 15.
	21	Edith Wilson: Memoirs, p. 297.
160	3	New York Times, March 9, 1920.
	12	Houston II, p. 41.
	14	Grayson, p. 106.
	24	Edith Wilson: Memoirs, p. 303.
	29	Butler II, p. 201.
161	1	Grayson, p. 106.
	7	*Ibid.*, p. 113.
	18	Houston II, pp. 69-70.
162	3	Hatch, pp. 220 ff.
	7	Grayson, p. 116.
	12	*Ibid.*, pp. 114-117.

Page	Line	Source
	22	Tumulty and the Wilson Era, pp. 242-243.
	24	Gene Smith, pp. 160 ff.
	25	Tumulty and the Wilson Era, p. 244.
	26	Grayson, pp. 116-117.
163	4	Starling, p. 157.
	24	Smith and Beasley, pp. 205-216.
	30	*Ibid.*, pp. 207-208.

VIII . . Harding, Coolidge, Hoover

BIBLIOGRAPHY

Adams, Samuel Hopkins, *Incredible Era*. Boston, Houghton Mifflin Company, 1939. (Incredible Era)

Allen, Frederick Lewis, *Only Yesterday*. New York, Harper and Brothers, 1931. (Only Yesterday)

———, *Since Yesterday*. New York, Harper and Brothers, 1940. (Since Yesterday)

"As One President to the Next," *American Heritage*, XI no. 5 (August, 1960) 106. (American Heritage)

Britton, Nan, *The President's Daughter*. New York, Elizabeth Ann Guild, Inc., 1927. (Britton)

Coolidge, Calvin, *Autobiography*. New York, Cosmopolitan Book Corporation, 1929. (Coolidge)

Daugherty, Harry M. and Dixon, Thomas, *The Inside Story of the Harding Tragedy*. New York, the Churchill Company, 1932. (Daugherty)

Harding, Warren G., *Last Speeches and Addresses of Warren G. Harding*, ed. James W. Murphy. Washington, D.C., for the U.S. Senate, 1923. (Murphy)

———, *Our Common Country: Natural Goodwill in America*. Indianapolis, Bobbs-Merrill Company, 1921. (Harding)

Hoover, Herbert, and Coolidge, Calvin, *Campaign Speeches of 1932*. Garden City, New York, Doubleday, Doran and Company, 1933. (Campaign Speeches 1932)

———, *The New Day*. Stanford University, California, Stanford University Press, 1928.

Jaffray, Elizabeth, *Secrets of the White House*. New York, Cosmopolitan Book Corporation, 1927. (Jaffray)

Johnson, Willis Fletcher, *The Life of Warren G. Harding*. Philadelphia, John C. Winston Company, 1923.

Joslin, Theodore G., *Hoover Off the Record*. Garden City, New York, Doubleday, Doran and Company, 1934. (Joslin)

Lorant, Stefan, *The Presidency*. New York, Macmillan Company, 1951. (Lorant)

McKee, John Hiram, *Coolidge Wit and Wisdom*. New York, Frederick Stokes Company, 1933. (McKee)

Moos, Malcolm, and Hess, Stephen, *Hats In the Ring*. New York, Random House, 1960. (Moos and Hess)

Reeves, Earl, *This Man Hoover*. New York, A. L. Burt Company, 1928. (Reeves)

Roosevelt, Franklin D., *Public Papers and Addresses of Franklin D. Roosevelt*. 13 vols. New York, Random House, 1938-1950. (F. D. R.: Papers and Addresses)

Shankle, George Earlie, *American Mottoes and Slogans*. New York, The H. H. Winston Company, 1941. (Shankle)

Starling, Edmund W., and Sugrue, Thomas, *Starling of the White House*. New York, Simon and Schuster, 1946. (Starling)

Stevenson, Burton Egbert, editor, *The Home Book of Quotations*. Philadelphia, The Blakiston Company, 1949. (Home Book of Quotes)

"Times of Trial," *American Heritage*, ed. Allan Nevins. New York, Knopf, 1956. (Times of Trial)

White, William Allen, *Masks In a Pageant*. New York, Macmillan Company, 1928. ("Masks")

Wood, Clement, *Warren Gamaliel Harding: An American Comedy*. New York, William Faro Inc., 1932. (Wood)

VIII NOTES

Page	Line	Source
166	15	Incredible Era, p. 171.
	22	*Ibid.*, p. 91.
	24	*Ibid.*, p. 216.
	26	*Ibid.*, p. 171.
167	1	Jaffray, p. 81.
	3	Murphy, p. 293.
	6	Incredible Era, p. 224.
	9	Britton, pp. 25-27.
	18	*Ibid.*, p. 284.
	20	Wood, Appendix A.
	26	"Masks," pp. 422-23.
	32	Wood, Appendix A.
168	5	Incredible Era, p. 223.
	12	Wood, Appendix A.
	20	Incredible Era, p. 194.

Page	Line	Source
	23	Harding, p. 125.
	25	Wood, Appendix A.
	31	Britton, pp. 172-173.
169	7	Wood, Appendix A.
	13	Daugherty, p. 121.
	16	Wood, Appendix A.
	22	Incredible Era, p. 347.
	25	Wood, Appendix A.
170	1	"Masks," p. 432.
	7	Coolidge, pp. 173-174.
	14	American Heritage, August, 1960, p. 106.
	21	"Masks," p. 446.
	22	Starling, p. 209.
	24	Ibid., p. 210.
	27	Times of Trial, p. 228.
	29	McKee, p. 121.
	30	Starling, p. 205.
	32	Jaffray, p. 105.
	34	Home Book of Quotes, p. 2231.
171	1	Starling, p. 264.
	3	McKee, p. 111.
	5	Shankle, p. 86.
	10	Ibid., pp. 27-28.
	11	Reeves, p. 215.
	13	Only Yesterday, p. 214.
	24	Reeves, p. 227.
	30	Time Magazine, June 25, 1928.
172	1	Joslin, p. 315.
	4	Ibid., pp. 49, 175.
	8	Reeves, p. 237.
	10	Campaign Speeches, 1932.
	12	Since Yesterday, p. 81.
	17	F. D. R.: Papers and Addresses II, pp. 11-15.

IX . . Franklin D. Roosevelt

BIBLIOGRAPHY

Arnold, Henry H., *Global Mission*. New York, Harper and Brothers, 1949.
  (Arnold)

Beard, Charles A., *President Roosevelt and the Coming of the War 1941.* New York, Yale University Press, 1948. (Beard)

Burns, James Mc, *Roosevelt: The Lion and the Fox.* New York, Harcourt Brace, 1956.

The *Congressional Record,* Pts. 2 and 13, vol. 87; 77th Congress, 1st Session. (Congressional Record)

The *Congressional Record,* Pt. 1, vol. 84; 76th Congress, 1st Session. (Congressional Record)

Gantenbein, James W., editor, *Documentary Background of World War II.* New York, Yale University Press, 1948. (Gantenbein)

Laurence, William L., *Men and Atoms.* New York, Simon and Schuster, 1946. (Laurence)

Namier, L. B., *Diplomatic Prelude.* New York, Macmillan, 1948. (Namier)

Roosevelt, Franklin D., *The Public Papers and Addresses of Franklin D. Roosevelt.* 13 vols. New York, Random House, 1938-1950. (F.D.R.: Papers and Addresses)

Sherwood, Robert E., *Roosevelt and Hopkins.* New York, Harper and Brothers, 1948. (Sherwood)

Sinclair, Upton, *I, Candidate for Governor and How I Got Licked.* Farrar Straus and Company, 1935. (Sinclair)

United States Executive Branch of the Government, Commission on the Administrative Management, *Report to Congress.* 3 vols. Washington, D.C., Government Printing Office, 1949. (Administrative Management Commission)

United States Congress, Joint Committee on the Investigation of the Pearl Harbor Attack, *Hearings, before, persuant to S. Cong. Res. 27 and 49.* Washington, D.C., Government Printing Office, 1946. (Hearings: Pearl Harbor)

United States Senate, Committee on Military Affairs, *Hearings on H. R. 3791.* Washington, D.C., Government Printing Office, 1939. (Hearings: Military Affairs)

Warren, Sidney, "How to Pick a President," *Saturday Review,* XLVII, no. 27 (July 4, 1964), 10-13. (Saturday Review)

IX NOTES

Page	Line	Source
174	8	Administrative Management Commission, pp. 3-5.
175	34	F.D.R.: Papers and Addresses V, pp. 288-291.
176	31	F.D.R.: Papers and Addresses VI, pp. 410-411.
177	13	Ibid., pp. 422-445.
178	20	New York Times, March 13, 1938.

Page	Line	Source
179	7	Congressional Record 76th Congress, p. 2134.
	15	Hearings: Military Affairs, pp. 64-69.
180	10	Arnold, pp. 184-186.
	17	Hearings: Military Affairs, pp. 92, 106.
	23	New York Times, February 3, 1939.
	31	New York Times, February 13, 1939.
181	1	Sinclair, p. 78.
	6	Laurence, pp. 57-58.
	30	Gantenbein, pp. 1025-1026.
182	7	*Ibid.*, pp. 1037-1038.
	16	F.D.R.: Papers and Addresses VIII, p. 457.
	23	*Ibid.*, pp. 512-522.
183	6	Gantenbein, p. 759.
	11	D.S.S. Form 150.
	20	F.D.R.: Papers and Addresses IX, p. 415.
	28	*Ibid.*, p. 517.
184	11	*Ibid.*, pp. 607-608.
	25	Congressional Record 77th Congress, p. 3507.
	29	Beard, p. 20.
	31	*Ibid.*, p. 17.
185	1	"An Act Further to Promote the Defense of the United States" (U.S. Statutes).
	12	Sherwood, pp. 291-292.
	22	Hearings: Pearl Harbor, Pt. 5, pp. 2292 ff.
	33	F.D.R.: Papers and Addresses X, pp. 133-315.
186	16	New York Times, April 30, 1941.
	23	F.D.R.: Papers and Addresses X, p. 181.
187	4	*Ibid.*, pp. 133-135.
	16	Hearings: Pearl Harbor, Pt. 5, pp. 2294 ff.
	23	Beard, pp. 71, 75.
	29	F.D.R.: Papers and Addresses X, pp. 272-277.
188	13	Congressional Record, 77th Congress, p. 6572.
	17	*Ibid.*, p. 6573.
	21	*Ibid.*, pp. 6676-6677.
	28	Sherwood, p. 367.
189	1	Selective Service Act, 1940.
	11	F.D.R.: Papers and Addresses X, pp. 384-385.
	26	Congressional Record, 77th Congress, p. 8518.
190	1	*Ibid.*, p. 8315.
	17	F.D.R.: Papers and Addresses X, p. 322.
	20	Hearings: Pearl Harbor, Pt. 16, p. 2209.
	26	Beard, pp. 440-441.
	32	F.D.R.: Papers and Addresss X, p. 464.
191	6	Hearings: Pearl Harbor, Pt. 16, p. 5432.

Page	Line	Source
	22	F.D.R.: Papers and Addresses X, pp. 500-502.
	32	Hearings: Pearl Harbor, Pt. 16, p. 5433.
192	10	Beard, p. 525.
	25	F.D.R.: Papers and Addresses X, pp. 508-510.
193	5	Hearings: Pearl Harbor, Pt. 16, pp. 5437-5438.
	33	Beard, p. 555.

X .. Harry S Truman

BIBLIOGRAPHY

Batchelder, Robert C., *The Irreversible Decision*. Boston, Houghton Mifflin Company, 1961.

Compton, Arthur H., *Atomic Quest*. New York, Oxford University Press, 1956. (Compton)

Craven, W. F., and Cate, J. L., *The Army Air Forces in World War II*. Chicago, University of Chicago Press, 1953. (Craven and Cate)

Osada, Arata, editor, *Children of the A-bomb*. Tokyo, Uchida Rokakuho Publishing House, 1959. (Osada)

Rossiter, Clinton, *The American Presidency*. New York, Harcourt Brace, 1956. (Rossiter)

Truman, Harry S, *Years of Decision*, in *Memoirs*. 2 vols. New York, Time Inc., 1955. (Truman Memoirs)

————, *Mr. President*, ed. William Hillman. New York, Farrar, Straus, Company, 1952. (Mr. President)

United States States Special Committee on Atomic Energy, *Hearings . . .* pursuant to S. Res. 179. Washington, D.C., Government Printing Office, 1945. (A.E.C.: Hearings)

X NOTES

Page	Line	Source
194	7	Atomic Energy Commission Archives.
195	21	Saturday Review, July 4, 1964, p. 12.
	25	Truman Memoirs I, p. 5.
196	7	Press Dispatches.

Page	Line	Source
	12	Truman Memoirs I, pp. 9-10.
	21	Ibid., p. 85.
	28	Ibid., p. 10.
197	1	Ibid., p. 11.
	4	Mr. President, p. 143.
	24	Rossiter, p. 125.
198	16	Compton, p. 219.
199	13	Truman Memoirs I, p. 415.
	15	Ibid., p. 420.
	19	Ibid., p. 419.
	25	Craven and Cate V, pp. 697 ff.
200	14	A.E.C.: Hearings.
	29	Ibid., pp. 385-386.
201	21	Osada, pp. 3-5.

Index

ABOUT THE AUTHOR

Arthur T. Hadley is a writer-journalist-historian, a combination coming to the fore in a society that is interested both in itself and its antecedents. Forty-one years old, he has seen two of his plays produced and among his books is the celebrated *Nation's Safety and Arms Control*, a pioneer work that was both a Book-of-the-Month Club alternate and recommended by President Kennedy as a basic work on national security.

Graduating from Groton in 1942, he enlisted in the Army, and as a tanker was twice decorated for bravery, rising to the rank of captain. After the war he entered Yale, graduating as a Scholar of the House with Highest Honors. A book published while in college led to the Washington Bureau of *Newsweek*, where he covered first the Pentagon and later the White House for that magazine. In Washington he was known among his fellow journalists for his familiarity with the inner workings of the National Security Council and his understanding of the effects of military power on diplomacy and policy. In 1956 he became an editor of the *New York Herald Tribune*, but disliked the prolonged separation from his typewriter and in 1960 returned to full-time writing. In addition to his books, his articles have appeared in such publications as *The Reporter* and *The New York Times*.